EDUCATION AND MILITARY LEADERSHIP

A Study of the ROTC

EDUCATION AND MILITARY LEADERSHIP

GENE M. LYONS AND JOHN W. MASLAND
WITH A FOREWORD BY JOHN SLOAN DICKEY

A STUDY OF THE R.O.T.C.

PRINCETON, NEW JERSEY
PRINCETON UNIVERSITY PRESS
1959

Copyright © 1959 by Princeton University Press

ALL RIGHTS RESERVED

The Library of Congress catalog entry for this book appears at the end of the text.

Publication of this book has been aided by the Ford Foundation program to support publication, through university presses, of works in the humanities and social sciences.

GENE M. LYONS AND JOHN W. MASLAND are members of the Department of Government at Dartmouth College. Mr. Lyons served with the Infantry during World War II. He was in the secretariat of the International Refugee Organization and the United Nations Korean Reconstruction Agency. Mr. Masland has served in the Department of State, the headquarters of the Supreme Commander for the Allied Powers in Japan, and the faculties of Stanford University and the National War College. He is co-author, with Laurence I. Radway, of *Soldiers and Scholars, Military Education and National Policy* (Princeton University Press, 1957).

Printed in the United States of America
by Princeton University Press, Princeton, New Jersey

FOR

CATHERINE, MARK, AND DANIEL

AND

JOANN, JAMES, THOMAS, AND ANDREW

FOREWORD

BY JOHN SLOAN DICKEY, PRESIDENT, DARTMOUTH COLLEGE

ROTC is a familiar brand name. It is not, however, one of those brand names which guarantee uniform ingredients in all packages bearing the brand. The ROTC is not what it was in pre-World War II days; it is not now the same for the three services; it varies from campus to campus; and almost certainly the future holds more change for ROTC than the past.

The story Professors Masland and Lyons tell portends changes for the ROTC, but the same story also reveals a record of resistance to change that cautions against expecting very much very quickly if the initiative for change is to come from within the existing setup. All of which is simply to say that the ROTC, like other human institutions, can absorb many new needs and variations without changing very much. As the French have told us: *"la plus. . . ."*

Whatever else the ROTC is or is not, it is not an example of what unification of the armed forces can accomplish. Today three ROTC programs grow where in earlier years only one flourished. The three services maintain separate ROTC programs, policies, and staffs both in the Pentagon and on most of the larger college campuses of the country.

Leaving aside the critical issues of economy and effectiveness in this tripartite setup of the ROTC, so long as it prevails it almost certainly means two things: first, that the ROTC will continue to be regarded and operated by the separate services as essentially a training and recruitment device rather than as an educational program; secondly, that this traditional concept of the ROTC is not likely to suffer bold or swift reexamination

FOREWORD

through the tortuous processes of multilateral diplomacy of three independent sovereigns.

The central issue of the whole business seems to me to focus squarely on whether the traditional concept of the ROTC is adequate to the national security requirements of this nation in the foreseeable future. If there is real doubt about this, then, I think, there can be little doubt about the need for some very fundamental changes in the entire setup with a strong educationally oriented lead being given from above and outside, and the sooner the better.

If, on the other hand, the existing ROTC concept is reasonably adequate for providing the kind of manpower our national security establishment is going to need in the space age, there is, I think, good reason to believe that the ROTC as we have it today will solve its own problems as it goes.

Professors Masland and Lyons have undertaken a frontal attack on this question. They began with the inestimable advantage of being able to draw on the deep and pervasive understanding of the basic problem acquired by Professor Masland in the earlier study he did in collaboration with Professor Laurence Radway on the professional education of officers for the armed forces. (See *Soldiers and Scholars*, Princeton University Press, 1957.) The existence of this earlier work undergirds the present study both because of its inquiry into the nature of the professional demands made on officers today and because it lays a solid foundation for the proposition that our officer manpower cannot be wholly, or even primarily, provided through the governmental military academies. The only other source for this manpower is our civilian colleges and this brings us around to the other side of the same question: is the ROTC, as we now have it, the best way to harness our civilian educational resources for this critical manpower need of our federal government?

In an effort to keep their investigation rooted in all the realities of this question, Professors Masland and Lyons arranged in June 1958 to have Dartmouth College sponsor a conference where for two days interested private and public authorities discussed the problem from, one might almost say,

FOREWORD

every conceivable angle. This informed, candid, and comprehensive discussion provided the authors of this book with a unique opportunity for pre-testing their approach to the problem.

The Dartmouth conference took no concerted actions; indeed, divergences of view or emphasis were expressed on almost all questions, but the very great benefit of these discussions is reflected at many points in this book. Some idea of the range of realities to be kept in mind as each of us makes his own approach to the basic questions of the ROTC is found in the following list of the participants in the Dartmouth conference:

Major General John W. Bowen, Assistant Chief of Staff for Reserve Components, Department of the Army

Colonel Joseph Chabot, Director, Reserve Affairs Policy Office, Office of the Assistant Secretary of Defense

Brigadier General T. J. Conway, Director of Research, Office of the Chief of Research and Development, Department of the Army

Reverend Dr. Thomas C. Donohue, Academic Vice President, St. Louis University

Dr. Buell G. Gallagher, President, The City College of New York

Brigadier General Bertram C. Harrison, Deputy Director, Personnel Procurement and Training, United States Air Force

Rear Admiral John T. Hayward, Assistant Chief of Naval Operations for Research and Development, Department of the Navy

Mr. L. Eugene Hedberg, Staff Director, Reserve Forces Policy Board, Office of the Secretary of Defense

Dr. Frederick L. Hovde, President, Purdue University

Mr. Raymond F. Howes, Staff Associate, American Council on Education

Dr. Barnaby C. Keeney, President, Brown University

Colonel George A. Lincoln, Department of Social Sciences, United States Military Academy

Mr. William W. Marvel, Executive Associate, Carnegie Corporation of New York

FOREWORD

Dr. Earl J. McGrath, Executive Officer, Institute of Higher Education, Teachers College, Columbia University

Mr. Walter Millis, The Fund for the Republic; author

Dr. J. L. Morrill, President, University of Minnesota

Mr. James A. Perkins, Vice President, Carnegie Corporation of New York

Major General Turner C. Rogers, Commandant, Air Force ROTC, Air University

Mr. David S. Smith, Assistant Secretary of the Air Force for Manpower, Personnel and Reserve Forces

Mr. Russell I. Thackrey, Executive Secretary, American Association of Land-Grant Colleges and State Universities

Dr. M. H. Trytten, Director, Office of Scientific Personnel, National Research Council

Dr. O. Meredith Wilson, President, University of Oregon

This undertaking, including the conference, has been made possible by a grant from the Carnegie Corporation of New York to Dartmouth College.

Needless to say, none of the above persons or organizations is responsible for anything that appears in these prefatory words or in the book itself, but neither can they be absolved from some responsibility for the answers that America gives to the question this book raises.

November 13, 1958

PREFACE

THIS ANALYSIS of the Reserve Officers Training Corps programs is a study of the relationship of higher education to the national defense. Indeed, the ROTC represents the single area where there has been a continuing historical relationship between the federal government and our colleges and universities. The nature of the officer requirements of the armed services is changing, however, under the impact of weapons development and the complexities of our international commitments. The services are looking more and more to civilian colleges and universities, not for reserve officers as before, but as a primary source of long-term active duty and career officers.

There are two sets of limitations on the relationship between the federal government and colleges and universities: one stems from the diffusion of authority within the American system of higher education; the second from institutional arrangements and attitudes which have developed within and outside the government in response to earlier demands but which now inhibit the process of change. Any reasonable adjustment to meet new requirements will have to make serious inroads into established patterns. The present situation is as full of danger as it is of opportunity.

The present ROTC programs have been accepted for too long without the asking of some really critical questions. Recently, however, a number of developments have created considerable concern among many college administrators and military planners. These developments include the failure of the federal government to provide continuous and meaningful support for legislation authorizing aid in the construction of ROTC facilities, the reexamination at several institutions of the requirement for compulsory basic ROTC instruction, the high turnover rate of officer personnel from ROTC and other

PREFACE

procurement sources, and the general decline in enrollment in ROTC courses.

Beyond these are a number of other developments that transcend the programs themselves but clearly influence their future: the passage of legislation, such as the military pay bill, designed to create a greater degree of professionalization in the armed forces, the evolution of strategic doctrine that calls for a professional military capability, and the impending debate on the future of the draft.

Both these sets of developments have greatly contributed to the need for an inquiry into the ROTC programs. This book represents an attempt to make such an inquiry. It makes no pretense of being a comprehensive catalogue and examination of the ROTC programs. Rather, it is concerned with a clarification of the objectives of the programs, both in the past and at the present time; the differences that characterize the programs of the Army, Navy, and Air Force, their relationship to other manpower needs and to the search for national policies for manpower and education, and their relationship to the purposes and structure of American higher education. Many ROTC problems—problems of credit, academic time, and instruction—are peculiar to individual campuses and are best threshed out by local administrators and service representatives. It is, however, the purpose of this book to try to develop a framework within which these problems can be looked at against the changing objectives of the programs and the national interest in the broadest sense.

While seeking to focus sharply and constantly on this purpose, we have also sought to maintain a broad perspective on the problems discussed. Nevertheless, perspective might often be lost in the attempt to examine only a single plot in the wide field of American higher education. It would therefore be well for us to make clear at once the way we ourselves look at this problem.

The purposes of higher education are twofold: the treasuring, enrichment, and transmission of pure knowledge; and the application of pure knowledge to practical problems. The sec-

PREFACE

ond purpose is shaped by the nature of the contemporary environment, by what society needs. We begin this study with the assumption that our society, at the present time and for some time to come, will need armed forces of considerable size and strength. This is a practical problem with which we are faced. It is neither an inherent demand of society nor, for that matter, even a desirable one. Nevertheless, it must be met.

We recognize that the officer requirements of the military services are not the only serious obligations facing American colleges and universities. They must produce specialists in all scientific and professional fields. They must prepare to meet these growing demands for higher education under harsh financial burdens. And, above all, they seek to continue to raise their standards and to preserve and develop in young men and women a deep sense of basic ethical values and a thirst for knowledge for the sheer sake of knowledge. These goals should not be disregarded, no matter how pressing the immediate need.

Our investigations of these matters have been made possible by a grant to Dartmouth College from the Carnegie Corporation of New York. That Corporation is not, however, the author, owner, publisher, or proprietor of this publication, and is not to be understood as approving by virtue of its grant any of the statements made or views expressed herein. We are particularly indebted to John W. Gardner, president of the Carnegie Corporation, whose own interests in these matters stem from a deep concern for the quality of higher education in the United States. James A. Perkins, vice president of the Carnegie Corporation, and William W. Marvel, executive associate, have been helpful throughout the undertaking with advice and encouragement. We are also grateful to John Sloan Dickey, president, and Donald H. Morrison, provost, of Dartmouth College, for their personal interest in our work and for facilitating its completion. Mr. Dickey served as host and chairman of a conference held at Dartmouth in June 1958 at which college and university administrators, representatives of the armed services, and specialists in military and educational affairs

PREFACE

discussed current problems arising from the ROTC programs. The names of these individuals are listed in Mr. Dickey's Foreword to the book. We are indebted to all of them, not only for the contributions that they made during the conference, but for the additional comments and suggestions that they have transmitted to us.

We were fortunate to have the research assistance of Dr. James F. Tierney for several months at an early stage in the project. Mrs. Anne C. Tonseth has been a devoted and unbelievably understanding secretarial assistant. The reference staff of Baker Library at Dartmouth was not only helpful, but patient with our demands. Many others, too numerous to mention by name, have made this study possible. We are particularly grateful to the officers and officials of the armed services who have discussed ROTC matters with us and have helped us with our research, to the many college and university administrators and faculty members on the campuses that we have visited who gave us their time, and to all those who commented in detail on portions of the manuscript. Miss R. Miriam Brokaw, of the Princeton University Press, has graciously and skillfully guided the manuscript through publication. Needless to say, none of these, nor Dartmouth College, has any responsibility for what we have written. We alone are responsible.

Portions of this book have appeared in *The Educational Record* and the *Bulletin* of the American Association of University Professors and are reproduced with permission of the editors.

GML
JWM

Hanover, New Hampshire
January 1959

CONTENTS

	Foreword by John Sloan Dickey	vii
	Preface	xi
	PART ONE. The Problem	
I.	The Nature and Sources of Officer Requirements	3
	PART TWO. A Brief History of the ROTC	
II.	The ROTC through the Second World War	27
III.	Changing Concepts in the Postwar ROTC	64
	PART THREE. Current Issues in the ROTC	
IV.	The Nature of Current Issues in the ROTC	101
V.	The ROTC and National Policies for Education and Manpower	131
VI.	The ROTC on the College Campus	166
	PART FOUR. The Future of the ROTC	
VII.	Principles and Proposals	209
	A Note on Method and Sources	243
	Statistical Appendix	245
	Index	273

CHARTS AND TABLES

CHARTS

		Page
1.	Officers commissioned through the Army and Navy ROTC programs: 1920-1945	53
2.	Army officer production by sources: 1950-1957	113
3.	Navy officer production by sources: 1950-1957	114
4.	Air Force officer production by sources: 1953-1957	115
5.	Army ROTC General Military Science curriculum	182
6.	Navy ROTC Standard curriculum	186
7.	Air Force ROTC Generalized curriculum	190-191

TABLES
(in Statistical Appendix)

1.	Officers commissioned through the Army and Navy ROTC programs: 1920-1945	246
2.	Army officer production by sources: 1950-1957	246
3.	Navy officer production by sources: 1950-1957	247
4.	Air Force officer production by sources: 1953-1957	247
5.	Annual costs of Army, Navy, and Air Force ROTC programs by major items of expenditure: 1954-1957	248
6.	Army, Navy, and Air Force personnel on ROTC duty: 1957-1958	249
7.	Officers commissioned through the Army, Navy, and Air Force ROTC programs by civilian institutions of origin: 1955-1957	250

PART ONE

THE PROBLEM

CHAPTER I · THE NATURE AND SOURCES OF OFFICER REQUIREMENTS

1. The Changing Military Strategy
2. The Changing Nature of the Officer Corps
3. The Sources of Talent for the Officer Corps

THE PRESENT PROBLEMS of the Reserve Officers Training Corps programs involve, at their core, an ability to respond effectively to new requirements for the security of the nation. The programs were originally designed for the preparation of reserve officers available to lead a citizen army and navy mobilized in an emergency. They have also come to be used as a source of temporary active duty and permanent career officers of all three services.[1] Present trends suggest a diminishing role for reserve forces, and a different kind of role for those which are retained. They also indicate a rising demand in the career service for officers trained in colleges and universities. These new requirements have been shaped by two sets of factors: the changing nature of war and the increasing military commitments and vulnerability of the United States.

1. THE CHANGING MILITARY STRATEGY

The defense of the United States is a much more pressing concern than it was when the basic form of the ROTC took shape during and after the First World War, and the require-

---

[1] The Marine Corps secures both regular and reserve officers from the Naval ROTC program. It also conducts its own platoon leader officer training program for the procurement of college graduates. It conducts no ROTC program of its own.

ments of the situation are very much different. Defense against attack no longer depends on the traditional mobilization of reserve troops to fill in and support the active forces. It depends, in the first instance, on possession of a retaliatory capability of sufficient power to deter an attack on the United States, and an air defense system that can search out and destroy enemy aircraft and missiles if an attack occurs. In this situation the defense of the nation depends either on active forces in being or on reserve forces which are as highly trained as the active forces and are almost as quickly available for commitment.

Beyond the threat to the United States itself lies the commitment to resist aggression wherever it may occur. To do so without necessarily provoking the outbreak of a major war and a nuclear attack on the United States itself has been a major dilemma in American policy since the Korean conflict. In partial response, a theory of limited war has been advanced which involves a veritable revolution in American military doctrine. This policy calls for armed forces that can be immediately committed almost anywhere in the world: forces of high mobility, possessing a high unit ratio of firepower, and physically and psychologically prepared for prompt action. The proposition is advanced that such forces will deter limited war, just as a capability of massive retaliation will deter nuclear attack on the United States.

Behind these calculations is a conviction that any future war, intercontinental or limited, will require instantaneous reaction. What is left unanswered is whether any future conflict can in fact be limited with respect to weapons, objectives, or geographical area; whether the logical consequences of any war over vital national interests will not lead to general war. Whatever the answer, the impact of changing weapons systems and both strategic and tactical concepts raises basic questions about the role of reserve forces. It is clear that if there is indeed a place for reserve forces within the broad spectrum of American strategy, that reserve must be in existence, trained and organized to handle weapons and instruments of up-to-date complexity, even though it may not be committed immediately. There may also be a need for a new kind of reserve whose functions would be directed to civil affairs in the event of attack upon the United States, including the restoration of essential services and the maintenance of order.[2]

The nature of modern weapons and the commitments and vulnerability of the United States have thus drastically changed the concept of reserve forces. First, the reserves exist behind a standing force of between two and a half and three million men. It is somewhat anachronistic to consider the National Guard to be in "the first line of defense," a concept that was valid when the federal standing force numbered less than half a million men and the United States Army could not have taken the field against a major power without the immediate calling up of the Guard. Second, the reserves must be at a high degree of readiness at all times. In point of fact, it is no longer possible to count on a mobilization period. These changes are underscored by the statement of the Secretary of Defense that "training programs [for the reserve forces] will have to be improved and adjusted to changing concepts of warfare."[3]

The Reserve Plan of 1955 was, to a large extent, originally conceived as an adaptation of traditional military policy to modern requirements, but there is already some question if, as a military manpower policy, it kept pace with the development in weapons systems and in strategic and tactical concepts. The plan itself was foreshadowed by the Universal Military Training and Service Act of 1951 which accepted the principle of universal military training. At the time, Secretary of Defense George Marshall suggested that the 1951 Act "will make possible, for the first time in the history of the United States, the attainment of Washington's ideal of a citizens' army in which

[2] The relation of the reserves to civil defense was particularly underscored in an address by General Willard G. Wyman, Commanding General, U.S. Continental Army Command, before the National Association of State and Territorial Civil Defense Directors on April 9, 1958. For a résumé of his remarks, see *Army*, July 1958, Vol. 8, No. 12, p. 51.

[3] Department of Defense, *Semiannual Report of the Secretary of Defense*, January 1 to June 30, 1957, p. 22.

each member is trained and ready to fulfill a definite military assignment when the Nation needs his help."[4] Since 1951, the Armed Forces Reserve Act of 1952 and the Reserve Forces Act of 1955 have provided the basis for a variety of training and organizing arrangements for the reserves.[5] Prior to 1951 the reserves were almost wholly made up of men who had seen prior service and subsequently volunteered to accept reserve status or who, in the case of National Guardsmen, had volunteered directly into a Guard unit. Two basic changes have developed out of the legislative and implementing arrangements drawn up since 1951: first, there is a distinct obligation for those who are drafted for two years to continue in reserve units for specified periods after their active duty; second, there is an obligation of six months' active duty training for those who enter directly into the reserve components. These arrangements have been developed to insure that all reserve forces have some period of active duty training and that reserve units are in a continual state of training in order to be ready for almost immediate deployment.

Despite these arrangements, the reserve forces have been increasingly reduced as all three services have more recently stressed the need for professional standing forces and smaller but better trained reserve units. Within the role and mission of the Army, there is conceivably a larger part for the reserves to play than in the case of the other services, and more likelihood of their mobilization over a period of time. The Army has maintained that "reserve component units, even those well manned and highly trained, will, upon mobilization, still require various periods of time for mobilization and training prior to entry into combat"; they "cannot provide the immediate readiness capability required to implement national policy and

[4] Department of Defense, *Semiannual Report of the Secretary of Defense*, January 1 to June 30, 1951, pp. 18-19.
[5] See Eilene Galloway, *Reserve Forces Legislation, A Legislative History of the Reserve Forces Act of 1955*, prepared for the Committee on Armed Services, House of Representatives, 84th Congress, 2nd Session, May 1956.

OFFICER REQUIREMENTS

approved war plans."[6] In order to minimize the gap between the state of readiness of its reserves and present military requirements, the Army embarked in March 1958 upon a program to convert all reserve units to the pentomic organization. This is expected to provide greater mobility and atomic firepower and require more stringent training standards. If the results, projected into 1960 and 1961, promise a more readily available and powerful Army reserve, they also mean a smaller reserve, either in numbers of active divisions or in active strength within presently constituted divisions.[7]

In the case of the Navy, the need for reserves at a high state of readiness has tended to emphasize the training of coastal reserve units that are available to man designated ships or planes for antisubmarine duty in a matter of hours. Naval reserve units in the interior states are clearly of less utility in meeting the Navy's mission. Their status has therefore been made secondary, to provide replacements and meet special requirements. With the Navy's current policy of training units rather than individuals, reserve forces that are not in position for immediate commitment have been relegated a low priority, particularly with respect to the important question of distributing available budgetary resources in order to achieve maximum effectiveness. Like the Army, the Navy is planning on a smaller but more efficient reserve.[8]

---

[6] This statement was included in a reply to the Congress on the question: "Whether or not it is better to spend more money with your Reserve and your Guard Establishment than it is to spend that money in the Regular Establishment, or rearrange it?" See Hearings before Subcommittee No. 1, Committee on Armed Services, House of Representatives, 85th Congress, 2nd Session, *Proposed Reduction in the Strength of the National Guard*, p. 5,888.

[7] In 1958, the Army planned to reduce the number of existing divisions from 27 to 21 in the Guard and 10 to 6 in the Organized Reserves. Under pressure from the state governors and adjutant generals, particularly, the decision was taken to retain the total of 37 divisions, but with no increase in cost or personnel beyond current program levels. The consequences will be "skeletonized" divisions of questionable effectiveness.

[8] The emphasis on coastal reserve units came up for discussion during the meeting of the Naval Reserve Association in December 1957. For a review of this discussion, see *Navy Times*, December 21, 1957. See also

THE PROBLEM

In the Air Force, the tendency to eliminate those Air Reserve and Air National Guard units which cannot be effectively made ready for immediate deployment has been even more marked. Indeed the reduction of Air Force reserves to thirty-nine wings announced late in 1957 forced the abandonment of eighteen Reserve squadrons and three National Guard squadrons. If there is a place for reserves in the extreme notion of forces-in-being which characterizes Air Force strategic doctrine, it exists only in their complete integration into an active duty mission such as the Air Defense Command.

In actual practice, therefore, the spirit of a citizen army that lay behind the 1955 reserve arrangements is giving way before the need for active and reserve forces of high proficiency and selectivity. Perhaps a basic difficulty is that the reserve arrangements were, to a large extent, responsive to traditional concepts and to past problems, particularly those encountered in the Korean conflict, rather than to changing manpower requirements of new technology and warfare. In his message to Congress on January 13, 1955, for example, the President stressed that "the program will go far toward assuring combat veterans that they will not be called in an emergency until younger men who have not had combat duty are called, thus alleviating an inequity made apparent during the Korean conflict." The President also resurrected historical arguments against the idea of a large standing army when he warned that the "inescapable burdens" of keeping "armed and in uniform the total forces that might ultimately be required in all-out war . . . would endanger the liberties and the economic system we are determined to defend." Finally, he offered the prediction that "the new national Reserve plan, selective service and the Reserve forces, in conjunction with our Regular establishment, will fulfill our security needs with the least possible disruptive impact on the life of the individual citizen and the civilian economy."

New York Times, May 7, 1958, for a later announcement of the Navy's "selected Reserve" program.

OFFICER REQUIREMENTS

Despite the President's hopes, all three services have, for all intents and purposes, rejected what his statement added up to: a constant turnover of manpower, particularly in the active forces, but in reserve units as well. Rapid turnover means less proficiency in the handling of weapons and equipment and less dedication to the role of the particular service in the national defense. What the services want is a large stable professional military service. Under this concept, selective service is no longer primarily a democratic method of distributing the burden of military obligation but a technique for broadening the military manpower base. Selective service standards are, therefore, becoming more selective as draft calls are becoming smaller but military needs more complex and demanding. It is becoming increasingly the function of selective service to select out rather than to select in. There is some speculation that selective service can, in fact, be abandoned as military personnel needs are increasingly met on a career basis. Whether, without the draft, a sufficiently large manpower procurement base can be maintained to fill both active and reserve requirements is still highly questionable. There is, moreover, the traditional attachment to the concept of the citizen soldier, especially championed in the Congress, which operates against the complete acceptance of a system of military professionalism.[9]

Nevertheless, in what must be considered a reversal of the President's position in 1955, the Secretary of Defense publicly stated early in 1958 that it is the policy of the Eisenhower Administration "to try to get to a point where we have a

[9] For a critical analysis of the draft situation, see John Graham, *The Universal Military Obligation*, The Fund for the Republic, New York, June 1958. This particular study advocates the end of the draft in favor of a highly paid professional career service. Against this viewpoint, there is the continued support of the citizen army thesis. One of the strongest advocates of this latter view is Lieutenant General Lewis B. Hershey, Director, Selective Service System, who sees not only a continued need for large reserve forces but also great failings in our democratic system if citizens give up the privilege of serving in their own defense. See General Hershey's editorial, "Professional Forces Concept Holds Pitfall for Nation," in *Selective Service*, Vol. VIII, Number 6, Washington, D.C., June 1958.

THE PROBLEM

military force that is entirely based on volunteer enlistment."[10] At the time, the Secretary was testifying before the Congress on behalf of a bill to revise military pay scales to put more emphasis on merit and proficiency as criteria for advancement and less on longevity. The bill was the product of considerable study of the effect of manpower turnover on the efficiency of the armed services carried out particularly, during 1956 and 1957, by the Defense Advisory Committee on Professional and Technical Compensation under Ralph J. Cordiner, president of the General Electric Company, as chairman.[11] In testifying on behalf of the bill, Mr. Cordiner emphasized the technical nature of modern warfare, the need to eliminate any but technical competence as a basis for advancement, and the almost complete uselessness of reserve forces in waging war. In accepting a revised pay bill, both the Administration and the Congress rejected this extreme position of looking at future warfare as a "push-button" affair. Nevertheless, the pay bill was explicitly and implicitly recognized as an important step in eliminating the need for the draft to provide a broad military manpower base, in increasing the dependence for national defense on the professional military, and of retaining a sizeable portion of the nation's skilled manpower in the military services.

2. THE CHANGING NATURE OF THE OFFICER CORPS

The military pay bill is but one in a series of actions in recent years that reflect the response of the armed services to the need for a more professionalized career officer corps. Other important measures are the Officer Augmentation Act of 1956, authorizing the services to enroll up to fifty percent of their

[10] Statement of Secretary McElroy before Subcommittee No. 2, Committee on Armed Services, House of Representatives, 85th Congress, 2nd Session, *Method of Computing Basic Pay*, February 20, 1958.

[11] *A Modern Concept of Manpower Management and Compensation for Personnel of the Uniformed Services, Volume I—Military Personnel*, A Report and Recommendation for the Secretary of Defense by the Defense Advisory Committee on Professional and Technical Compensation, May 1957.

OFFICER REQUIREMENTS

officer ranks as regulars, and the interest of the services in the retention of non-regulars on active duty for fixed terms. These steps, taken deliberately over the last few years, suggest several developments: the shaping up of a new kind of professional officer corps composed of a much larger proportion of regulars and long-term non-regulars; greater selectivity of those who are retained; the reduced utilization of short-term active duty reserve officers; and increased professionalization throughout the services. Moreover, as the relative importance of reserve forces as a whole diminishes, the significance of the ready reserves within these forces increases. Accordingly, among reserves as well as regulars, there is a greater need for a high level of skill and talent among officers.

The qualitative aspect of these developments is perhaps the most significant. It is clear that the armed forces must secure and retain officers of the highest caliber. These men must, of course, possess the traditional military attributes and skills and the expected qualities of character, loyalty, dedication, patriotism, and leadership. But as large complex organizations, involving intimate association with almost every aspect of our national political, economic, and social life, the Army, Navy, and Air Force must have officers who transcend these fundamental soldierly qualities. Broadly defined, there appear to be two kinds of additional capabilities called for. The first relates to technical competence; the second to breadth of outlook, judgment, and wisdom.

In the first place, a very high level of technical knowledge and skill is required to plan for the use of and to operate complicated weapons systems and supporting organization and equipment, and to direct the research and development activities that will bring further advances. The armed forces can no longer meet these essential needs by borrowing skill and talent on the basis of short-term loans. They must retain men of skill and of leadership qualities in their ranks without returning them to the civilian economy after only relatively short tours of active duty.

A case in point is the Navy's program in nuclear power propulsion. Training in this program is carried on in two phases: young officers preparing for billets on nuclear-powered vessels undergo twenty-one weeks of academic training after which they spend twenty-four weeks of practical work on a land-based operating prototype reactor plant. After this total of forty-five weeks of formal training, they are then ordered to report to shipyards where nuclear-powered vessels are being constructed. Here they remain for approximately one year prior to the actual commissioning of their vessel, receiving further training in the actual reactor plant being installed and assisting with the installation and testing of the plant components and systems.[12] Before filling his billet, the young officer has therefore had almost two years of specialized training which has followed a reasonable period of active service during which he has presumably demonstrated a high degree of command potentiality and technical proficiency. To lose his services even within the five years following the end of his specialized training would be more than a waste of time, money, and human resources. It would be potentially crippling to a program which is rapidly gaining momentum but for which there are few trained officers. This same reasoning applies to pilots, missile commanders, and a wide variety of other positions in all three services requiring similar degrees of specialized training and skill.

There is of course danger in thinking of the problem of officer requirements primarily in terms of scientific and engineering talent. Weapons development has given rise to more than just a need for increased technical proficiency on the part of officers. As complicated and intricate as the weapons themselves are the problems of decision-making and leadership: the decision to use nuclear weapons, the morale of the men in a nuclear-powered submarine that remains submerged for days or weeks at a time, the task of holding together men who have suffered the shock of their first atomic attack, and, at a higher

[12] *Hearings before a Subcommittee of the Committee on Appropriations, House of Representatives, 85th Congress, 1st Session, Department of the Navy—Appropriations for 1958,* pp. 387-388.

level, the whole complex of policy development. The military services need their share of the talented and educated young men as leaders as well as technicians. Studies made by the services, as well as the independent observations of many individuals, have emphasized the need for officers with a rich store of general knowledge as well as specialized knowledge of military affairs. These men must understand the role of the military establishment in a democratic society and be sensitive to political, economic, and social developments at home and abroad. They must have the executive talent to manage large operations. They must have analytical skill and good judgment of high order. Perhaps of greatest importance is the need for wisdom and a broad perspective, not only among officers who advance to higher levels of responsibility but among officers at all levels, in peacetime and in war.[13]

What is happening in the military profession is what is happening throughout American society. As the complexity of our social organization has increased, so has the demand for highly skilled talent, particularly in the professions and areas of specialization. As John Gardner has observed, "We are just beginning to understand that one of the distinguishing marks of a modern, complex society is its insatiable appetite for educated talent. It is not just technologists and scientists that we need, though they rank high in priority. We desperately need our gifted teachers, our professional men, our critics, and our seers. There is no present likelihood that this trend will reverse itself."[14] Of significance to the armed forces not only is that they need superior career officer talent, but that they must compete in a highly competitive market for this talent, and that this situation will become more rather than less intense.[15] These developments indicate the need for a broader

[13] For further comment on this aspect of military leadership see John W. Masland and Laurence I. Radway, *Soldiers and Scholars, Military Education and National Policy*, Princeton University Press, 1957, particularly Chapter Two.
[14] John W. Gardner, "The Great Talent Hunt," *Annual Report, Carnegie Corporation of New York*, 1956, pp. 11-12.
[15] See *The Pursuit of Excellence, Education and the Future of America*,

concept of the military profession. Such a concept would include changes both in the structure of the profession and in the sources of membership.

On the first point, the need for more regular career officers potentially qualified for advancement to the highest ranks is supplemented by a requirement for a substantial portion of officers, particularly in the technical specialties, who will serve on extended active duty, but not on a lifetime career basis. This is, perhaps, most striking in the case of combat pilots whose efficiency begins to diminish at about the age of thirty-five. Not all the available pilots in any one age group can move into command and staff positions and higher rank. Out of necessity, the pyramid of the rank structure of each of the services gets narrower and narrower as it reaches the top. A consequence of taking in too many officers of the same age group is to create what has come to be known as "the hump" in the rank structure; that is, a large number of officers who are grouped at a particular grade level because there is not sufficient room for all of them at the next level and the age group below them has begun to catch up. This very situation has occurred as a result of the large number of officers accepted as regulars at the end of World War II. One of the peculiarities of the military profession is the relationship between age and level of advancement. If a man has not advanced to a given level at a certain age, there is no place for him in the profession and he must leave.

One possible solution to the problems brought on by the characteristics of the military rank structure is to offer a combination of long-term contracts and high separation bonuses in lieu of a career. This is to say, young officers might be guaranteed retention in the services until they reach the age of thirty-five and then be discharged with unusually generous cash payments. Any such arrangement does not, of course, eliminate the infinite difficulties inherent in beginning a new

---

Panel v of the Special Studies Project, Rockefeller Brothers Fund, New York, 1958.

OFFICER REQUIREMENTS

career at even this early age. The thought of these difficulties would certainly cause a college generation that is presently apt to be overly concerned with problems of security to shy away from accepting any proposition from the armed services that did not offer the possibility of a career or the opportunity to leave in order to take advantage of a career elsewhere. If the armed services ask more officers to spend longer periods on active duty, they must be prepared to make adjustments in their own system that will offer these men reasonable opportunities. On the one hand, these opportunities would have to include the fair chance of rising to the very highest positions of command and responsibility and, on the other, the understanding that there will be no abrupt and arbitrary dismissal and that a man will be given the necessary means to re-establish himself in a new career.[16]

Another major problem involving the nature of the rank structure is the role of the technical specialist in uniform. For many years advancement to the higher ranks has been the prerogative of the line officer. Yet specialists are needed in uniform. Many of the specialized needs of the services can and are being met by hiring civilians to work in the military establishment. This does not fully meet the needs of the military, however. Civilians in the services are pretty well restricted to the role of expert technicians or advisers. Authority continues to reside in their military chiefs. In many areas, particularly in research and development, this authority should be exercised by men fully as expert as their advisers. Such a degree of expertise can be achieved only by years of study and specialization with the prospect of advancement to the higher ranks.

The military profession is thus being fundamentally altered by the new capabilities that its membership must possess: technical competence and wider intellectual breadth. Changes

[16] For recent thinking on term retention, see the Hearings before Subcommittee No. 1, Committee on Armed Services, House of Representatives, 85th Congress, 2nd Session, *Consideration of Active Duty Agreements for Reserve Officers*, July 1958.

are required at the point of entry into the profession and at the levels of advancement. There is clearly a relationship here. There will be a reluctance for young men with a potential in these areas to enter the profession if the channels of advancement are restrictive. At the same time, these channels will never be fully broadened, if entry into the profession is not well opened to allow such young men to enter in the first place. One is as important as the other.

3. THE SOURCES OF TALENT FOR THE OFFICER CORPS

One of the keys to changing officer requirements is the search for highly qualified talent. Increasingly the tasks to be performed and the leadership to be provided require a high level of educational preparation. Estimates at the Military Academy, to cite one recent example, suggest that fifty percent of all regular Army officers in the combat arms and one hundred percent in the technical branches will attend graduate school, for which they must be adequately prepared by their undergraduate studies.[17] The situation is similar in the other services. Perhaps of greater importance is the relationship of an appropriate educational background to the development of the broad perspective and understanding demanded of officers as they advance to progressively higher levels of responsibility.

The changing nature of these requirements indicates the importance to the armed services of institutions of higher education as sources of officer personnel. Civilian colleges and universities constitute but one source which the services have tapped in their search for talent, however. There are other sources, and it would be well to consider them briefly at this point. They are few. An expanded academy system? An expanded officer candidate program? An expanded system of

[17] A survey conducted in 1958 by the Military Academy of 60 percent of its graduates in the classes of 1900 to 1954 inclusive indicated that already almost one half (48 percent) have done postgraduate academic study. One quarter hold master's degrees, *Report on Graduate Questionnaire*, July 1, 1958.

military colleges? It is important to point out that these alternatives involve an expansion of the system of military education as contrasted with increased reliance on civilian educational institutions as a source of career officers.

All of these sources have merit. All should be retained and qualitatively strengthened. But there is a grave risk in utilizing them to the exclusion of the nation's colleges and universities, its civilian institutions of higher education. If the services were to limit their procurement of career officers to the academies, officer candidate programs, and the military colleges, they would be narrowing their procurement base at a time when the scope of their requirements is broadening. A substantial portion of young men entering the professional military service should experience the kinds of educational opportunities available in the great state and private universities and the leading colleges of the nation. This is not to say that the educational experience gained at the academies and military colleges is not satisfactory; it is rather to suggest that it is not sufficient to meet the full range of personnel requirements of the services.

Each alternative source of professional officers needs to be considered in the light of this situation. The first alternative is an expanded academy system. There is some sentiment in military circles for this solution to the officer procurement problem, but it appears that there are no present plans to go beyond a modest increase in the present enrollments at West Point and Annapolis of about 2,400 and 3,700 respectively. The Air Force Academy, when it is settled in its new facilities at Colorado Springs, will be about the same size as the Military Academy. It will graduate its first class in 1959. At that time the agreement of the Air Force with the Army and the Navy, whereby it commissioned twenty-five percent of the graduating class at West Point and Annapolis, will terminate, permitting an increase to that extent in the production of regular officers from the academies for these two services. Even so, the academies will be inadequate to meet the quantitative requirements for active duty and regular officers.

Enlargement of the Military and Naval Academies, moreover, would be difficult because of the restrictive physical limitations of their present sites. The new barracks now being constructed at each of these institutions should do no more than alleviate the already excessive crowding in present facilities. While the Air Force Academy's magnificent site appears to be limitless, stretching for miles along the front range of the Rockies, the cost of further construction there, as at West Point and Annapolis, would be extremely high. Any considerable enlargement of these schools, moreover, would inevitably change their character, and this would be unfortunate. The establishment of a second academy for each of the services on other sites might be undertaken, but the costs would be extreme and the possibility of Congressional approval slight.[18]

There are, moreover, more fundamental reasons for rejecting the substantial enlargement of the academy system. There is clearly a very real and permanent place for the academies.[19] But the effectiveness of the armed forces would be diminished if they were to draw upon the academies, or any other single source, for a larger proportion of their career and active duty officers. In the first place, there is the practical problem to be considered. Since the long-term career expectations of academy graduates are high, and since not all officers, given prevailing promotion and retirement practices, can rise to the highest ranks, a substantially greater input of academy graduates would be likely to cause a serious situation at the middle rank and age levels. This can be minimized by maintaining an appropriate balance in the input of academy and non-academy graduates. For it can be assumed that non-academy men would be more prepared, psychologically at least, to leave the services for lateral transfer into civilian life at midpoint in

[18] Estimates of the cost of the new Air Force Academy range from the Congressional construction authorization of $135,000,000 upward to a construction and equipment total of $300,000,000, and have aroused severe criticism in the Congress. See Hearings before Subcommittee of the Committee on Appropriations, House of Representatives, 85th Congress, 2nd Session, *Military Construction Appropriations for 1959*, pp. 95-147, 983-1,144, 1,230-1,241.

[19] See Masland and Radway, *op.cit.*, pp. 232-234.

OFFICER REQUIREMENTS

their careers. Secondly, although the charge that the academies contribute to undue service parochialism among their graduates is often exaggerated, there is nevertheless a risk in this respect involved in greater reliance upon them to fill the officer ranks. Thirdly, the academies alone cannot satisfy the range of talent, skill, and outlook required in an officer corps to meet the complex demands of modern warfare—from the broadly gauged and experienced generalist to the highly trained specialist. Lastly, and perhaps of greatest significance, is the fact that exclusive reliance upon the academies would involve risk of creating an inbred military elite, a situation to be avoided if our democratic values are to be preserved.

Proposals have been made from time to time that the service academies be converted into advanced schools, providing specialized military preparation to men who have completed two or three years in civilian institutions, or even into postgraduate schools for this purpose. While there may be some advantages to such arrangements, the services have rejected them whenever they have been seriously pressed, and for this and other reasons the possibility of their achievement, at least in the foreseeable future, is too slight to warrant practical consideration.[20]

A second alternative would be increased utilization of such programs as the officer candidate schools and the aviation cadet and similar programs. The former has the advantage of a short lead time. The course is of short duration and the program can be expanded promptly to meet changing officer needs. At least a modest program, moreover, is essential to provide opportunity for able and promising enlisted men to enter the officer ranks. Many of these men aspire to be career officers. But the OCS does not appear to be a suitable vehicle for attracting substantial numbers of college and university graduates into the professional military service. Its relatively short duration minimizes the opportunity to stimulate an interest in a military career in these graduates. Aside from a means of opening the officer ranks to carefully selected enlisted

[20] *Ibid.*, Chapter Six, particularly pp. 106-117.

men, it lends itself more readily to the production of non-career junior officers for active duty in times of emergency when the armed forces are expanded. While the probability of mass mobilization is hotly contested, the OCS should be held available principally for this purpose, if the need should arise.

The aviation cadet programs of the Air Force and the Navy present at least one very substantial advantage—a relatively high proportion of the graduates of these programs appear to be career-minded. But this motivation seems to be oriented toward a technical specialty. Because of the lower educational requirements of the programs, they do not attract the sort of individual who is likely to achieve high rank and responsibility, the sort needed at these levels by the armed forces of the future.

These programs do lend themselves, on the other hand, to a definite need of the services that might be more fully developed. This is the need, to which reference was made above, for officers to serve on active duty for extended periods. While on active duty, they will perform certain functions of a rather specialized technical nature for which high levels of specialized technical training are required, but they will not anticipate promotion to the higher ranks and to the broad command or managerial responsibilities attached to these ranks. Perhaps undue concern that these men possess a college degree should be avoided. For such officers, however, there is need for increased attractions to active duty of a term character supplemented by rather generous separation allowances, facilitating their transfer to civilian life at an age at which they can either commence another vocation or profitably transfer their service training to a civilian job. Along this line, the present and projected programs of the services in sending carefully selected enlisted men to civilian institutions in return for an extended active duty obligation appear to offer possibilities for increased use. The active duty motivations of these men are relatively high. Many of them are of potential officer quality.

A third alternative is an expanded system of military colleges.

OFFICER REQUIREMENTS

Actually Virginia Military Institute, the Citadel, Norwich, and the others in this category participate in the ROTC programs. ROTC units are maintained on their campuses by the Army and the Air Force in the same manner as at other colleges and universities. The general requirement that students enroll in basic ROTC, the imposition of military organization and discipline, and the maintenance of other military features are the responsibility of each institution and not of the Army or the Air Force. Except for the fact that students enrolled in these institutions need not register with selective service and that they receive somewhat larger allowances for uniforms, they are treated by the services just like those in ROTC programs elsewhere. In practice, proportionately more of them have accepted regular commissions under the Distinguished Military Graduate programs than have those from civilian institutions, but the Army has rejected the plea of the heads of these schools that it agree to accept a substantially larger number of their graduates into the regular service. The Army has opposed this suggestion as a delegation of its responsibility for the selection of its officers, and has preferred to retain maximum selectivity from all sources. Students in these institutions, as in others, are encouraged toward a professional military career, but not put in a preferred position with respect to those of other institutions of higher education. At the undergraduate level the need is not for more military training, but for more and better general education and specialized scientific and technical preparation. The expansion of the military college system would not meet this requirement as effectively as increased reliance upon civilian colleges and universities.

These comments indicate that the services cannot meet their needs from the aforementioned sources alone. Inevitably they must rely also on the nation's colleges and universities. These institutions perform first a selective and then a preparative function that no potential employer of high quality talent can afford to ignore. Arrangements whereby the armed services can secure their share of the annual crop of college and university graduates are essential. A substantial portion of these graduates should be encouraged to make a career of the military profession, some advancing to the highest ranks, others filling the need for officers serving on extended active duty.

The need of the armed services for high quality talent, however, is but a part of the need of our entire society for such talent. As the panel on education of the Special Studies Project of the Rockefeller Brothers Fund has emphasized, there is a long-term upward trend in the demand for all trained manpower. This is a consequence of "the constant pressure of an ever more complex society against the total creative capacity of its people." Thus "we must prepare ourselves for a constant and growing demand for talents of all varieties, and must attempt to meet the specific needs of the future by elevating the quality and the quantity of talented individuals of all kinds."[21] This situation underscores the importance of the colleges and universities as sources of talent in all areas of productive, managerial, professional, and creative leadership.

John Gardner's words again are relevant here: "The immensely increased demand for educated talent has placed a wholly new emphasis upon the role of colleges and universities in our national life," he has written. "Virtually the total future leadership of our society—political, cultural, industrial, technical, professional, educational, and agricultural—is today being channeled through the colleges and universities and, increasingly, through our graduate and professional schools. It follows that these institutions will play a far more weighty and powerful role on the American scene than anyone had anticipated. As the cradle of our national leadership, their vitality and excellence become a matter of critical importance."[22]

The aspirations of the colleges and universities of the country to meet this challenge are reflected in the spirit of dedication to the service of society that has distinguished American higher education. It is reflected also in the diversity of educational opportunities offered, extending far beyond the traditional fields of law, medicine, theology, and the arts that have charac-

---

[21] *The Pursuit of Excellence, Education and the Future of America,* op.cit., p. 10.
[22] Gardner, op.cit., p. 11.

terized European universities, to the inclusion of engineering, agriculture, business, education, journalism, nursing, public health, and many other specialized fields.[23] But there is still another aspect of higher education relevant to its ability to meet social needs. This is the inherent worth and importance of institutions of higher education in themselves, quite apart from their function as sources of talent. These institutions are a principal repository of our knowledge and wisdom, of the qualities that have made our civilization great. They provide the libraries, laboratories, and classrooms in which these heritages are transmitted to each new generation and in which the frontiers of human knowledge and understanding are pressed outward against the unknown. Freedom in the pursuit of learning and in the transmission of ideas, cherished by all those who honor learning, is one of our essential liberties. It must be cultivated as a wellspring of our strength and vitality. Programs designed to utilize colleges and universities for some specific purpose, no matter how important, must not be permitted to compromise this aspect of their existence.

The relevance of these matters to each other is obvious. On the one hand, it is essential that the armed forces maintain a competitive position in attracting college and university graduates in relation to other professions and occupations. On the other hand, the demands of the services must be kept in balance with those of other social needs. And throughout, the essential integrity and independence of institutions of higher education must be preserved. It is within this context that we examine the principal means now available for bringing college and university graduates into professional military service. This is, of course, the Reserve Officers Training Corps programs.

[23] John S. Brubacher and Willis Rudy, *Higher Education in Transition*, New York, Harper and Bros., 1958, pp. 376-379.

PART TWO

A BRIEF HISTORY OF THE ROTC

CHAPTER II · THE ROTC THROUGH THE SECOND WORLD WAR

1. Nineteenth-Century Origins
2. The Emergence of a Military Policy
3. World War I and the Interwar Years
4. World War II
5. In Retrospect

THE EVOLUTION of the Reserve Officers Training Corps programs has been in the American pragmatic tradition. In its origins, no less than today, the ROTC represented a method of drawing upon college-educated men to produce a trained officer corps. In the past it was a corps built on citizen army foundations. Today it serves a highly professionalized military establishment that requires a variety of skills and carries broad national responsibilities. The programs have grown to meet these new requirements and have been forced to adjust to changing circumstances without prior design or total plan. It is our purpose here to show how the ROTC was first created as part of the slow development of a federal reserve, what problems were involved in the early operations of the program, and what contributions the program made to the national defense during the First and Second World Wars.

The memories of two world wars and the interwar period still plague any real clarification of new objectives for the ROTC programs. It is perhaps necessary to understand this period in the ROTC history in order to comprehend the true extent of the changes that the programs are presently undergoing and some of the problems involved in meeting new requirements. College faculties still think of the programs in terms of substandard courses and close order drill; college administrators are still concerned with the effect of military obligation on continued enrollment and are convinced that the armed services do not know how to use talent; and many military planners are still thinking in terms of stockpiling manpower. All these attitudes were born in the years prior to 1945.

1. *NINETEENTH-CENTURY ORIGINS*

The concept of the citizen army is deeply rooted in American experience. It is a product of the early political development of the country and is closely associated with the principle of the decentralization of power. In the case of the citizen army, this principle was expressed in the militia system, derived from colonial origins and written into the law of 1792. That early law, sometimes called the "Infamous Militia Act" by military analysts, made all free white male citizens between eighteen and forty-eight, liable for military obligation. Literally everyone was in the militia, which was, practically speaking, a military manpower pool. Calls into the federal service, however, were limited to specific conditions enumerated in the Constitution. Training, discipline, and inspection, moreover, were left to local decision.

It was in fact the desire to provide professionally trained officers for the militia that motivated the establishment of the first non-professional military college, in many ways the spiritual grandfather of all the ROTC programs that followed. This was the American Literary, Scientific, and Military Academy (now Norwich University), founded in Vermont in 1819 by Captain Alden Partridge, a former Superintendent of the United States Military Academy. Its mission was to provide officers for the national defense who would be "identified in views, in feelings, and in interests, with the great body of the community." Partridge was looking toward a balance between the militia and the Regular Army, a balance that would bring the popular support and allegiances of the militia system into harmony with the training and discipline of an efficient army.

THROUGH WORLD WAR II

Many of Partridge's students volunteered for the Regular Army and tended to broaden the educational base of the professional corps. But his main purpose was to offer professional training to future officers of the militia.[1]

The southern military colleges were established after Norwich, the Virginia Military Institute in 1839 and the Citadel in 1842. Here there was less than a conscious relationship to the militia system. They and the many military schools set up before the Civil War sprang rather out of the southern military tradition, and the belief that military training was a good way to teach discipline and self-restraint. It was also a practical means of preparing young men for duties of supervision and protection on the estates of the southern ruling class.

During the Civil War the northern forces were plagued by an insufficiency of professional officers. When the war broke out, there were 684 graduates of the Military Academy on the rolls of the Regular Army. Although the total officer corps numbered 1,098, more than 300 chose to resign their commissions and serve with the Confederacy. The rest remained to serve with their Regular Army units, leaving the mobilized divisions of state forces to be trained and led by officers appointed by the governors. The majority of the troops in the Civil War were thus officered by non-professionals, although in some cases state-mobilized units were in fact led by Regular Army officers who had previously resigned their commissions. In the south the caliber of the citizen-officers was strengthened by the training many had received in the private and state military schools. In the north the caliber was less high, although Norwich University for one furnished 523 officers for the Union Army, almost as many as West Point.[2]

[1] The Academy was renamed Norwich University in 1834; it was removed to Northfield, Vermont, in 1866. For the early history, see William A. Ellis, *Norwich University, 1819-1911, Her History, Her Graduates, Her Role of Honor*, Montpelier, Vt., Capital City Press, 1911. Also of interest is *Captain Partridge's Lecture on National Defense*, n.d.; this privately published pamphlet seems to be a reprint of a lecture the Captain gave to promote interest in the Academy shortly after it was founded.

[2] Marvin A. Kriedberg and Morton G. Henry, *History of Military*

A BRIEF HISTORY

The experience of the Civil War, and the lack of trained military leadership in the north, particularly, were directly responsible for the inclusion of military instruction in the curriculum of the colleges and universities founded under the terms of the Land-Grant Act of 1862. There had been no provision for military instruction in an earlier version of the Land-Grant bill which President Buchanan had vetoed in 1857. It was, however, included in the version presented to the Congress five years later.

The major supporter of the bill was Justin Morrill, a Vermont friend and neighbor of Alden Partridge. Advocating its passage in June 1862, Mr. Morrill told the House of Representatives that "something of military instruction has been incorporated in the bill in consequence of the new conviction of its necessity forced upon the attention of the Loyal States by the history of the past years." Mr. Morrill made it clear that he did not consider an expansion of West Point to be a practical solution to the problem of providing adequately prepared officers. He presented his proposal as a necessary condition "if we ever expect to reduce the army to its regular dimensions. . . ." This theme articulated the fear that a large centrally controlled standing army commanded by professional officers was a danger to a free society. Like Partridge, he offered the alternative of military training in civilian educational institutions as a means by which a democratic people could gain a competent officer corps for a military reserve without endangering their basic liberties.[3]

In brief, the Land-Grant Act of 1862 offered to each state tracts of federally controlled public lands, or scrip in lieu thereof. The funds derived from their sale were to be devoted to "the endowment, support, and maintenance of at least one college where the leading object shall be, without excluding other scientific and classical studies, and *including military*

Mobilization in the United States Army, 1775-1945, Department of the Army Pamphlet No. 20-212, June 1955, pp. 115-116.

[3] *Congressional Globe*, 37th Congress, 2nd Session, Vol. 4, Appendix, June 6, 1862, p. 256.

tactics, to teach such branches of learning as are related to agriculture and the mechanic arts. . . ." This represented a significant change in American higher education. No longer was the education of a small number of spiritual leaders and scholarly gentlemen adequate to serve the needs of a bursting national economy after the Civil War. The development of the West, the growth of industry, the application of science to the needs of living—all these required a concept of education dedicated to the public service. The land-grant measure provided for the establishment of colleges in the new areas where people were settling, and broadened the opportunities for higher education. In all these ways, it contributed to the decentralized, egalitarian pattern of American higher education that has distinguished its development.[4]

Each land-grant school conducted its military program differently. There was no organization and little enthusiasm for the training in the War Department. There was equally little agreement anywhere on the meaning of the Morrill Act itself. It was not clear in these early years, for example, whether the Land-Grant Act called for military training to be a compulsory or optional course of study. Nor did the Congress or the War Department make it clear, leaving the colleges to decide for themselves what role military training was to play in the life of the students. Some made military instruction a four-year requirement, others for three years, others for two, and still others did not, at first, require it at all. The number of hours of instruction per week also varied. The controlling factor seemed to be the degree to which the authorities of the colleges considered it important to use military instruction to achieve good posture and bearing among the students and to train a discipline of the mind that had formerly been the task of the rigid classical curriculum. The instruction itself generally consisted only of drill. Even when the War Department sent an officer to a college as professor of military science and

[4] For a brief history of the land-grant colleges, see Edward D. Eddy, Jr., *Colleges for Our Land and Time*, New York, Harper and Bros., 1957. A good deal of the discussion in the next few pages is based on this book.

tactics, he was not given study outlines or lengthy instructions but was left to his own devices to work out a program with the local administrators.

The Morrill Act itself had not provided for assistance from the federal government to the land-grant colleges in carrying out their military courses. Most colleges pushed off the military courses as an added burden onto faculty members who had retired from the Regular Army or had been volunteer officers during the Civil War. In a series of supplementary acts in 1866, 1888, and 1891, however, the Congress authorized the War Department to detail Regular Army officers to the institutions and to military colleges like Norwich, as military instructors. During the years prior to the Spanish-American War, the number of officers assigned was progressively increased to one hundred. In 1870, Congress also authorized the War Department to issue small arms and artillery to these schools. The officers and equipment which could be sent to the colleges were generally considered to be surplus to the Army's immediate needs. The War Department was not placed under any compulsion to service the colleges but was left to decide for itself whether or not officers and equipment could be furnished.

The implementation of the military provisions of the Morrill Act was thus left to be worked out through general cooperation between the land-grant colleges and the War Department. Set up, in many ways, to meet the trained manpower needs of an expanding nation, the colleges began to develop a sense of public service that was later to strengthen their conception of the military instruction program as a contribution to the essentially federal purpose of national defense.

There was consequently a general agreement among the colleges that the War Department was not fully supporting the program as it should have. Neither instructors nor equipment arrived despite Congressional authorization. The Department insisted, as it was to do for many subsequent years, that its poverty in men and money prevented it from doing more. Only in 1889 did the Department make a move to formalize its relationship with the colleges by proposing that the professor of military science and tactics be granted full faculty status, that a uniform be worn by students while taking military instruction, and that the compulsory feature be made standard. These proposals do not seem to have been followed up until the military training programs of the land-grant colleges were absorbed into the ROTC system set up under the National Defense Act of 1916. Yet by 1898 there were organized military departments in forty-two institutions. The contribution of *college* military training to the Spanish-American War effort cannot, however, be properly evaluated, for the War Department kept no record of the students who had received training.

2. THE EMERGENCE OF A MILITARY POLICY

The development of military policy from the Spanish-American War until the First World War revolved around two constants: the establishment of a rational system of military preparedness; and the creation of a federally controlled reserve force to implement plans. Out of the first grew the General Staff organization; out of the second, the increasing federalization of the National Guard and the establishment of an organized federal reserve corps. As one of the elements of the reserve system, the Reserve Officers Training Corps emerged to provide a steady supply of young college-trained reserve officers.

The first landmarks were the Acts of 1903, the work of Secretary of War Elihu Root. The first of these, the General Staff Act, provided for a Chief of Staff and a military planning group, offering a means for constantly revitalizing the military command and a system for drawing up advanced preparedness programs. The second, the Militia Act, permitted the federal government to undertake certain aspects of the training and discipline of state National Guard units, organized under the militia clause of the Constitution, in order to achieve a predetermined minimum state of readiness among all state troops called into national service in case of emergency.

A BRIEF HISTORY

During the early years of the century, a good deal more attention than previously seems to have been given to the military training being offered in the land-grant colleges. While there were no illusions about what could be accomplished, the Chief of Staff stated in his report of 1909 that "with serious application the student may obtain a clear idea of the fundamental principles and essential details of a company officer's duty."[5] Shortly after the Spanish-American War, a practice had been adopted of granting "distinguished institution" ratings to ten of the land-grant and military colleges every year on the basis of War Department inspection reports. One outstanding student from each such college was then recommended for a commission in the Regular Army. Moreover, by 1912, an attempt was made at a conference of college officials called by the War Department at the Army War College to set up minimum training standards in land-grant and military colleges. A more comprehensive program of training in colleges and universities awaited the development of a federal reserve.

In 1912 the War Department General Staff came up with a mobilization plan that called into play the full force of the reforms inaugurated by Root in 1903. It grew out of the enthusiasm of two men, Henry Stimson and General Leonard Wood, the one Secretary of War and the other Chief of Staff. In his annual report in 1911, Wood had reluctantly accepted the role of the National Guard and the limits on a standing army. He had pointed out that, within this framework, a reasonable state of preparedness could be assured only if these elements were supported by a federal reserve trained in time of peace. The reserve was the key to Wood's military policy.

The 1912 plan was based on the premise that the preparation of "great armies of citizen soldiers to meet the emergency of modern war" involved "the partial organization and training of citizen soldiers in peace" as well as "provisions for prompt and orderly expansion on the outbreak of war."[6] Particular em-

[5] Report of the Chief of Staff, *War Department Annual Reports, 1909*, Vol. I, p. 218.
[6] "A Report on the Organization of the Land Forces of the United

THROUGH WORLD WAR II

phasis was given to the training of officers and detailed provisions were laid down for going to the land-grant colleges for reserve officers for the citizen army. The plan recognized that under the existing system graduates of the land-grant colleges "may in some cases go into the National Guard, some of them may enter the regular service, and some of them, no doubt, may find a place in the volunteer armies of the future." This was hardly a satisfactory arrangement. Implicit in the movement to create and develop the General Staff system was the assumption that emergencies could be anticipated and plans made for the mobilization of manpower and matériel to protect the nation once an emergency arose.

The 1912 report therefore suggested that "upon their graduation opportunities could be given [to these students] to serve with regular organizations at camps of instruction or maneuvers." Following this service (which resembles the summer camp training later provided for ROTC graduates) the young men would be commissioned as reserve lieutenants in the Regular Army. They could then be allowed to serve with the Regular Army for short training periods and "on the outbreak of war" would provide a trained, definite cadre of officers for the mobilized army. The report also suggested that this "class of reserve appointments should be open to other suitable classes, such as former members of the Regular Army, Volunteers, and National Guard. . . ." Here then, in essence, was the Officers Reserve Corps later provided for in the Act of 1916, with a training program in the colleges forming the major source of young reserve officers.

The General Staff plan of 1912 did not gain very much political support and General Wood himself began to turn in other directions to create a reserve of citizen soldiers. Among his efforts was the establishment of the famous Plattsburg movement, a program of summer training camps that was initiated with college students in 1913. The story of the Platts-

---

States," reprinted as Appendix A to the Report of the Secretary of War, *War Department Annual Reports, 1912*, Vol. I.

burg movement has been told many times and need not be repeated here. It need only be emphasized that Wood, and others, looked upon college students as the best starting point to build a reserve officer corps. This was also obvious in Wood's annual report for 1913 when he suggested that four hundred graduates of the land-grant colleges be selected each year for commissioning as "provisional" second lieutenants and assigned to Regular Army units for one year's training.[7] It was not until 1916 that a federal reserve was actually created, however.

The National Defense Act of 1916 developed out of a General Staff study presented to the Secretary of War in 1915 as "A Statement of a Proper Military Policy for the United States."[8] Three assumptions were particularly important to the thesis of the "Proper Policy": first, that the objective of American military planning was protection of the United States against a hostile invading force; second, that the Navy could only delay, not defeat, a threatening armada, and accordingly the mobile land force that would meet invading troops had to be trained in time of peace; third, that the reserve elements of this mobile land force had to be made up of federal and not National Guard troops, since, in the view of the General Staff, the militia clause did *not* insure the immediate availability of Guard units in time of emergency nor uniformity in the standards of their training. These three assumptions were equally pertinent to the development of plans that were soon to be used in establishing the Reserve Officers Training Corps, plans that were an integral part of the Proper Policy.[9]

[7] Report of the Chief of Staff, *War Department Annual Reports, 1913*, Vol. I, pp. 151-152.

[8] *A Statement of a Proper Military Policy for the United States*, reprinted as Appendix C to the Report of the Secretary of War, *War Department Annual Reports, 1915*, Vol. I.

[9] These staff studies of the War Colleges Division, General Staff Corps, were: (a) *Organization, Training and Mobilization of a Reserve for the Regular Army*, wcd 8106-15, Nov. 1915. (b) *Organization, Training and Mobilization of a Force of Citizen Soldiery*, wcd 7541-12, Nov. 1915. (c) *Organization, Training and Mobilization of Volunteers under the Act of April 25, 1914*, wcd 8160-25, Nov. 1915. (d) *The Recruitment of Officers in Time of Peace in the Principal Armies of Europe*, wcd 9278-1,

In many ways an ROTC program was only a feasible alternative, so far as the General Staff was concerned, to a greatly expanded military academy. It was, indeed, considered that West Point would have to be enlarged to meet officer needs under the Proper Policy but that the Congress would not agree to as large an increase in the professional officer corps as would be necessary to meet all requirements. In the consideration of other alternatives, the number of selected enlisted men who would make good officers was limited and the number of National Guard officers available for federal reserve assignments was unknown and uneven in quality. This left the colleges and universities, with the land-grant institutions as a nucleus, as the most promising source to tap. In developing its plans, the General Staff anticipated many of the major areas of conflict that have since complicated the task of the ROTC program: whether the program is fundamentally an obligation of the federal government or of the institutions of higher education; the extent to which the land-grant schools should consider military training compulsory for all male students; the status of ROTC courses in relation to other courses of instruction; and the extremely complex problem of imposing a standard course of instruction upon a highly diversified system of higher education.

In devising a Reserve Officers Training Corps, the General Staff was motivated by the same purposes that supported its concept of a *federal* reserve. There was thus an insistence that the Corps be trained under "a standard course of military instruction" under centralized direction. The need for central control was also fortified by misgivings about the lack of cooperation on the part of the educational authorities in the land-grant schools, especially prior to the War College conference in 1912. School administrators did not provide "sufficient funds for the upkeep of the military department to in-

---

Nov. 1915. (e) *Study on Educational Institutions Giving Military Training as a Source for a Supply of Officers for a National Army*, WCD 9053-121, Nov. 1915. (f) *The Standardization of Methods of Military Instruction at Schools and Colleges in the United States*, WCD 9089-8, Nov. 1915.

sure its efficiency" and failed "to allot proper time and opportunity for the work of the [military] department when getting up the college schedule." There is also little doubt that the War Department was, at the time, operating on the theory that the 1862 Act, despite the lack of clarity in the text, required all male students in the land-grant colleges to take military instruction. Indeed, a General Staff study spoke of "the evident requirement of the law for compulsory instruction."

The staff studies of the General Staff also indicated a concern that the ROTC course would probably prove attractive only to a limited number of students and that tangible incentive might have to be offered. It was thought desirable, even if it were not immediately possible, that "military scholarships" be provided by the federal government. This idea seems to have been encouraged and was, perhaps, originated by the organized agencies of the land-grant and military colleges. In point of fact, an alternative proposal for producing reserve officers through a program of subsidized education had been presented by Representative McKellar of Tennessee as early as 1913. In a bill which went so far as to pass the House Committee on Military Affairs two years later, Mr. McKellar sought to provide federal aid to build a military college in each state of the union, or, alternatively, to provide benefits to existing institutions that agreed to train and graduate one hundred reserve officers per year.[10] Early in 1915, before the General Staff had completed its own study of a proposed ROTC program, Secretary of War Garrison had recommended passage of the bill as a "commendable" method to meet "the lack of trained officers to supplant those in our small Regular Army." He indicated particular enthusiasm for the federal supervisory clauses contained in the bill, while somewhat pointedly asserting that "the absence of this effective control in the case of the land-grant institutions created by the Morrill Act of 1862 and amendments thereof have very strongly militated against their

[10] Report No. 243, House of Representatives, 64th Congress, 1st Session, *Military Training Schools.* Existing military colleges such as Norwich, the Citadel, and Virginia Military Institute enjoyed no more support from the federal government than did the land-grant institutions.

usefulness in this respect."[11] As the General Staff began to develop a different kind of officer-training program in conjunction with drawing up the "Proper Military Policy," the War Department reconsidered its position on the McKellar bill. A report of the General Staff commented on the excellence of the provisions of the McKellar bill, but suggested "that existing agencies should be used before attempting to provide new ones for training officers. . . ."[12]

The Reserve Officers Training Corps program that was presented to the Congress by the War Department and incorporated in the National Defense Act of 1916 was, therefore, essentially the program developed by the General Staff. Other parts of the General Staff plan did not fare so well. The Chairman of the House Military Affairs Committee, Representative James Hay of Virginia, did not agree with the General Staff's interpretation of the militia clause. He insisted, in the committee report, that there was "no doubt of the Constitutional authority of Congress to provide for the discipline, organization, training, and pay of the militia. . . ."[13] Moreover, after receiving a concurring opinion from the Attorney General, President Wilson, who had formerly gone along with the General Staff's thinking, now switched his position and agreed with the politically wise Hay that it was possible to federalize the National Guard to the extent of controlling its peacetime training. The War Department was thus forced to accept a National Defense Act that reflected the essential compromise between the army and militia clauses found in the Constitution.

Under the Act the federal government assumed responsibility for providing equipment, training, and duty pay for the National Guard which would be held to federal standards of efficiency and liable to federal service when called. Under these conditions, the Guard was to continue to be the first

---

[11] Quoted in *ibid.*, p. 3.
[12] Hearings before the Committee on Military Affairs, House of Representatives, 64th Congress, 1st Session, *To Increase the Efficiency of the Military Establishment of the United States*, Vol. 2, p. 844.
[13] Report No. 297, House of Representatives, 64th Congress, 1st Session, *Increasing the Efficiency of the Military Establishment*, p. 3.

line of defense behind the Regular Army. But the idea of an exclusively federal reserve was not entirely lost. The Act also created an Organized Reserve Corps for which officers would largely be trained in a Reserve Officers Training Corps established in accordance with the proposals of the General Staff. While the Proper Policy was considerably watered down under the pressure of the Guard's political power, the ROTC system was accepted intact. If anything, the scope of the system was expanded, for the continuance of the Guard as a federal component provided ROTC graduates with a third possible source of commission in addition to the Regular Army and the Organized Reserve, as originally considered in General Staff planning.

3. WORLD WAR I AND THE INTERWAR YEARS

The ROTC provisions of the National Defense Act of 1916 were passed too late to allow complete preparations for many new units during the school year 1916-1917, and by the time the fall semester opened in 1917 the United States was at war. The War Department, beginning the hasty and confused mobilization that almost unbelievably was to lead to victory, was forced to recall to their contingents all active officers then on duty with ROTC units. A number of retired officers were found to serve as ROTC instructors, but for all intents and purposes the program did not get underway until the war was over. Nevertheless, a survey of 39 of the 48 land-grant institutions where military training had been part of the curriculum before 1916 later disclosed that over 50,000 of their graduates had served in the First World War, with over 28,000 of these as officers.[14]

Whatever the Defense Act of 1916 accomplished, it had not provided the machinery that the nation was going to need to mobilize the full force of its manpower resources. Almost as soon as the Act was passed, the General Staff was sent back to

[14] Arthur J. Klein, *Survey of Land-Grant Colleges and Universities*, Office of Education Bulletin No. 9, 1930, Department of the Interior, pp. 318-319.

prepare a plan for universal military training. Briefly, the plan, as drawn up, proposed that all male citizens be called up in their nineteenth year for eleven months of continuous training. This would be followed by two training periods of two weeks each in their twentieth and twenty-first years, after which they would remain in reserve status for a stated period.[15]

It is easy to see how such a program would have affected the ROTC. All young men would have had an intensive period of military training either before they entered college or after their freshman year. It would have thus been difficult to sustain a compulsory program of military training in institutions such as the land-grant schools. Any ROTC program maintained simultaneously with conscription would have been a limited program of advanced military instruction. The universal military training plan was not adopted, however, and the ROTC had not been in operation long enough to have any real effect on the organization and training of American troops in World War I.

The United States started pretty much from scratch when war was declared in 1917. Within a few weeks Congress passed the first Selective Service Act in American history, making all males from twenty-one to thirty-five subject to draft into the armed forces. The colleges and universities stood still in uncertainty as faculty members and students rushed to volunteer. Even though the minimum draft age of twenty-one continued to leave the bulk of college-age men to higher education, enrollment had dropped by about twenty percent throughout the country by the opening of the school year 1917-1918, with some colleges suffering up to a fifty percent loss.

Right after the declaration of war, the General Staff estimated that there was no time to use the colleges for the training of officers. Alternatively, the War Department opened the first of a series of officer-training camps through which most Army officers were processed. The Navy, too, trained its war-expanded officer corps at its own installations, the Naval Academy and "officer material" schools organized in the naval

[15] Senate Document No. 10, 65th Congress, 1st Session, *Universal Military Training*.

districts. Neither service had, in all their planning, provided means for harnessing the institutions of higher education to the war effort. Educators, brought to Washington by a growing sense of public duty and a growing fear of decreasing enrollments, confronted utter bureaucratic confusion in their efforts to put their facilities at the disposal of the government.

It was not until very late in the war that both the Army and the Navy opened training units in more than five hundred colleges and universities. This was the Students Army (and Navy) Training Corps. The purposes of the Corps were several: to maintain sources of technical skill which the armed services needed if the war went on; to provide additional training camps to accommodate new draftees called up after the age limit was lowered to eighteen; and, as a byproduct, to support American higher education during a period when its normal student body was lost to military demands. The results of the Corps were disastrous, however. College administrators gave over their institutions to young military officers who, for the most part, had little experience in directing large-scale activities and no appreciation for the educational process. Moreover, the war ended within months of the establishment of the Corps, which was immediately abandoned, leaving most institutions in complete chaos in the middle of the academic year. The poor relations between the services and higher education during the war undoubtedly contributed to much of the tension to which the ROTC was subjected in the following years.

Within days after the end of the war, the War Department announced that "about one hundred of the 115 [ROTC] units in existence before the war were being reestablished and that applications had been received for about 200 new units."[16] A few schools were permitted to delay dissolving their SATC units until January 1919, so that they could begin their new ROTC programs without a break. The reasons why colleges and universities asked to have ROTC units established on their campuses were undoubtedly varied. The fervor of patriotic

[16] Quoted in Parke R. Kolbe, *The Colleges in War Time and After*, New York, D. Appleton & Co., 1919, pp. 80-81.

cooperation was still very high. Also, despite the pitfalls inherent in having no advance planning and despite the general confusion of the wartime mobilization, the war had undoubtedly heightened the sense of public responsibility which had already been a developing characteristic of American higher education. Some weight must also be given to less idealistic motivations rooted in the financial pinch which had compelled many institutions to accept military training on their campuses during the war and in the chaotic situation created by the sudden disruption of federal aid the moment the war was over. In the confusion of the demobilization period, an ROTC unit seemed a source of federal support during a trying period of readjustment. By June 1919, Army ROTC units had been established in 191 colleges and universities, almost twice as many as had been operating when war was declared. A good many of these units seem, however, to have been little more than a temporary fancy, for within two years the number of participating colleges was reduced to 124 as life began to settle into its normal pattern, even on college campuses.

The net result of these developments stemming from World War I was to broaden the association of the military with higher education. Army officers assigned to ROTC duty now were posted to more institutions than previously. The majority of cadets were still in the land-grant and military colleges, where it was a familiar sight to see students drilling and where the spirit of public service was often strong enough to support military training against popular disapproval.[17] But the land-grant schools themselves were changing, growing broader in scope as their curricula developed to include the fine arts and social studies as well as practical arts and physical sciences. Units were now being operated in privately endowed colleges and universities, where the utilitarian movement in higher education had not been as widely accepted. As established in

[17] Military colleges like Norwich, the Citadel, and Virginia Military Institute were also brought into a formal relationship with the Army through the ROTC program. Although placed in a special "military college" category, they have never enjoyed any special support or privileges, but have been subject to the same regulations as wholly civilian colleges.

A BRIEF HISTORY

this period and maintained to the present day, the program was organized into two distinct parts, basic and advanced, each normally covering two years of college. Enrollment in basic ROTC was compulsory in the land-grant institutions and some of the private schools. Advanced ROTC was on a selective and completely voluntary basis, and it led to a reserve commission.

During the interwar years there developed a good deal of antagonism between military men and educators on the problem of accepting the ROTC courses as legitimate educational programs.[18] Basically, the ROTC courses had two lessons to teach, the techniques of soldiering and the obligations of citizenship, and neither was academically appealing. The first was geared to the world war training camps, where the rate and depth of instruction had been lowered to meet the abilities of men generally below accepted college caliber. The second suggested a presumption on the part of the military that they knew what obligations citizens should accept. For the officer steeped in the traditions of his country as taught at West Point, it was undoubtedly difficult to comprehend that there was a difference between indoctrination and education, between having a code of ethics thrust upon a student and allowing him to develop his own philosophy of living through inquiry and examination.

[18] Much of the discussion on how professional officers approached the ROTC program is based on a review of military publications, particularly the *Infantry Journal* and the *Journal of the United States Artillery* (later the *Coast Artillery Journal*), during the interwar period. A considerable number of articles were written on the ROTC, many of them by officers while on or shortly following tours of duty as PMST. Several studies of the Civilian Military Education Fund, a private organization set up to support the ROTC programs, are also of interest. See particularly *Orientation for ROTC Duty*, A Compilation of Experiences of Military Instructors at Educational Institutions. It is perhaps significant that this same 1934 study is today being distributed by the Corps of Engineers to officers assigned to engineering ROTC units, on the assumption that the attitudes of civilians and the problems they will encounter are still fundamentally the same. Another important study of this organization is Ralph Chesney Bishop, *A Study of the Educational Value of Military Instruction in Universities and Colleges*, Pamphlet No. 28, Office of Education, U.S. Department of the Interior, Washington: GPO, 1932. See also the comments of the Chief of Staff, General Douglas MacArthur, on the Bishop study in his annual report for 1934.

The military were, in fact, suggesting, during the early Twenties, the imposition of military ethics on American higher education. Indeed, the Chief of Infantry seemed exceptionally pleased to note in 1923 that the ROTC instructors "bring to bear at numerous points of contact, the ethical influence of Army traditions and ideals." It is doubtful that many educators approved. For example, that same year Abraham Flexner, then secretary of the Carnegie Foundation for the Advancement of Teaching, wrote that "insofar as training for citizenship or training in character is concerned, the present disorganized college surely makes little or no specific instructional effort toward either." He nevertheless went on to say that he found it "difficult to conceive of college courses aiming in cold blood to train students to be good citizens."[19]

The military reaction to this difference in approach was most unfortunate. Opponents of the ROTC, and particularly active anti-ROTC demonstrators and pacifist sympathizers, were accused of being manipulated by Bolshevik conspirators if they were not Bolsheviks themselves. This was especially evident in the public controversy over the issue of compulsory military training in the land-grant colleges. Although the Morrill Act was not explicit on this point, the War Department, in negotiating ROTC contracts in 1916, had stipulated that units could be opened in land-grant schools only if military training was required of all male students for at least two years. This interpretation by the War Department was generally accepted in 1916 and, later, in 1919 when the ROTC was reestablished after the war. Because of the compulsory feature, the student agitation against ROTC was particularly strong in the land-grant schools. Indeed, in the case of the University of Wisconsin, feeling grew so strong that, in 1923, the state legislature voted that ROTC be put on an elective basis. The War Department did not choose to contest the decision but continued to maintain the unit at the university, even though the enrollment began to fall until by 1927 it had dropped to 648 from the high of 1,528 in 1922.

[19] Abraham Flexner, *A Modern College and A Modern School*, Garden City, N.Y., Doubleday, Page & Co., 1923, p. 70.

Despite the Wisconsin decision and the acquiescence of the War Department, no other land-grant institution followed suit immediately. Most of them continued to favor compulsory ROTC and succeeded in passing a number of resolutions through the Association of Land-Grant Colleges and Universities in support of military training. Wisconsin was the exception. Indeed, when the University of Minnesota followed the Wisconsin example in 1933, the decision was taken by the Board of Regents only after it had been reorganized by a governor elected on a maverick Farmer Labor ticket.[20]

In choosing not to contest the Wisconsin and Minnesota decisions, the War Department had thrown the burden of responsibility onto the state legislatures or the institutions themselves. Several attempts were made, nevertheless, to eliminate the compulsory feature through federal legislation, mainly under pressure from the Committee on Militarism in Education. This was a private organization founded in the mid-1920's, by a group of liberal educators and pacifists, some of Quaker belief, who sincerely considered that military training was incompatible with the ideals of peace and international cooperation that they thought should motivate the United States in its foreign policy. In 1925 the Committee published a study by Winthrop D. Lane which alleged to prove that the War Department was militarizing the youth of the country through the ROTC program without the knowledge or approval of the American people.[21] The Lane pamphlet attacked the claim that the ROTC program had educational value and warned colleges and universities that by accepting the standard curriculum they were relinquishing control over part of their teaching.

In 1926 this group was instrumental in bringing a bill to abolish compulsory military training at schools and colleges

[20] It should perhaps be noted at this point that the University of Wisconsin reverted to compulsory ROTC after World War II; ROTC continues on a voluntary basis at the University of Minnesota, however.

[21] Winthrop D. Lane, *Military Training in Schools and Colleges of the United States*, published by the Committee on Military Training, New York, 1925.

before the House Committee on Military Affairs.[22] The supporters of the bill emphasized that they were not advocating the complete abolition of the ROTC but only putting before Congress the question "whether compulsory training gives the country better defense than voluntary training." The effectiveness of their argument was, however, weakened by being put forward in the main by men who under questioning admitted that they themselves were against military training *in principle* without reference to its being voluntary or compulsory.

Although the Committee on Militarism in Education was able to boast of the support of eminent educators such as John Dewey, the organized educational associations were generally against the bill. They argued that compulsory military training was not necessarily inconsistent with the concept of public interest found in American higher education and pointed out that it was, in fact, a matter for the states or the institutions themselves to decide. The opposition to the bill that came from military-oriented groups was considerably less reasonable and was substantially predicated on the presence of a conspiracy against the best interests of the United States. A representative of the Reserve Officers Association, for example, insisted that "the purpose of the bill is entirely in accord with the declared purposes and objects of every pacifist, defeatist, socialist, and communist organization in the United States." It seemed obvious that "when that aggregation are unanimous on any question affecting the welfare of the nation, we believe the rest of us can well afford to be against that which they support."

The bill never got beyond the hearings stage. The campaign against the compulsory feature continued, however, and by the mid-1930's could point to seventeen colleges that had dropped ROTC altogether since 1921 and seven that had changed from compulsory to elective.[23] The responsibility of the states and

[22] Hearings before the Committee on Military Affairs, House of Representatives, 69th Congress, 1st Session, *Abolishment of Compulsory Military Training at Schools and Colleges.*

[23] Taken from a compilation issued by the National Council for Prevention of War, 532 17th Street, Washington, D.C. (1934?) Those colleges which had changed from compulsory to elective were: Boston University,

the land-grant institutions themselves for deciding whether or not military training should be compulsory or elective had, however, been confirmed by an opinion of the Attorney General in 1930. The opinion found that "an agricultural college which offers a proper, substantial course in military tactics complies sufficiently" with the Morrill Act "even though the students at the institutions are not compelled to take that course."[24] The position of the War Department was also upheld in the Supreme Court's ruling in the Hamilton case in 1934, involving the right of the Regents of the University of California to force conscientious objectors to take ROTC courses. The court concluded that a state could not only decide whether military training would be required, but because the training (in Justice Cardoza's concurring opinion) was "unaccompanied . . . by any pledge of military service," could also require that it be taken by students regardless of religious belief.[25]

Despite these legal obstacles, a new bill was submitted in the Senate by Senator Gerald Nye in 1936 to eliminate compulsory military training through federal action.[26] This, too, failed. The anti-ROTC opposition was, moreover, already beginning to split between liberals who, with the rise of Hitler's Nazi Germany, began to question their earlier acceptance of the strength and rightness of peace as an absolute truth, and isolationists who, even if they recognized the signs of impending disaster, were determined that the United States could and should keep out of any crisis that might erupt.

Throughout these years the military themselves and military

1926; City College of New York, 1926; University of Cincinnati, 1931; Georgetown University, 1927; University of Minnesota, 1934; Rose Polytechnical Institute, 1932; University of Wisconsin, 1923. (Minnesota and Wisconsin were land-grant institutions.)

[24] See *Federal Laws and Rulings Relating to Morrill and Supplementary Morrill Funds for Land-Grant Colleges and Universities*, Federal Security Agency, U.S. Office of Education, Pamphlet No. 91, 1940, p. 6.

[25] Hamilton et al. vs. the Regents of the University of California, 239 U.S. 245 (1934).

[26] Hearings before a Subcommittee of the Committee on Military Affairs, Senate, 74th Congress, 2nd Session, *Compulsory Military Training*.

associations had responded to the anti-ROTC campaign with warnings that the program was vital to a strong reserve and that a strong reserve was vital to the national defense. Nevertheless, the War Department found it difficult to offer really effective support to the program. Part of the difficulty lay, of course, in continual budget cuts. But beyond this, the War Department did not seem to be convinced that the ROTC product was of immediate practical use in time of emergency. In his annual report for 1930, for example, Chief of Staff Summerall was forced to conclude that "with all due acknowledgment of the splendid quality of Reserve Officers Training Corps graduates, it must be recognized that they will require a further period of training on mobilization to fit them for the performance of their duties."[27]

There is, perhaps, a direct relationship between this conclusion and the mobilization plans of the 1930's. The plans did not include the Organized Reserve units in the emergency defensive force available on mobilization day. They were, as always, based on the defense of continental United States and depended on forces in being, the Regular Army and the National Guard, as the main defensive element. Provision was made for augmenting the initial force after mobilization was undertaken, presumably implying that the Organized Reserve Corps could be trained during the emergency to be brought up to a state of combat readiness. Organized reserve units had, in fact, a difficult time in holding ROTC graduates. Unlike the National Guard, the Reserves had no political machine that could fight to insure adequate funds for training purposes. They were dependent on what part of the small military budgets the Regular Army was willing to set aside for reserve training. As a result, practical training was minimal and often dull, and correspondence courses for reserve officers took considerable free time with few compensating incentives. Moreover, local reserve officer groups were many times only social clubs for

[27] *Report of the Chief of Staff*, War Department Annual Reports, Vol. I, 1930, p. 92.

veterans of World War I and consequently unattractive to the younger ROTC-trained men.

The opportunities for active training widened, however, in 1935 with the passage of the Thomason Act. This Act provided that up to one thousand reserve officers could train with the Regular Army for one year and that fifty could be offered Regular Army commissions at the end of the training period. It was through this Act that many ROTC graduates who, by then, constituted the greater part of the reserve officers eligible for such training, came to augment the Regular Officer corps. Another opportunity for ROTC-graduated reserve officers to assume leadership responsibilities for an extended period in the 1930's was offered when the War Department took over organizational duties in connection with the Civilian Conservation Corps. Reserve officers, especially in the junior grades, were called in for active duty with the Regular Army to help administer the CCC camps.

Although the opportunity existed for ROTC graduates to join National Guard units, they do not seem to have been encouraged to do so. The Guard remained tied to local traditions, loyalties, and interests, and each division undoubtedly preferred officers who had come up through its own ranks and were part of the local scene. There was a certain pride in later remembering that "National Guard officers . . . commenced their military careers as privates and usually served quite an apprenticeship as enlisted men before being made officers. . . ." A common Guard complaint about reserve officers who had gained commissions via the ROTC route was that they "lacked the sense of round-the-clock responsibility for their men which was, as a rule, a good point among National Guard officers of like grades who had come up through the ranks and who, year after year, in summer camps and field maneuvers, had gained experience in leadership and administration. . . ."[28]

The difficulties the War Department encountered in support-

[28] *Official Proceedings*, the National Guard Association, Sixty-Sixth Annual Convention, Baltimore, Maryland, 1944, pp. 84 and 85, and p. 236, especially.

ing the ROTC program succeeded in bringing on only more difficulties in the Department's relations with higher education, particularly the land-grant schools. Year after year the Department admitted that it had cut instructional staffs below a level compatible with efficiency, and it also turned down requests for new units. It insisted, however, that it had been forced to this action because of Congressional parsimony. The Land-Grant Association began to suspect that the true cause was again military indifference to the ROTC program. Indeed, by 1936, the Association was sufficiently incensed by lack of federal support to report that "no . . . explanations, or alibis, can persuade anyone that the Army is not indifferent toward ROTC if, with the all-time high appropriations in peacetime, there is no evidence of sincere and vigorous effort to provide for ROTC."[29] In 1939, the Association threatened "to consider the possibility of no longer giving credit toward a degree for ROTC courses" unless the Department brought the "courses, in equipment and teaching personnel, more nearly up to the standards maintained in all other departments of instruction."[30]

Despite these problems, the number of ROTC graduates annually accepting reserve commissions ranged from a low of 4,838 to a high of 6,686 during the 1930's and reached 7,000 by 1941. This was undoubtedly due to a number of factors: the maintenance of the compulsory feature by almost all the land-grant institutions, the establishment of some new units, and the general increase in college enrollments in the late 1930's. The small Navy program that had been established in six institutions in 1926 under legislation passed the previous year also began to expand in the late Thirties. Two more units were added in 1938 and as the United States then moved into its prewar mobilization stage, the number of NROTC units was again increased until it reached twenty-seven. As a result, when the United States turned to the task of rearming, over 100,000 reserve officers were available for active duty with the Army and more than 2,000 with the Navy, almost all of them products

[29] Quoted in Eddy, *Colleges for Our Land and Time*, p. 165.
[30] Quoted in *ibid.*, pp. 223-224.

A BRIEF HISTORY

of the ROTC system. For all its weaknesses, inadequacies, and inconsistencies, the system provided a manpower pool that could be immediately tapped. It would, nevertheless, be wrong to conclude that the mere availability of these men made the program a success. Yet perhaps its worth need only be expressed in the words of General George Marshall: ". . . without these officers the successful rapid expansion of our Army . . . would have been impossible."[31]

4. WORLD WAR II

Planning for mobilization involved two goals during the interwar period: the organization of an initial protective force made up of the Regular Army and the National Guard; the mobilization of total manpower resources under a compulsory selective service system with the organized reserves as a nucleus for the expanded force. Under the National Defense Act of 1920, the General Staff had been authorized to "prepare plans . . . for the mobilization of the manhood of the Nation . . . in an emergency." On the basis of this authority, a Joint Army-Navy Selective Service Committee was appointed in 1926. This committee, building on the experience of the First World War, functioned continually from its inception until the passage of the Selective Service Act by the Congress in 1940. It provided the key to the organization and training of the millions of men the United States put under arms during World War II.

As written in 1940, the Selective Service Act exempted ROTC students from registering for military service. The Congress was assured by Administration witnesses during the hearings on the bill that they did not, however, comprise a preferred class since a young man of twenty-one or over who left his ROTC status for one reason or another would then have to register with his draft board immediately. Although this provision preserved the ROTC program during the initial stages of mobilization, a number of factors soon developed to hasten

[31] *The War Reports of General Marshall, General Arnold, and Admiral King,* Philadelphia and New York, J. B. Lippincott Co., 1947, p. 53.

CHART 1

Officers Commissioned through the Army and Navy Programs: 1920-1945

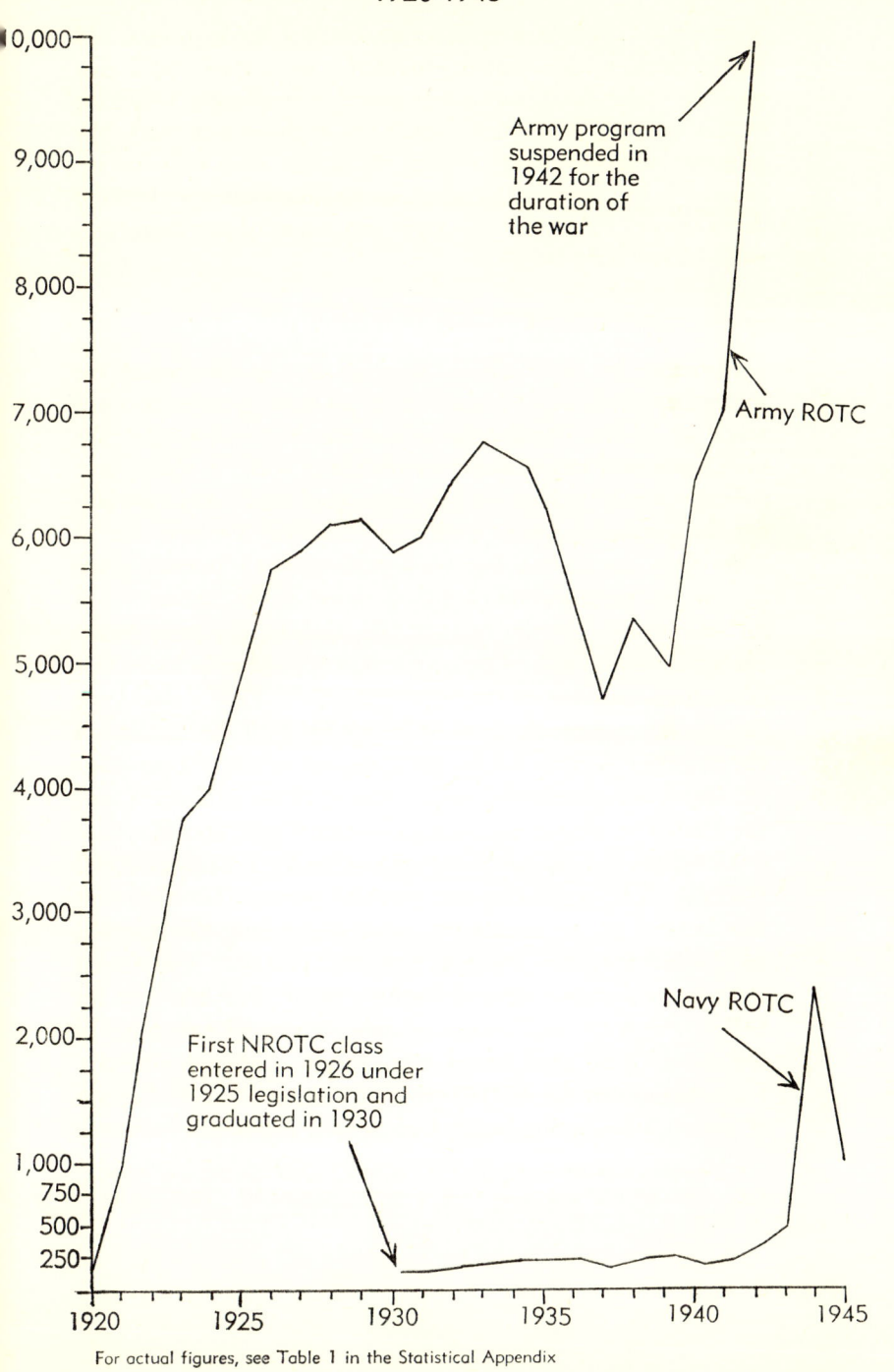

Army program suspended in 1942 for the duration of the war

Army ROTC

Navy ROTC

First NROTC class entered in 1926 under 1925 legislation and graduated in 1930

For actual figures, see Table 1 in the Statistical Appendix

A BRIEF HISTORY

the establishment of Officer Candidate Schools and the subsequent curtailment of the ROTC.

Early in the mobilization, the General Staff had vetoed proposals from within the Army to increase the number of ROTC units because of the number of Regular officers such an expansion would require. With the multitudinous duties the Army suddenly undertook in 1940, it was considered impossible to detail officers to the production of ROTC graduates with a four-year lead time. For the moment, too, the reserve of junior officers seemed ample, with over 100,000 eligible for duty as of the autumn of 1940 and 8,000 more due to be commissioned out of existing units by the following June. The officer situation seemed so favorable that the Chief of Staff, General George Marshall, had to establish the Officer Candidate Schools (OCS) over the objections of many of his senior staff. Marshall was concerned not only with creating a method of producing officers quickly but also with the high disciplinary value of training in the ranks and with the broad objective that commissioning from the ranks would increase the popularity of the Selective Service Act.

Despite the officer reserves and the new Officer Candidate Schools, an impending officer shortage faced the Army by mid-1942, so rapid was the mobilization after Pearl Harbor. ROTC students over twenty-one (the minimum draft age at the time) still remained a deferred class, and requests reached the War Department to expand the program as a method of meeting the shortage. Two factors principally argued against such a plan. First the needs were too immediate and the ROTC program too slow for wartime emergencies. Second, the Army Ground Forces, with the experience of seven months of actual combat conditions, now concluded that OCS graduates with similar education were more valuable than recent products of the ROTC. AGF mainly contended that three months of intensive training under war conditions were far superior to the full ROTC course.[32]

[32] Robert R. Palmer, Bell J. Wiley, and William R. Yeast, *The Procurement and Training of Ground Combat Troops*, Historical Div., Department of the Army, Washington, 1948, pp. 94-95.

Within several months, by November 1942, the draft age was lowered to eighteen and the major contribution of the ROTC to the wartime mobilization came to an end. To have maintained a full ROTC program with ROTC students in deferred status would, in fact, have created a stockpile of the best young talent in the country. This could not be done when the OCS was being geared to meet the officer requirements and the branches of the service were in desperate need of intelligent young men in enlisted-man status. The ROTC was, therefore, to all intents and purposes abolished for the duration of the war. Only the basic course was retained, but there were few students to enroll. Under political pressure, the War Department was forced to provide the opportunity for officer training to students who had already entered advanced ROTC training. Students who were to complete their college requirements by June 1943 and, under the wartime accelerated program, by the following September, were allowed to stay in college and then sent to OCS on graduation. By the time they were commissioned, the basic officer needs in the combat arms, particularly, had been met and replacement machinery was working through the OCS. They thus largely contributed only in creating an officer surplus.

The wartime experience of the ROTC demonstrated the complexity of adjusting an officer procurement program with a relatively long lead time to a rapidly fluctuating bill of manpower requirements. Only an OCS in which the supply of candidates could be increased on a moment's notice or turned down almost as quickly met the spectacular speed of mobilization from Pearl Harbor until mid-1943 and the leveling of officer requirements after that. But beyond this time factor there was the conclusion of the Army Ground Forces that three months of intensive training could produce a better combat leader than four years of ROTC courses. Did this mean that what was required was not an elaborate system of training imposed upon American higher education, but only a method whereby a substantial number of college-educated young men would be immediately available to the armed services in an emergency? The essential contribution of the ROTC lay in the availability of 100,000 reserve officers who, even if they required a period of training to reach a state of combat readiness, did not have to be enlisted under the emergency conditions of wartime mobilization.

The curtailment of the ROTC and the reduction of the draft age to eighteen, brought the colleges and universities closer toward the drying-up that had been threatening ever since the Selective Service Act had been passed in 1940. The situation was more hopeful than it had been in 1917-1918, for this time selective service had been in operation for over a year before the actual declaration of war and agencies for harnessing higher education to the war effort already were organized. Shortly after Pearl Harbor, for example, Samuel P. Capen had pointed to the differences between the status of institutions of higher education then and what he remembered to have been the case in 1917: "We have now . . . the American Council on Education, which represents us all; and we have a fortified Office of Education which is something more than a reporting agency, as it was in 1917, and which has direct and clear channels to the other operating agencies of the government. We have a roster of scientific personnel already more complete than anything we ever had during the whole course of the last war. We have a splendid organization of the research program of the government. And we have also a Selective Service System which is a year and a quarter old, which is a going concern and not something improvised on the spur of the moment, and which recognizes the necessity of providing through deferments for the complete preparation of skilled specialists."[33]

High among the purposes of educators was a determination that the experience with the Student Army Training Corps of World War I should not be repeated. Shortly after selective service began to operate, the American Council on Education had sponsored the first of a series of wartime conferences in

[33] Samuel P. Capen, "The Experiences of Higher Education in 1917-1918," in American Council on Education Studies, Series I, No. 16, *Higher Education and the War*, Washington, D.C., February 1942, p. 22.

which this determination was given positive expression.[34] While the facilities of higher education were offered to the government, the hope was expressed that a "sane balance" be maintained "between immediate and long-range defense needs." The burning questions were, of course: What is a "sane balance"? and How can it be rationally determined? A reply supposed more accurate an assessment of future military manpower needs than, unfortunately, the Army particularly ever achieved. Moreover, the development of the war into a total conflict, the purpose of which became the unconditional and uncompromising surrender of the enemy, soon dropped the priority of "long-range needs" far below that of "immediate needs."

The problem which had to be solved was really what part of the manpower pool should be left in a training status in order to insure a steady flow of skilled talent into the military services and industry for so long as the war lasted. Unfortunately, the record of this early conference does not indicate that many educators assessed the situation as realistically as this. Those representing the large private and municipal universities expressed the view that "the educational and scientific preparedness which colleges and universities supply is an indispensable part of national preparedness"; those from liberal arts colleges stressed that "in this crisis the emphasis on intellectual and moral training for civil life should be greatly increased"; and those from teachers' colleges suggested "that the recognition of the more immediate and emergency aspects or phases of the present situation, while real, will not require or indeed permit any serious impairment of the sound and substantial programs of teacher education now under way." Taken in sum, these interpretations of what was important added up to leaving higher education virtually intact. This, of course, was impossible.

Although civilian agencies had been set up to direct the allocation of total manpower resources, the crux of responsi-

[34] American Council on Education Studies, Series I, No. 13, *Organizing Higher Education for National Defense*, Washington, D.C., 1941.

A BRIEF HISTORY

bility on how the institutions of higher education could be best used in organizing and training the manpower resources of the nation lay with the armed services. If this was not evident earlier, it became unchallengeable with the announcement of the War Manpower Commission on August 19, 1942, that "all able-bodied male students are destined for the armed forces" and "the responsibility for determining the specific training for such students is a function of the Army and the Navy."[35]

Unfortunately, the Army and Navy plans were largely developed independently of each other and the Army program, by far the larger of the two, was poorly related to the actual manpower requirements of the service. It was also unfortunate that the early advice of the Department of War to educators, meeting under American Council auspices immediately after Pearl Harbor, had been both misleading and uninformative.[36] In the first place, the Army had announced that while no new ROTC units would be established, "the War Department intends to continue ROTC training as it is now functioning." This, presumably, was Army policy one month after the declaration of war when it was also acknowledged, in the same statement, that the officer candidate schools would be increased because they were "the shortest and most practical route to a commission." As has already been pointed out, a few months later the Army faced an officer shortage which, under the conditions of war, could be met only by an acceleration of the OCS and a subsequent curtailment of the ROTC. At the same time, the Army spokesman informed the educators that "the War Department believes in the continuation of the educational processes with as little disruption as possible" and "does not feel that we should temporize with the situation." Clearly, the Army was making neither a realistic projection of its own manpower requirements nor a realistic assessment of the effect of war on American higher education.

[35] Quoted in George Zook, "How the Colleges Went to War," American Academy of Political and Social Science, *The Annals*, Vol. 231, January 1944, p. 4.

[36] American Council on Education Studies, Series i, No. 16, *Higher Education and the War*, Washington, D.C., 1942.

In contrast, the Navy told educators at this same conference one month after Pearl Harbor that it needed 2,500 aviation cadets per month "with a minimum of two years of college work satisfactorily completed," 7,000 juniors and 7,000 seniors for general line and engineering duty, and an indefinite number of graduate engineers. If in meeting these requirements it was necessary to disrupt colleges and universities, then the Navy simply accepted the fact that "these are abnormal times!" and suggested that the colleges do likewise. Since these figures were estimates, the Navy spokesman further counselled the college administrators "to assume that the actual requirements may prove to be larger . . . rather than smaller."

It was, of course, possible for the Navy to assess its manpower needs more scientifically than the Army: the Navy's mission was narrower and the smaller number of men needed could largely be tied to seagoing and shore facilities in operation or under construction. Yet the differences in the nature and mission of the two services do not explain the more realistic approach taken by the Navy in understanding the effect of the war on the colleges. This very understanding and the preciseness of naval requirements made the colleges and universities come to prefer a wartime Navy program on their campuses to an Army program. With the Navy, the contribution of the institution to the war was known and satisfying and the contribution of naval students to the institution was a stable source of income not subject to sudden and unexpected change. Moreover, the Navy wisely set up its much larger wartime programs initially on the basis of the peacetime NROTC units, thus providing continuity of great benefit to its own operations and to participating colleges. Part of the Navy's good relations with higher education may be attributable to the commissioning of about two hundred educators as reserve officers and the assignment of these men to posts with Navy units on college campuses and in the Bureau of Naval Personnel.

Both the Army and Navy had established programs immediately after Pearl Harbor under which students could enlist in the reserves and then return to their colleges on inactive status in order to perfect skills which the services needed. The quotas set by the services were never filled and, in September 1942, the Army announced that reservists of draft age would have to be called to active duty whether or not they had finished their training. When the draft age was lowered, therefore, only the smaller Navy reserve programs (V-1 and V-7) remained as a source of students to reduce the impending losses. Within weeks the War and Navy Departments issued a joint statement which set out plans for new service-sponsored training programs to be established at selected colleges and universities. The Army Specialized Training Program (ASTP) was consequently established in March 1943 and the Navy V-12 program the following June.

The two programs followed different patterns. The V-12 program absorbed the students in the NROTC, V-1 and V-7 programs and was essentially geared to meet the officer needs of the service. Unlike the ASTP, which was not essentially an officer-producing program, the V-12 did not require that the students pass through a basic training course before joining the program. The ASTP, on the other hand, was fundamentally a program to develop technical skills among enlisted men to insure their continuing availability to the Army. The program was not, unfortunately, drawn up with any definite relationship to the projected manpower requirements of the Army. As a consequence, few of the students ever used the skills they managed to acquire and many lost the opportunity to go to OCS because of their ASTP duty. The needs of the infantry for intelligent, strong young men in 1944 proved so great that the Army disbanded the program prematurely in order to make the ASTP students immediately available for reassignment. General Marshall himself explained to the Secretary of War that ASTP had to be broken up because "we are no longer justified in holding 140,000 men in this training when it represents the only source from which we can obtain the required personnel, especially with a certain degree of intelligence and training...."[37]

[37] Memorandum from Chief of Staff to Secretary of War, Feb. 10,

At the height of the operation of ASTP, enrollment approached 150,000. By April 1944 most of these student-soldiers had been transferred to the combat arms. The Navy V-12 and aviation (V-5) programs continued and, the next year, provided continuity from the wartime programs to the reestablishment of the NROTC units. Their enrollment never totaled more than half the Army total and was considerably decreased by mid-1944. The Army's ASTP program had the major impact on higher education. The end of the program, together with the impending reduction in naval projects, brought the almost 250 participating institutions to the critical financial precipice over which colleges that had had no service contracts were already hovering.[38]

The relations between higher education and the War Department were thus full of misunderstandings. To a certain extent, these misunderstandings can be attributed to the inability of many college administrators, concerned with their own financial problems, to comprehend the needs of the armed services realistically. But, primarily, the poor relations stemmed from the inability of the Army to project its own manpower requirements with reasonable accuracy and foresight. All other problems, curriculum, assignments, training, were secondary and, indeed, dependent on the personnel requirements of the service. Nevertheless, the Army administered the ASTP fundamentally as a training rather than a personnel procurement program. Men were trained or, more usually, partially trained for jobs they rarely undertook. Within the Army itself opposition to the program developed as the field commands looked on the ASTP only as a means of hoarding the ablest young men in uniform. Some attempts were made to relate the training of the students to the technical needs of the Army but these were

---

1944. Quoted in *History of Training; Army Specialized Training Program to 31 Dec. 1944*, unpublished MS., Office of the Chief of Military History, Department of the Army, p. 24.

[38] The effect of the cut-back of the service programs was analyzed in Report No. 214, House of Representatives, 79th Congress, 1st Session, *Effect of Certain War Activities upon Colleges and Universities*, pp. 20-21.

not very successful and were finally frustrated by the overwhelming demands for front-line manpower in the final big push of the war in Europe. Not even an acceptance of the truth that war is wasteful could entirely explain the complete ineptness with which the program was handled.

Nevertheless the war was won and was ended. Most of the ASTP students proved themselves in battle and many earned battleground commissions and honors. It is, of course, difficult to estimate whether there was a correlation between a man's educational level and his ability to withstand the tensions of the war and apply himself with coolness under fire. It may nevertheless be observed that when the war ended most Americans had a deeper appreciation of the contribution of higher education to the national defense.

5. IN RETROSPECT

The relationship of the ROTC to the development of American military policy comes through clearly in this brief historical review. It also raises questions for the future. Can the programs respond effectively to the new development in American military policy, the change from a strategy based on a reserve citizen army to one based on professional forces-in-being? The experiences of the past still lie fresh in the minds of many military men and many educators. To military men, the availability of ROTC-trained officers is something that can be counted on. They are therefore often reluctant to consider changes that might disturb the *status quo*. The ROTC remains a stockpiling operation and it seems sufficient to them to assure *quantity*. They are also used to treating the ROTC in relation to reserve policy and there is an automatic tendency to retain problems within this framework, administratively and politically, without actually realizing that basic policy changes have affected these arrangements.

Unfortunately, most educators contribute to this tendency to retain the *status quo*. To a great extent the battles they fight with the military and the solutions they seek are more responsive to their early frustrations with the ROTC than to present military requirements. The land-grant schools bear the burdens of early military negligence. The private schools bear the scars of fighting for wartime military programs to avert empty classrooms. These are burdens and scars not easily forgotten. Nor are the fears of creeping militarism easily forgotten. No matter how realistically men of intellect and liberal views accept the need for strong armed forces, they continue to find it difficult to reconcile the authority and discipline of the military profession with the spirit of open inquiry that is essential to a free educational system. Yet it is this very reconciliation that is a key to the survival of democracy today.

CHAPTER III · CHANGING CONCEPTS IN THE POSTWAR ROTC

1. The Period of Postwar Planning
2. The Implementation of the Postwar Programs
3. The Development of the ROTC as an Active Duty Officer Procurement Program

THE ROTC programs which are the particular focus of this study largely took their present form during the postwar years from 1945 to 1950. At an early stage the programs became involved in the controversies that raged over two major issues of military policy: unification of the armed forces and universal military training. Indeed controversy still runs high and both issues have had important repercussions on how the services have developed their separate programs. A review of the five years from 1945 to the Korean conflict shows, in considerable relief, the relationship of the ROTC programs to basic elements of military policy. In each of the services the ROTC is part of a training system. Training, in turn, is related to weapons, weapons to roles and missions, and roles and missions to strategy. These relationships are at the heart of the postwar history of the ROTC.

1. *THE PERIOD OF POSTWAR PLANNING*

Planning for a postwar ROTC was carried on during most of 1944 and 1945. In both the Army and the Navy it reflected the different conceptions of the services as to their future roles in war. The War Department fell behind a move towards a single Department of the Armed Forces which would operate, in many ways, as a unified command operates in a theatre of active military operations. Oriented towards the methods and organization that were bringing the war in Europe to a victorious end, the War Department was already building its postwar military policy on the twin foundations of a unified department and a citizen army trained in peacetime through a system of universal military training. The ROTC program which fitted into this pattern was geared to the reserves, to provide the officer corps for the citizen army, rather than primarily to meet the precise and limited needs of the active duty forces. Within this framework, a variety of suggestions were developed within the War Department. Most plans eliminated the basic ROTC program for those students who had completed their UMT training and called for a two-year advanced course during the junior and senior years to provide reserve officers. The combat arms, reflecting the wartime experience, sought to provide for both UMT and an OCS-type training period after graduation from college as prerequisite for a commission. All the Army's plans for improving the quality of the program and of the product depended on UMT, however they differed in detail.

As for the Navy, the war in the Pacific had emphasized the flexibility and variety of naval power. No longer was the Navy to be confined to starving the enemy and protecting the supply lines to our own and allied forces. In the Pacific, the Navy had participated directly and destructively in the attacks upon the enemy's land forces, as well as upon his seapower. The Navy thus began to resist, at an early stage, any unification plan that would absorb its Marine forces into massive land armies under War Department direction and its naval aviation corps into a separate Department of the Air Force. In meeting the War Department's proposals for the unification of the armed services under a single department and General Staff, the Navy offered a counterproposal for a coordinated system of three separate services to maintain the identity of naval power and, it was argued, enhance flexibility in American military policy.

A BRIEF HISTORY

A special Navy board, headed by Admiral William S. Pye, thus based its study of the naval educational system on the assumption that there would be a well-defined naval service no matter what kind of unification was eventually undertaken. On the basis of this assumption the Pye Board, in July 1944, calculated that the Navy would need between 2,800 and 3,400 ensigns each year and that an enlarged Naval Academy with twice the prewar capacity would produce 1,600 ensigns against this total requirement. The Board rejected the idea of a combined service academy. The principal source from which the remaining junior officers would be obtained was a Naval Reserve Officers Training Corps in civilian colleges and universities. The NROTC would thus primarily serve as a procurement program to meet calculated manpower requirements.

Although the Navy had not as yet developed all the details of a postwar program, it was in a position to approach colleges and universities about its plans early in 1945.[1] As a first step, the Navy planned to reconvert its best V-12 units into NROTC units without interruption, even though the war was not yet over. This would allow the Navy to continue to produce officers needed so long as the war went on and, then, to begin to develop the bottom layer of the peacetime naval officer corps. The Department received authorization from the Congress in February to enroll 24,000 students in NROTC units while the wartime emergency continued, and to increase the enrollment in the NROTC from the prewar level of 7,200 to 14,000 after the war. It is clear that the Navy did not want to break off relationships with higher education as the Army had done in disbanding ASTP, but sought to build up its NROTC program as the V-12 was reduced. While the Navy was on record as favoring UMT, it considered it a desirable but not essential sifting process in the procurement of junior regular and reserve officers for the postwar fleet. It felt no compunctions in ap-

[1] Building on the basis of the Pye Report, a Navy Board under the direction of Rear Admiral James L. Holloway, Jr., later recommended a program for the postwar NROTC in a report to the Chief of Naval Operations in October 1945. The work of the Holloway Board is discussed in Section 2 of this chapter.

proaching the problem of a postwar NROTC without particular reference to the Army or other federal educational plans for veterans. As Navy witnesses insisted during hearings before a House subcommittee on appropriations in March, it was their "responsibility to seek to insure the welfare of Navy training, ... not to insure coordination with the Army and the Veterans' Administration program." Basic to the Navy position was the assertion, often to be repeated by all three services in the years to come, that "the training of a naval officer is different from the training of an Army officer" and that "the Navy necessarily must set up their own standards, which are different from the standards for training Army officers."[2]

In order to build up toward the postwar levels set up by the Pye Board, the Navy planned to establish some 50 NROTC units. This was a substantial increase over its earlier program which, until 1938, had operated on only six campuses and then been increased to 27 units by the time of Pearl Harbor. The Bureau of Naval Personnel began to circulate information on the Navy's plans for expansion as early as February and March 1945, as a preliminary step to establishing new NROTC units. In theory, the establishment of new units was, under an executive order issued in December 1942, subject to approval of a joint Army-Navy board and was supposed to cover as wide a geographical distribution as possible in order to satisfy Congressional interests. In practice, the joint board had been set up to insure a measure of interservice coordination with respect to the wartime ASTP and V-12 programs and did not, it turned out, pass on the expansion of the NROTC units. Also, the Navy's standards, both quantitative and qualitative, in fact restricted the colleges and universities eligible for an NROTC unit to the largest and best institutions in the country despite the concern given to geographical distribution.

In approaching the colleges and universities during the

[2] Testimony of Captain Arthur Adams and Rear Admiral Randall Jacobs, Hearings before a subcommittee of the Committee on Appropriations, House of Representatives, 79th Congress, 1st Session, *Navy Department Appropriation Bill for 1946*, pp. 194-195.

first half of 1945, initially through correspondence and then through the visit of a team of naval officers, the Navy emphasized the purposes and needs of its expanded program in terms that were bound to appeal to the institutions. High among the Navy's purposes were the promise to select qualified officers as instructors and the willingness to sponsor legislation that would authorize the federal government to share the expense of providing and maintaining NROTC facilities on the campuses. These promises went far in meeting the major objections of higher education to the Army's ROTC program before the war. They were particularly reassuring in early 1945 when the wartime educational programs of both services had drastically declined even though the war itself was continuing. Moreover, the adjustments that higher education would have to make when peace came were still largely speculative and a matter of unsure chance.

The prospect of a stable NROTC program on the campus as a positive and continuing source of students was thus most desirable, especially when viewed against the strong possibility that some kind of universal military training program would be enacted by the Congress at the end of the war. This was particularly noted in the study of the effect of the war on colleges and universities completed for the House Committee on Education in February 1945. One observation made was that the income from Army and Navy contracts had, during the previous school year, "accounted for 50 percent or more of the income of certain men's colleges and to a lesser degree but still of a substantial amount of the income in many coeducational institutions." The study went on to report that this source of income had considerably declined for the year 1944-1945 and "will soon be totally withdrawn except in those few institutions that *will be fortunate enough to participate in plans that the Army or Navy has for ROTC....*"[3]

The Army, however, had no plan that it was prepared to

[3] House Report No. 214, Committee on Education, House of Representatives, 79th Congress, 1st Session, *Effect of Certain War Activities upon Colleges and Universities*, pp. 20-21. (Italics added.)

propose to the colleges until the future of UMT was determined. Those institutions which had formerly had Army ROTC units and which now received information on the Navy's program hurriedly addressed inquiries to the War Department asking what the Army had to offer to meet the Navy's proposition. The problem was whether the Army could inform these institutions that they would participate in an Army program that had at least the advantages of the Navy's proposals. Otherwise, "the likelihood is that the Army will lose some of its best ROTC institutions to the Navy."[4] General Brehon Somervell, commanding Army Service Forces, pointed out in March to the Chief of Staff that "although the number of degree-granting institutions is about 1,720, only a small percentage of them have large enough student bodies to provide a source of proper candidate selection, and have the facilities, faculties, and curricula necessary to integrate academic and technical training with desirable military training."[5] Both General Somervell and Brigadier General Edward W. Smith who, as Executive for Reserve and ROTC Affairs, had direct responsibility for the program recommended that the Army reactivate the advanced course by September 1945 and that steps be taken to coordinate the postwar plans of the two services.

The possible political repercussions of the Army-Navy competition for the best colleges and universities seem to have provoked a number of members of the House Military and Naval Affairs Committees to write to the Secretary of War in early March.[6] They expressed the growing Congressional

[4] Memorandum for the Chief of Staff from Brigadier General E. W. Smith, Executive for Reserve and ROTC Affairs, Subject: *Reactivation of ROTC*, 27 March 1945, WD Br. file 326.6, DRB, TAGO. Note that the Executive for Reserve and ROTC Affairs is now identified as the Chief of Army Reserve and ROTC Affairs (CARROTC).

[5] Memorandum for the Chief of Staff from General B. Somervell, Commander ASF, Subject: *Training of Officer Personnel*, 30 March 1945, WD Br. file 326.6, DRB, TAGO.

[6] The Congressmen who signed the letter represented some of the most influential members of the committees. They were: Andrew May, Democrat of Kentucky; Sterling Cole, Republican of New York; Carl Vinson,

sentiment that coordination between the armed services was essential and suggested three factors that should govern the postwar ROTC policies of both the Army and the Navy: (1) that units be established over as wide a geographic area as possible; (2) that, wherever possible, Army and Navy units not be established at the same institutions; (3) that, wherever possible, units be established at all-male colleges only. The implications of these suggestions seem clear. Their realization would require the closest cooperation between the two services. The elimination of coeducational institutions and the restriction of a single service to any one all-male college or university might well have insured that every eligible institution in the country would, in fact, have had an ROTC or NROTC unit if it wished.

The threat to the Army's position on the campuses and the pressure of the Congressional recommendations prompted Secretary of War Stimson to write to Secretary of the Navy Forrestal on April 4. He suggested that "it is questionable whether the two services should compete for institutions" and that a conference be arranged "to agree upon certain principles as between the two Departments." Forrestal agreed and a meeting was held later that month. The Navy representatives pointed out that their postwar plans were not completely formulated and that their current activities were primarily directed to continuing their temporary wartime program on an expanded basis. On this premise, the Army posed no objections to the Navy's contacting institutions which had previously had Army ROTC units. At the same time, it was mutually acknowledged that "at such time as . . . educational institutions are to be selected for the *permanent* Army and Navy programs, it will be necessary for the two Departments to agree upon specific institutions either to be utilized jointly or separately in their respective postwar programs."[7]

Democrat of Georgia; W. G. Andrews, Democrat of New York; R. E. Thomason, Democrat of Texas; James Wadsworth, Republican of New York.

[7] Memorandum for the Record by Brigadier General Edward W. Smith,

THE POSTWAR ROTC

The distinction between the Navy's wartime and postwar officer procurement plans was not as sharp as the Army seems to have accepted. Indeed, there was a deliberate continuity in the programs which made the distinction somewhat unreal. The Navy had, in fact, continued the NROTC program as an integral part of the V-12 throughout the war although no new students were initially enrolled as NROTC trainees after the V-12 started. When all NROTC men had been graduated by March 1944, some V-12 students were transferred to NROTC status. To all intents and purposes, the two programs were the same and constituted a method whereby the Navy, in peace or war, could meet the active duty officer needs that could not be met through the Naval Academy. Also, it is difficult to imagine that either the Navy or an educational institution in which an NROTC unit was established during the war would easily consent to disrupting a mutually advantageous relationship in the future. The Navy wound up in an extremely strong position despite its agreement to consult with the Army prior to setting up units under its "postwar" program. It could get a foothold on the best campuses in the country with little chance, short of a major reduction of the anticipated peacetime officer requirements and an accompanying reduction in NROTC units, that the Army would be able to force it to give up a unit which was proving productive.

The Army was understandably anxious to get back on the campuses in order to avoid being completely frozen out by the Navy. A "transitional" program to reinstitute the prewar system was drawn up by the Executive for Reserve and ROTC Affairs to act as a stop-gap measure until the Congress had acted on the UMT bill which the Administration was preparing to present.[8] The program was justified in three ways: first, it was pointed out that the program could begin training the junior

---

Executive for Reserve and ROTC Affairs, 3 May 1945, WD Br. file 326.6, DRB, TAGO. (Italics added.)

[8] Memorandum from Brigadier General Edward W. Smith, Executive for Reserve and ROTC Affairs, Subject: *Establishment of transitional ROTC program*, 12 April 1945, WD Br. file 370.01, DRB, TAGO.

reserve officers who would be needed under the anticipated postwar UMT system; second, in awareness of the growing concern of many educators that the United States was in danger of falling behind other major nations in scientific and technical education, development, and research, it was suggested that the "transitional" program offered an opportunity to help keep talented youngsters in college and, as a byproduct, to begin to close the breach that had developed between the Army and higher education over the ASTP program; and, finally, it was clearly imperative to keep up with the Navy's expansion, especially since the Navy was including among its solicitations colleges and universities which, during the period from 1920 to 1942, had produced more than 80 percent of the ROTC graduates commissioned in the Officer Reserve Corps.

The "transitional" program was opposed by the operations and planning divisions in the War Department as a revival of the ASTP. Having disbanded the ASTP a year earlier in order to make young men of college caliber available to the combat arms, the Army was inviting criticism in suggesting that a program that would exempt such young men from service now be reinstated. Thus when the ROTC advanced course was reactivated in those colleges and universities which previously had had Army units, it was restricted to a total of 10,000 students and particularly geared to attract returning veterans. Under legislation passed by the Congress at War Department request these men, because of their prior military service, received credit for the basic, or first two-years course. They also were eligible for the ROTC allowances and summer camp pay in addition to their benefits under the GI Bill of Rights.[9]

When the war ended, both the Army and Navy were thus again prepared to conduct officer-training programs in the colleges and universities. As the first peacetime classes in four years opened in September 1945, the Army's program, deliber-

[9] See War Department Circular No. 300, October 1945, *Reactivation of Advanced Course, ROTC*; also, War Department Press Release dated October 7, 1945, *War Department Lifts Suspension of ROTC Advanced Course*.

ately termed "interim," was extended to 129 campuses, while the Navy's combined V-12/NROTC program was operating at 66 colleges and universities. Both services had by this time already developed permanent postwar programs. There was one essential difference. The Army's program was inextricably tied to the success of UMT, while the Navy's plans were deliberately designed to stand on their own if necessary. A good deal depended, from the Army's viewpoint at any rate, on what action was taken by the Congress on the problem of peacetime conscription.

2. THE IMPLEMENTATION OF THE POSTWAR PROGRAMS

With the end of the war, War Department planners approached the problem of UMT with pessimism and caution. The production of nuclear weapons, now finally known to the world, and the possibility of missiles patterned after the V-bombs that Germany had showered on Britain in the last year of the war, were neither assurance that war had become too terrible to break out again nor reason for concluding that trained manpower would not be needed in future battles. What they did mean, the Army contended, was that trained manpower would be needed as soon as hostilities began, that there would have to be well-prepared and disciplined forces in being to take retaliatory action the moment the enemy attacked. In terms of traditional military formulae in the United States, the War Department sought to achieve this goal of readiness by maintaining a relatively small but highly skilled Regular Army, a National Guard with a full complement of efficient officers in a state of immediate call, a large Organized Reserve, and a general pool of citizens who had passed through a universal military training program. It was within this framework that the Army presented its permanent postwar ROTC program during the hearings on UMT the fall after the war was over.[10]

[10] See, particularly, Hearings before the Committee on Military Affairs,

A BRIEF HISTORY

The Army planned on having two kinds of ROTC students: one who would pursue two years of advanced ROTC courses in college after having completed a year of basic military training; a second who, after several months of basic training, would be chosen for his outstanding qualifications for a military assignment and sent to college with government financial aid after agreeing to serve on active duty for a prescribed period following graduation. UMT was related to the postwar ROTC in three ways. First, UMT would provide all ROTC students with basic training off the campus, eliminating the need for sub-college training and considerably reducing the total time ROTC would take from the student's chosen course of study. Second, it would provide a testing and screening process to choose, from among UMT trainees, those young men who, possessing a good balance in technical qualifications and in positive motivation towards the military service, would later serve on active duty as junior officer instructors. Third, it would create a situation wherein all ROTC graduates could have experience in leading troops. On the latter point, it was envisaged that ROTC students whose education was not subsidized would be commissioned as reserve second lieutenants at the completion of their sophomore year and allowed to volunteer, with the incentive of full pay and allowances for the period, for active duty during the two summer vacations prior to their graduation.

The Navy, on the other hand, had proceeded on the basis of either having UMT or not. Indeed, in some respects, it seemed preferable, from the Navy's viewpoint, to have a young man go right into college in NROTC status than to spend a full year in trainee status under UMT. The broad basis of a postwar NROTC program was contained in a report prepared by a special board under Rear Admiral James L. Holloway, Jr. and approved by the Secretary of the Navy on October 30, 1945.[11] The recommendations of the Holloway Board were

---

House of Representatives, 79th Congress, 1st Session, *Universal Military Training*.

[11] See Rear Admiral James L. Holloway, Jr., "The Holloway Plan—A

based on the premise supplied by the Pye Report that the Naval Academy would produce only one half of the active duty officer requirements for the postwar Navy. During its deliberations, the Board examined and rejected a plan developed by Rear Admiral Randall Jacobs (the Jacobs-Barker plan) of appointing men to the Naval Academy after two years at a civilian institution, thus doubling the production of the Academy without enlarging its capacity. Not only would such a scheme disrupt the pattern of four years at a single undergraduate institution, but also, and perhaps most importantly, it would eliminate the tradition of the four-year pattern at the Naval Academy. The Board also rejected the idea of building a second Naval Academy on the grounds that it was not politically feasible. Basically the Board was reluctant to take any action that would weaken the esprit and discipline produced by the traditional Annapolis experience.[12]

The Holloway Board was, in fact, confronted with the task of producing more regular officers than could be produced at the Academy without losing or tempering the strong Academy-trained motivation that bound the Navy's officer corps to the service. The expansion of the NROTC to fill the officer ranks had the advantage of meeting junior officer needs with men who would not generally make a career out of the Navy but who would normally leave after two or three years of duty and go into reserve status. They would provide the Navy with

---

Summary View and Commentary," *United States Naval Institute Proceedings*, Vol. 73, No. 11, November 1947, pp. 1,293-1,303. The Board consisted of the following members: Dr. James P. Baxter, President, Williams College; Dr. Henry T. Heald, President, Illinois Institute of Technology; Captain Felix L. Johnson; Captain Charles D. Wheelock; Captain Stuart H. Ingersoll; Captain John P. W. Vest; Captain Arthur S. Adams (USN retired); Commander Charles K. Duncan; and Commander Douglas M. Swift.

[12] For a full discussion of the development of the service academies in the postwar period, see Masland and Radway, *Soldiers and Scholars*, Chapter 6. Generally, the Army and Navy sought to retain the essential character of the academy system, particularly against the movement to establish a "combined" service academy, as the best method of producing the core of career officers.

a competent and experienced reserve officer corps and, at the same time, leave advancement into the higher echelons of the Navy command almost entirely to the more highly motivated Academy-trained men.

The main features of the NROTC program recommended by the Board were twofold: first, that the Navy subsidize the education of NROTC candidates for the "regular" or active service; second, that these NROTC "regular" candidates be chosen through a system of nationwide examinations similar to those used successfully during the war in the V-12 program. As later presented to the Congress, the plan also provided for an additional ten percent (1,400) whose education would not be subsidized but who, under a "contract" with the Navy Department, would accept a reserve commission upon graduation without first entering on active duty. The remaining 14,000 students allowed under earlier legislation would, however, have their education paid for by the Navy.

There were thus two essential differences in the subsidized educational schemes developed by the Army and Navy to meet their active duty officer needs. First, the Navy adopted a system of general educational testing that did not, like the Army's plan to select candidates from among the ranks of UMT trainees, depend on Congressional approval on the explosive question of peacetime military training. Second, of great practical significance, the Navy program was designed to produce only about 1,500 ensigns per year against the Army's total requirement of 20,000. Quantitatively it presented itself as a reasonable venture in a period when the hope was high that the military budget could be lowered.

The first of these differences proved to be crucial, for with the defeat of UMT the Army had to rethink its whole scheme. It was forced to revert to an ROTC plan that was little more than a facsimile of the program that had been in operation before the war: two years of basic ROTC followed by two years of advanced courses leading to a reserve commission. A G-3 committee, under the direction of Major General James L. Bradley, reviewed the Army's curriculum and administration with educators and representatives of the various military arms and branches, their recommendations providing the basis for a *Statement of Policies Concerning the Postwar Reserve Officers Training Corps* issued by the Chief of Staff in June 1946.[13] The Committee proposed a number of adjustments to raise the quality of the curriculum and the instruction and to attract the better students into the program. It recommended that civilian educators be used in actually teaching those courses which were not technically military in essence, and that a good deal of authority be delegated to the Professor of Military Science and Tactics in order that he might adapt the program to meet the local situation and, particularly, to take advantage of the talent and facilities which could be made available by the host institution.

A number of recommendations of the Bradley Committee could not be put into operation without legislative approval. Undoubtedly challenged by the Navy's Holloway Plan, the Committee proposed that ROTC students receive the equivalent of a rations allowance during the basic course, although the Army had paid allowances only to advanced students before the war. The Committee also recommended, without specifying details, that assistance be granted to civilian institutions in providing facilities needed for ROTC units. While it was never made clear to what extent the Army should be prepared to support legislation in this field, the Army was obviously forced to move in this direction under the stimulus of the Navy's unequivocal promise to colleges and universities.

By early 1946 the two services were thus preparing to go to the Congress with separate programs. Last-moment attempts by the Army to achieve some kind of coordinated scheme on questions of emoluments, subsidization, active duty obligation, and entrance and instruction requirements failed. The Navy had already commenced to build up informal support in Congressional circles for the Holloway Plan and insisted that equality between the programs had to approach the level of

[13] *Report of G-3 Committee on Postwar ROTC Affairs*, 7 January 1946, WD Br. file 326.6, DRB, TAGO.

the Navy's proposals. The Navy pointed out that its program was directed initially towards the "regular" service rather than towards the reserves, and could therefore justify the higher per capita cost than a program that, like the Army's, was essentially a reserve program. Without UMT, the Army was in an especially weak position to justify the far greater cost that its total program would have meant had it adopted the subsidies and allowances proposed by the Navy.

The Navy, nevertheless, was forced to present the Holloway Plan to the Congress without the blessing of the Bureau of the Budget. Because the larger question of unification was still unsettled, the Bureau had returned the Holloway proposals without comment, simply stating that it was too early to decide whether they were in agreement or in conflict with the President's program. The Navy had already gone ahead with its plan; it had chosen 52 institutions in which it planned to inaugurate its new program in September 1946, and it had received authorization from the Congress to continue the V-12 program until the end of June so that there would be no break in the naval officer-producing system. Not all of the 131 colleges that had had V-12 units could be brought into the smaller postwar program. From among those schools which had participated in the wartime programs and those which had responded with interest to the Department's early solicitation, it had been possible for the Navy to choose institutions which would bring high quality talent into the program, while simultaneously insuring a general geographical distribution that would satisfy Congressional interests. Having thus arranged for the continuity of programs and encouraged if not committed the 52 institutions to the Holloway Plan, the Navy could not wait for the broader issue of unification to be settled, and proceeded to present its proposals to the Congress.[14]

While the Holloway Plan was being discussed in Congressional committees, a deliberate attempt was made by the Army

[14] See Hearings before the Committee on Naval Affairs, House of Representatives, 79th Congress, 2nd Session, *To Provide for the Training of Officers for the Naval Service, and for Other Purposes.*

to forestall its passage. Writing to the Director of the Budget, Harold D. Smith, in early March, Secretary of War Patterson suggested that legislation be developed to meet the essential reserve officer needs of both the Army and the Navy. Smith, in turn, wrote to Secretary of the Navy Forrestal, recommending that "the War and Navy Departments join in the preparation and presentation of a draft of legislation which would be equally applicable to both services."[15] As the legislative session moved towards adjournment, Forrestal, with Admiral Nimitz, Chief of Naval Operations, and their top aides, appeared before the Senate Naval Affairs Committee to urge the passage of the Holloway Plan as submitted by the Navy. When Senator Saltonstall suggested that a similar program would have to be approved for the Army, the Navy's Director of Training admitted that "the Army has expressed to the Budget a reluctance to have us proceed with this program." He emphasized, however, that the Army's opposition "is based on a misconception of the purpose of this bill" since "they seem to think that this program will only produce officers for the Reserve, which is not principally the purpose."[16]

The Navy's position on the Holloway Plan was completely consistent with the position it was taking on the unification issue. Secretary Forrestal was emphatic in opposing the bill then before the Congress to amalgamate the services into a single Department of Common Defense in which he felt the Navy would lose its identity and its proper strategic function. He especially argued that the education and training of naval officers were necessarily different from the education and training of Army officers and could not be developed or controlled under common standards. He and his associates agreed that it was both desirable and imperative that habits of cooperation and joint planning between the services be developed on the highest levels of policymaking. They nevertheless in-

[15] Memorandum from Harold D. Smith, Director, Bureau of the Budget, to Secretary of the Navy, James V. Forrestal, 15 May 1946, WD Br. file 326.6, DRB, TAGO.
[16] Hearings before the Committee on Naval Affairs, U.S. Senate, 79th Congress, 2nd Session, S 2304 (Holloway Plan), pp. 33-34.

sisted that the most effective cooperation and planning would be forthcoming from officers who were initially educated and trained in the skills and capacities of their own services.[17]

Forrestal undoubtedly realized that the Army's opposition to the Holloway Plan would at least have to be neutralized if the bill was to be signed by the President after passing the Congress. In early June, he wrote directly to Patterson asking for his views on the pending NROTC bill. Until then, the Army's comments had been transmitted through the Budget Bureau. In replying, Patterson pointed out that, with the ending of the war, it was necessary for the armed services to begin to tighten up their expenditures and provide "maximum training at minimum cost." He recalled that prior to the war "the facilities and emoluments of the Army and Navy ROTC units were established on a comparable basis" and suggested that "a coordinated plan, offering approximately equal opportunities and emoluments . . . would benefit both services." The Army's program, which provided "that 224,000 ROTC students will be enrolled annually to secure 28,000 officers," would cost more than the Congress would appropriate if the Army accepted the Holloway proposals. Patterson therefore suggested that a coordinated program be developed on the basis of the recommendations of the Bradley Committee for "an annual payment of $168 per trainee for the first two years . . . and $450 per trainee annually for the third and fourth years" with no provision for tuition. He pointed out that the Army, like the Navy, was planning to train officers for both its regular and reserve forces through the ROTC. This latter point seemed to minimize the Navy's contention that there was an essential difference in concept between the two programs.[18]

The Holloway Plan was passed by the Senate on July 20 and by the House three days later. The Army and Navy were

[17] Hearings before the Committee on Naval Affairs, U.S. Senate, 79th Congress, 2nd Session, *Unification of Armed Services*, Part I, pp. 31-55. For a full discussion of the relationship between unification and military education, see Masland and Radway, *Soldiers and Scholars*, chapter 21.

[18] Letter from Secretary of War to Secretary of Navy, 21 June 1946, WD Br. file 326.6, DRB, TAGO.

THE POSTWAR ROTC

nevertheless in almost complete disagreement on a joint approach to ROTC. The Army simply could not afford the Holloway Plan and the Navy felt anything less would not enable it to meet its postwar officer requirements. Even as the bill was on its way to the White House, Admiral Holloway met with Army representatives, seeking to gain their support for it. He indicated that its approval might well be an opening wedge which would make it easier for the Army to secure additional emoluments from the Congress under its own program. Holloway stressed that the Navy program was essentially different from the Army program. Its single objective was the procurement of officers. It was not, for example, concerned with students, such as those at land-grant schools, who took the compulsory basic course for two years and then dropped out. The Army representatives, nevertheless, disputed the assumption that the high emoluments of the Holloway proposals were necessary to meet officer requirements, even for the active forces. They pointed out that the Army's program for bringing ROTC graduates into the Regular Army under the provisions of the Thomason Act had always been oversubscribed. They also suggested that if the Navy wanted to procure officers for the regular service, it set up a procurement program separate from the ROTC and the Reserves and eliminate comparison with the Army's program. It was, of course, too late for any such change in concept, for the Congress had approved the Holloway Plan and the Navy was not willing to jeopardize the advantages to its position which this approval offered.[19]

It seems clear that there were definite pressures exerted on President Truman to veto the Navy's ROTC bill. Secretary Patterson obviously could not go along with a program which was infinitely more attractive than the Army's and which, on 49 out of 52 campuses, would be operating alongside an Army unit. It is unlikely that the Budget Bureau would have forwarded the bill to the President with a recommendation for approval without first gaining an understanding that the War

[19] Notes on *Conference on Army-Navy ROTC, 25 July, at Navy Headquarters,* 25 July 1946, WD Br. file 326.6, DRB, TAGO.

Department's needs would be reexamined. Finally, there seems also to have been opposition from influential reserve officers, in and out of Congress. They were bound to oppose a scheme that drained off the best talent and placed the Army and, ultimately, their own ranks under the handicap of losing the best of the new young officers.

Nevertheless, the President signed the bill on what seems to have been the personal and forceful intervention of Secretary Forrestal. He did, however, attach two conditions to his approval: first, the subsidized plan was to apply to only 7,000 students per year and not to the total 14,000 the Navy had intended to enroll as subsidized students; second, the Navy was to work with the War Department to develop a coordinated overall ROTC program. Both conditions were made clear in a letter Forrestal wrote to the President the day after the bill was signed: "With reference to our conversation last night regarding S. 2304, I wish to confirm our agreement. We will not take more than 7,000 in the program, this number to consist primarily of those men in the V-12 and V-5 programs and a small number of enlisted men. Further, that we will get together with the Army in working out with them a suitable ROTC program, and that no publicity will be given to this legislation. I wish to express to you my sincere thanks for your confidence in signing this important legislation."[20]

Despite these conditions, the Navy came out well ahead. It was authorized to undertake commitments which, in the case of entering freshmen, would continue for four years. Although it was too late to conduct nationwide examinations to choose candidates for the new college year, students were available in the wartime programs that had continued to operate through the end of June. With these and former enlisted men who could qualify as officer candidates, the Holloway Plan could be put into immediate operation. With limited failures, the lowered annual enrollment of 7,000 subsidized

[20] Reprinted in Hearings before the Subcommittee of the Committee on Appropriations, House of Representatives, 83rd Congress, 1st Session, *Department of the Navy Appropriations for 1954*, Part 1, p. 316.

students could still produce the requirement of 1,500 junior officers, while the enrollment of the remaining 7,000 on a non-subsidized or "contract" basis in addition to the planned 1,400 would contribute directly to the reserve program. The end purpose of the program could be accomplished even while negotiations continued with the Army on a coordinated approach.

In meeting with the Army, the Navy, as before, indicated that compromise was possible only at the level of the Holloway Plan. Great importance was attached to the support which the program was being given by educational institutions and, by implication, to the risks of losing such support if the provisions of the program were altered downward. The Navy therefore pledged its cooperation behind an Army staff plan drawn up in late October to adopt a subsidized program principally to meet its active duty needs.[21] What the staff proposed was to subsidize the education of 25,000 out of the projected total of 225,000 Army ROTC students in order to produce 5,000 junior officers yearly who would serve on active duty for two years on graduation. The remaining ROTC students would be enrolled under a program similar to that in operation before the war and would be commissioned, on graduation, into the reserves without being obliged to serve on active duty.

This partially subsidized plan seems to have been the closest the Army achieved in reaching a basis for agreement and coordination with the Navy. The position was not supported at higher echelons, however. The Chief of Staff decided that what had been agreed to by the Navy did not, in fact, amount to equality between the services since only about ten percent of the Army ROTC cadets would be on scholarship while ninety percent of the naval ROTC midshipmen would have their education subsidized. "The subsidization of ninety per-

[21] Letter from Vice Admiral Louis Denfeld, Chief of Naval Personnel to Major General W. S. Paul, Director of Personnel and Administration, 24 October 1946, and Memorandum for Lieutenant General C. P. Hall, Director of Organization and Training from Major General Edward S. Bres, Executive for Reserve and ROTC Affairs, 24 October 1946, WD Br. file 326.6, DRB, TAGO.

A BRIEF HISTORY

cent of the ROTC cadets" was not, moreover, "practical under budgetary limitations." The Army again reverted to the recommendations of the Bradley Committee and asked the Navy to "consider the amendment of the presently authorized NROTC plan to conform to the provisions of the War Department plan."[22] The Navy's reply was a foregone conclusion.

By December things had come to a point where it was virtually impossible for the Navy to carry out the directive of the President. The Navy remained steadfast in insisting that nothing less than the Holloway program could meet its needs and was determined to protect what it had. Secretary Patterson supported the Chief of Staff in arguing that only ninety percent subsidization of total ROTC enrollment would provide the Army with equality, but admitted that the cost of such a program was "beyond the anticipated budgetary limitations." Between the two stands, a situation was created in which compromise was impossible.[23] Forrestal, on behalf of the Navy, was determined that he would not go before Congress and recommend any basic change in the Holloway program. He attributed the failure to reach agreement to a fundamental "lack of full appreciation by the War Department that the Navy's new . . . program is primarily a method for the procurement and education of officers who will serve in the regular Navy, whereas Army plans . . . have been pointed primarily towards the provision of reserve officers who will serve little or no time with the regular Army except in times of emergency."[24]

The controversy between the Army and Navy now became reflected in a dispute that broke within the Army itself. Under the pressure of the continuing impasse in negotiations with the Navy, the War Department went ahead to translate the Statement of Policy adopted on the recommendation of the Bradley

[22] Letter to Chief of Naval Personnel from Lieutenant General C. P. Hall, Director of Organization and Training, 13 November 1946, WD Br. file 326.6, DRB, TAGO.

[23] Letter to Secretary of the Navy from Secretary of War, 16 December 1946, WD Br. file 326.6, DRB, TAGO.

[24] Letter to Secretary of War from Secretary of the Navy, 27 December 1946, WD Br. file 326.6, DRB, TAGO.

Committee into legislation in order to get something better than the "interim" program into operation. The Division of Personnel and Administration (G-1), however, now maintained that the Statement of Policy was no longer adequate as a guide for the Army's permanent postwar ROTC program. G-1 insisted not only that the Navy had gained a tremendous advantage over the Army in attracting the best talent with the Holloway Plan, but also that ROTC now had to become the major source for the Regular Army as well as for reserve officers. G-1 urged that the ROTC program be considered an integral part of the overall officer procurement plan and warned that worthwhile incentives had to be offered while students were taking ROTC and not at a later stage when the best students were already lost to the Navy.

A completely contrary view was taken by the Office of the Executive for Reserve and ROTC Affairs. This unit was responsible for maintaining the position of the reserves in the Department. It regarded the utilization of the ROTC to provide large numbers of active duty officers, many for the Regular Army, with considerable disfavor. The Executive for Reserve and ROTC Affairs therefore reverted to the arguments offered by the Chief of Staff in rejecting the subsidized plan concurred in by the Navy the previous October, and his views were supported at higher levels of authority. Until the period of the Korean conflict, the concept of the ROTC as essentially a reserve program prevailed in the Army against the continual opposition of G-1.[25]

The Army's bill, reflecting the "reserve" concept, was presented in the Senate late in April 1947 by Chairman Chan Gurney of the Senate Armed Services Committee after a final vain attempt on his part to achieve a coordinated Army-Navy ROTC program. Replying to Gurney's inquiry, Secretary of the Navy Forrestal repeated the argument he had previously put to Patterson that because "the term ROTC . . . is used in

[25] The above discussion on positions taken within the War Department is based on a series of memoranda in WD Br. file 326.6, DRB, TAGO for the months under review.

both programs, [the] difference in concept [between the Army and Navy] is frequently overlooked."[26] Patterson himself acknowledged that the Army would be at a disadvantage even if the pending legislation was approved. But he insisted that he did "not feel justified in requesting legislation which would increase Army ROTC benefits to parity with those authorized for the Navy, because of the extremely high cost involved." He concluded that insofar as a joint ROTC program was concerned, "I have no further solution to suggest."[27]

The Army's modest ROTC bill came up for hearing in both the Senate and the House late in the session and was principally defended by Major General Edward S. Bres, the Executive for Reserve and ROTC Affairs. Both in their testimony and in supplementary information furnished to the House Committee, General Bres and his colleagues made it clear that, in official War Department policy at that time, the provision of large numbers of active duty officers was not a primary function of the ROTC program. The Department therefore considered smaller benefits than those provided under the Navy plan to be completely adequate to meet the purpose of providing junior officers for the Organized Reserves and the National Guard, and also for the Regular Army under the provisions of the Thomason Act. The Army suggested that, in effect, there was no fundamental difference in purpose between the Army and Navy programs. The implication was, of course, that the Navy was paying a good deal more than the Army for a reserve officer.[28]

[26] Letter to Senator Gurney from Secretary of Navy, 11 March 1947, WD Br. file 326.6, DRB, TAGO.

[27] Letter to Senator Gurney from Secretary of War, 27 February 1947, WD Br. file 326.6, DRB, TAGO.

[28] In a letter to Mr. Bryce Harlow of the staff of the House Committee on Armed Services on 1 July 1947, R. M. Thurston, Chief of the Army's ROTC Branch said: "I have been informed that approximately 1,000 of each annual class of 3,000 NROTC graduates will be retained in the Regular Navy as career officers. Selection for retention will be made at the end of 15 to 24 months' active duty, which all subsidized NROTC graduates are obligated to serve. In comparison, the Army plans to assimilate, as career officers of the Regular Army, up to 2,000 ROTC graduates per year for the next ten years, and 1,100 to 1,200 annually thereafter.

Somewhat reluctantly the House Committee approved the Army bill, to enable the War Department to offer increased emoluments to advanced students and generally improve its program before the new college year opened. The Committee expressed concern at the inability of the two services to arrive at a common program and announced the intention of exploring the matter further with both the Army and the Navy in order to find a "middle ground" between their two concepts. In effect, action stopped at this point. Presented again in 1948 at the next session of Congress, the Army's proposals had to be viewed against a whole new background: an increasingly tense international situation and the assumption of new commitments by the United States in Europe and the Mediterranean under the Truman Doctrine and the Marshall Plan; the impetus to compulsory military obligation given by the growing threat of communist expansion and the report of the President's Advisory Committee on Universal Training; the establishment of a Department of Defense on the basis of three coordinated Departments of the Army, Navy, and the Air Force; and the emergence of the Air Force as a separate service and the doctrine of airpower as a touchstone for American military policy. The Army therefore requested the Congress to delay taking action on the bill until the ROTC programs of all three services could be reviewed against the broader reassessment of the role of the reserves in modern warfare being undertaken by a special committee under Assistant Secretary of the Army Gordon Gray.

3. THE DEVELOPMENT OF THE ROTC AS AN ACTIVE DUTY OFFICER PROCUREMENT PROGRAM

The deliberations of the Gray Committee on Civilian Components were held during the first six months of 1948. The Air

---

Except for individuals appointed as honor students, selection for career status will be made at the end of a 1-year 'competitive' tour of active duty with the Regular Army." (Letter available in DA Br. file 326.6, DRB, TAGO.)

Force had by now emerged as a separate service and American military policy was split in the controversy between the services over roles and missions. The strategic doctrine that had been developing in Air Force circles since 1917 now demanded a capability based on nuclear weapons and an air delivery system, and not on universal military training or a large naval building program.

To meet the demands of its doctrine, the Air Force needed more officers who were both technically qualified to handle increasingly complex equipment and adequately trained or naturally endowed to comprehend the scope of air capabilities. Except for academy graduates, the Air Force officer ranks, regular and reserve, especially at the junior and intermediary levels, were filled by men who had come into the service before and during World War II through the aviation cadet program and who rarely had college degrees. To remedy the situation, the Air Force embarked upon an ambitious program to raise the educational level of its officers. At first it advocated a combined service academy, a movement blocked by the Army and the Navy, both of which were intent on preserving their own individual academies. It then began a campaign for the establishment of a separate Air Force Academy as well as a subsidized Air Force ROTC similar to the Navy's Holloway Plan but considerably larger in numbers than the Navy program.

In 1946, while still technically under the War Department, the Air Force had already established its own ROTC units on seventy-eight campuses, but only within the modest framework within which the Army's postwar program operated. It was quick to recommend that the War Department request legislation that would extend the essential features of the Navy's subsidized plan to the Army (and, thus, to the Army Air Forces). The Air Force also suggested that provision be made for flight training under the ROTC program.[29] The provision for flight training was, in fact, included in the Army's

[29] Memorandum from Commanding General, Army Air Forces, to Legislative and Liaison Division, War Department Special Staff, 13 December 1946, WD Br. file 326, DRB, TAGO.

ROTC bill which received hearings in 1947. Like the other provisions of the bill, it was allowed to die as the Air Force prepared to present its own program to the Gray Committee.

The Gray Committee reported in June 1948.[30] At the core of its findings was the assertion that reserve forces had to be ready for immediate deployment in case of emergency. This state of preparedness could be accomplished only by the integration of the entire reserve structure under federal control and the continuous flow of pre-trained personnel, particularly officers, into the reserve components. The Committee recommended the complete amalgamation of the National Guard into the Organized Reserves, thus continuing a trend that had started with Elihu Root's reforms of 1903 and was as bitterly and successfully resisted in 1948 as it had been in 1903, 1916, and 1920. In the same vein, the Committee recommended not only a better coordination of the ROTC programs of the three services but also the elimination of the word "reserve" in the title in order to reflect the growing role of the program as part of the officer procurement system of the armed forces. Here the Gray Committee accepted the concept developed by the Navy in the postwar period, supported by the G-1 staff within the Army, and now being adopted by the Air Force in planning its expansion as a separate service.

The Army's presentation to the Gray Committee still essentially reflected the "reserve training" view of the ROTC, despite the preparation of a subsidized plan by G-1.[31] In contrast, the Navy and the Air Force both underscored the procurement nature of their ROTC programs. It was this very concept of integrating the ROTC into the officer procurement machinery

---

[30] *Reserve Forces for National Security*, Report to the Secretary of Defense by the Committee on Civilian Components, 30 June 1948. In addition to Assistant Secretary of the Army Gordon Gray, the Committee membership was: John N. Brown, Assistant Secretary of the Navy for Air; Cornelius V. Whiting, Assistant Secretary of the Air Force; Lieutenant General Raymond S. McLain, USA; Vice Admiral William M. Fechteler, USN; and Brigadier General John P. McConnell, USAF.

[31] See G-1 study dated 5 March 1948, signed by Lieutenant General W. S. Paul, Director of Personnel and Administration, DA Br. file 326.6, DRB, TAGO.

that the Gray Committee in fact favored. The Committee took the position that nothing less could provide an officer corps for the forces in being, and also insure that junior officers coming into the reserve components would have experienced the problems and responsibilities of leadership which would make them and the reserves immediately and effectively available in time of emergency.

The Committee acknowledged that the requirements of the three services, undoubtedly reflecting their different missions, "are completely different in emphasis." It nevertheless recommended that legislation be uniform for military training in civilian institutions, with provision being made for producing three categories of officers: regular, reserve, and reserve officers for extended active duty. Subsidized education would be offered to "regular" and "extended duty" candidates with each service determining the numbers it required in each category to meet its officer procurement quotas. The Committee also recommended a general improvement in the caliber of curricula and instruction and the coordination under a senior officer of the work of units of two or three services on the same campus.

The recommendations of the Gray Committee have never been translated into action, although the subsidized features have provided a basis for almost all subsequent attempts to pass new ROTC legislation. Responsibility for seeing a draft bill through the legislative machinery was delegated to the Air Force by the Secretary of Defense as early as 1949, but the bill was not positively supported by any of the services. The Army officially endorsed the bill, although the Executive for Reserve and ROTC Affairs still argued that there was no evidence to prove the need for special Holloway-type benefits to attract students into the regular or non-regular active duty forces. The Navy also went along with the draft bill but, comfortable in its prior possession of all the proposed legislation had to offer, felt no need to press the issue for fear the cost of applying the Holloway Plan to all three services might draw too much inquisitive attention toward the Navy program

THE POSTWAR ROTC

itself. The Air Force had the most to gain from the enactment of the omnibus bill, but did not press for its passage either. Practically speaking, the current economy drive soon made it evident that there was little chance of success. There was, in addition, some risk in exerting too much pressure at a time when the Air Force was putting major efforts behind the establishment of a separate Air Force Academy. Although the Air Force maintained that a subsidized AFROTC program was still essential, it therefore proceeded as an interim measure to expand its current program along the lines of the Army's operation.

The Air Force program had already been growing. From a total enrollment of 8,756 students in 78 institutions in 1946-1947, it increased to a total of 40,658 in 1948-1949 and was estimated to jump to 63,000 students in 139 institutions for the next school year. The Air Force was also now adopting a new training curriculum designed to produce a graduate who was basically qualified in a non-flying specialty, such as communications, or aircraft maintenance engineering, essential to Air Force needs. The purpose of the specialized curriculum was to attempt to produce reserve officers who, without benefit of training and practical experience from an active duty assignment, would be of immediate use to the Air Force in case of emergency. While the basic program for the first two years was to remain essentially the same as the Army's, the new advanced specialized curriculum was going to require completely separate handling and was undoubtedly bound to involve more administrative difficulties and educational questions in host institutions than previously.[32] The Air Force expansion and its deviation from the Army curriculum more than ever emphasized the differences of the programs of the services.

[32] For an explanation of the Air Force ROTC plans, see testimony of Brigadier General John R. McConnell, Deputy Special Assistant for Reserve Forces, Hearings before the subcommittee of the Committee on Appropriations, House of Representatives, 81st Congress, 1st Session, *National Military Establishment Appropriation Bill for 1950*, Part 2, Department of the Air Force, 1949, pp. 523-539.

The recommendations of the Gray Committee for greater coordination among the three programs gained little ground even though this was an internal matter that required no legislation. Early in 1949 Secretary of Defense Forrestal instructed the services to study the difficulties involved where more than one service was represented on a campus. Even as an *ad hoc* interservice committee met to take up the problem, stimulus for greater joint planning and administration throughout the educational systems of the services came from another source, the report of the task force on national security organization working under the first Hoover Commission as part of its review of the organization of the Executive Branch of the government. Referring to the ROTC, the task force pointed out that "there is urgent need for improvement in curriculum and instruction and better integration of the various ROTC systems now in use."[33] However desirable "integration" may have been, the reasons for separate programs separately administered were deep-rooted. They derived from the set of relationships mentioned at the beginning of this chapter: training related to weapons, weapons related to roles and missions, and roles and missions related to strategy. It was easier to recommend "coordination" and "integration" than to achieve them.

It is therefore not surprising that the representatives of all three services defended the thesis that the variations in desirable qualifications for officers precluded either a common curriculum or general administration. The *Statement of Joint ROTC Policies* agreed upon by the *ad hoc* committee and issued on June 21, 1949, was more a statement of good intentions than an instruction to the Army, Navy, and Air Force to work together. For example, the agreement that "the training of members of the respective ROTC programs will be conducted in common" was qualified in two ways: first, by pointing out that common training would be carried out only "when such action will

[33] *Task Force Report on National Security Organization* (Appendix G), prepared for the Commission on the Organization of the Executive Branch of the Government, January 1949, pp. 82-84.

promote economy or efficiency"; second, by concurring in joint courses only "to the full extent permitted by the ROTC curricula prescribed by the Departments of the Army, Navy, and Air Force." In effect, nothing could be accomplished unless there was a greater delegation of authority to unit commanders than actually existed.

No such delegation was made, although unit commanders were urged to cooperate with each other and with the college officials. It was, nevertheless, clear that the limits to cooperation were practically restricted by the minimum authority exercised by unit commanders and extended only to a point where the integrity and independence of each service had to be protected. Indeed, most officers, generally career men imbued with the spirit of their corps and keenly aware of the struggle for identity being waged by all three services at the very highest levels of government, were sure to be conservative in estimating how far these limits were from retaining complete independence of action.

In 1949 the ROTC programs were again reviewed, this time by the Service Academy Board, primarily established to reexamine the service academies. Here again the services presented a united front to retain distinct programs, even though there was a continued basic conceptual difference between the Army and the other services. The Military Education Panel of the Board had requested each of the services to reply to a number of specific questions.[34] High on the list were questions concerning the feasibility of establishing a common curriculum, of integrating ROTC courses with regular university offerings, and of relegating the purely military courses to summer camps and cruises. The Army, in replying, insisted that "because of the limited time which a junior reserve officer can spend on military training, due to the urgency of his business and desire to become well established as early as possible, a sound foundation of knowledge pertaining to his branch must be attained

[34] Memorandum from Lieutenant Colonel Arthur E. Boudreau, USAF, Acting Executive Secretary, Military Education Panel, *The Educational Program for the ROTC*, 31 August 1949, DA Br. file 326.6, DRB, TAGO.

prior to entering a business or professional field for his livelihood." The summer camp period was not sufficiently long to furnish an ROTC cadet all the technical training he needed to be militarily proficient. It was therefore necessary, from the point of view of producing reserve officers who would not see active duty upon graduation, to maintain an essentially military curriculum during the school year, taught by military officers; neither a common curriculum nor the integration of ROTC and regular civilian courses was possible if ROTC students were to be equipped "to perform as junior officers upon graduation."[35]

It was clear from the final report of the Service Academy Board that both the Navy and the Air Force had, likewise, recommended against compromising the single-service orientation of the ROTC curriculum. The rationale accepted by the Board, however, reflected the Air Force-Navy officer-procurement concept of the program more than the Army reserve concept. The Board suggested that the Navy purpose "to produce regular naval officers" and the needs of the Army and the Air Force "for a large number of non-regular officers on active duty dictate that the ROTC students be graduated as specialists in various fields to insure their immediate availability for use in their specialities." The Board went further in rejecting the Army's basis even though it came to similar conclusions. It speculated that "when conditions revert to those of normal peacetime and when there is *no longer a need for large numbers of reserve officers on active duty*, the ROTC curricula should be revised to provide the prospective ROTC graduate with a more general education rather than training in a speciality."[36]

In recommending that three separate ROTC programs and curricula be retained, the Service Academy Board was con-

[35] Memorandum for the Executive Secretary of the Military Education Panel of the Service Academy Board, *The Educational Program for the ROTC*, from Major General Clift Andrus, Director of Organization and Training, 11 October 1949, DA Br. file 326.6, DRB, TAGO.

[36] *A Report and Recommendation to the Secretary of Defense by the Service Academy Board*, January 1950. (Italics added.)

sistent with its recommendation to maintain separate service academies and proceed with the establishment of an Air Force Academy. It was evident that the Board, at least as a temporary measure, viewed the programs as part of the procurement operation for active duty officers, both regular and reserve. The Board endorsed almost without change the recommendation of the Gray Committee that ROTC students who agreed to serve on active duty upon graduation as either regular or reserve officers, should receive "tuition, fees, books, uniforms, and training equipment, together with an emolument of perhaps $25 per month." Also, while its Military Education Panel had indicated general approval of the Statement of Joint ROTC Policies, the Board seemed to recognize the essential weakness in the prevailing system of coordination between the services themselves and between the services and the educational institutions. In what seems to have been a criticism of the Army particularly, it suggested that control of the program be centralized within each service in order to simplify coordination at the policy-making level. It also suggested that greater authority be granted to unit commanders in matters of course credit, content, and instruction to enable them to solve their problems effectively in conjunction with the college authorities. Like the recommendations of the Gray Committee, the recommendations of the Service Academy Board remain unfulfilled.

By early 1950, the ROTC programs were thus conceived as active duty programs of three coequal and coordinate services. The colleges and universities had played little part in the impending development of the ROTC from a reserve to an active duty program. The change in program concept, however, came at a time when there was developing a parallel change in the pattern of relationships between the ROTC and higher education. The World War II experience and the establishment after the war of new naval and Air Force units as well as additional Army units had extended ROTC to include institutions, many of them private, that had not formerly been in the programs. The land-grant institutions were sensitive to this change, which was so much more distinct than in

A BRIEF HISTORY

the period after World War I. Indeed, the President of the Land-Grant Association noted, with some regret, late in 1948 that "the Land-Grant priority for peacetime officer training for the national defense was washed out by World War II—and the development of new naval and air force ROTC programs, widely spread in colleges the country over—has erased the Land-Grant identity, so conscientiously maintained, so proudly cherished, and defended with such difficulty against powerful pacifist protests before the war."[37]

By mid-1950, a total of 231 institutions of higher education, in which by far the great majority of male students in the country were enrolled, participated in the various Reserve Officer Training Corps programs. Of these, 30 institutions had units representing all three services, while 78 had units representing two of the services, and the remaining 123 had but one service represented. Applications for units were, however, pending from several hundred institutions, most of them private colleges and universities. The Army had not yet approached its annual projected production target of 22,000 junior officers principally for the reserves. The Department was planning not only to stimulate increased enrollment beyond the current 100,000 students in existing units on 190 campuses, but also to establish 55 additional units within the next few years. The Air Force expansion had missed its mark, enrolling only slightly more than 47,000 students in 127 institutions for the school year 1949-1950. It was, nevertheless, continuing towards the objective of producing a revised annual total of 6,500 junior officer-specialists. Operating on 52 campuses, the Navy had almost completely filled its quota of subsidized students by enrolling 6,800 under the Holloway Plan and had also enrolled an additional 4,000 on a non-subsidized basis. At the same time, the Marine Corps also conducted a Platoon Leaders Class, an officer-candidate program entirely carried on during two

[37] Address by J. L. Morrill, President, *Proceedings of the Association of Land-Grant Colleges and Universities*, Sixty-second Annual Convention, Washington, D.C., November 9-11, 1948, p. 37.

six-week summer training periods and projected to include approximately 1,800 students for the summer of 1950.

In total, the programs involved about 160,000 students and had produced some 10,000 regular and reserve officers in 1949 in contrast to 1,364 officers graduated from the academies. Moreover, enrollments were sure to rise under the impact of the Army and Air Force plans for expansion, the decrease in college and university enrollment of World War II veterans, the subsequent increase of non-veteran students, and, especially, the threatening possibility that the provisions of the Selective Service Act which had been passed in 1948 would be used if the international situation became more tense. The outbreak of hostilities in Korea in June 1950, and the almost immediate commitment of United States forces, quickened the pace both in the expansion of the programs and in the change in concept to the production of active duty and career officers.[38]

[38] A factual résumé of the programs, including a complete listing of all participating institutions, was published in *Higher Education*, Vol. VI, No. 16, April 15, 1950.

PART THREE

CURRENT ISSUES IN THE ROTC

CHAPTER IV · THE NATURE OF CURRENT ISSUES IN THE ROTC

1. The Response to the Korean Crisis
2. Changing Officer Requirements and the Scope of the ROTC Programs
3. The Question of Federal Purpose in the ROTC

OUR HISTORICAL analysis has shown how the ROTC programs reflected a merging of two characteristic themes in American development: the belief that a nation could rely upon a citizen army in time of emergency; the conviction that institutions of higher education, particularly those which are publicly supported, owe an obligation to provide certain services to society. Until the Second World War the programs of military training in civilian institutions functioned almost exclusively for the preparation of college graduates as officers for the reserve components of the armed services, to be called up only when crisis arose. Following the war, the ROTC programs began to constitute a principal source of regular and active duty officers as well. In the introductory chapter, we saw how the personnel needs of the services, particularly the Air Force and the Navy, are changing at a faster pace than ever before under new developments in the art of warfare. They now call for officers who will pursue their careers in the military profession. Fundamental to all current problems in the ROTC, therefore, is whether the programs can adjust to meet these new requirements.

CURRENT ISSUES

1. *THE RESPONSE TO THE KOREAN CRISIS*

The outbreak of hostilities in Korea in 1950 raised old, familiar questions on college campuses: What is the deferment policy for students? What are the military and industrial needs for scientists and engineers? Will it be necessary and practical to adopt an accelerated academic schedule? Are the armed services developing training programs that will be carried out in civilian institutions? And, most pertinently, will the ROTC programs continue to be the major source of junior officers for the armed services? These questions of immediate concern have become submerged in the more fundamental changes that have occurred since 1950. The impact and nature of these changes were not, however, fully appreciated at first.

The suddenness of the attack on the Republic of Korea and the speed which effective retaliation required made it impossible for the armed services to follow the usual practice of training troops for initial deployment after mobilization. In the absence of a large pool of manpower trained in the years between 1945 and 1950, veterans of the Second World War were called back and sent overseas again to support the skeletonized American forces that had been based in the Far East and immediately deployed in Korea. Because there was no full mobilization and because the greatest part of the fighting was over in the first year, it proved possible to indulge in training programs that had a longer lead time than would have been tolerated had a larger war materialized. Under the conditions of the Korean conflict, neither the Army nor the Air Force expanded their officer candidate schools appreciably. Rather, both services prepared to increase their officer reserves through their ROTC programs, even though this source involved the long lead time of four years. The services did, however, maintain their short-term OCS systems into which ROTC students and others presumably could have been diverted if a turn in military events required more officers sooner than had been originally anticipated.

A first reaction to the Korean conflict was, therefore, expansion of the ROTC by the Army and the Air Force. The Army's new ROTC production goal of 23,200 reserve officers was only slightly higher than the level it had set (although never achieved) before 1950. By the opening of the academic year 1951-1952, the Army had increased the number of institutions participating in the program from the pre-Korea total of 190 to a new high of 228 in order to increase the chances of meeting its goal. Moreover, the Army was in an advantageous position from which to continue its expansion if it so desired, for there remained approximately 250 applications for ROTC units on file.

Likewise, during the first year of the Korean war, Air Force planning boosted the AFROTC production target from 6,500 to 27,750 commissioned officers per year. The decision of the Air Force to increase the number of AFROTC units in order to meet this goal was announced to colleges and universities in January 1951 through the Office of Education. In response, the Air Force received formal applications from 487 institutions, of which 62 were chosen for new AFROTC units, bringing the total to 187.

The rush of colleges and universities to apply for ROTC and AFROTC units cannot be explained only in terms of the shock and sudden panic that must have hit many administrators when the Korean conflict broke open. There is also some explanation in the anticipation and then the passage of the Universal Military Training and Service Act in June 1951, and in the increasing dependence of most private institutions upon tuition income. The Universal Military Training and Service Act accomplished two things; first, it extended the provisions of selective service for an additional four years in order to provide a continuing method for furnishing manpower to the armed services; second, it confirmed acceptance, for the first time in American history, of the principle of peacetime conscription and established a National Security Training Commission to recommend a plan for implementing UMT. The Act now made it eminently clear that whatever the outcome of the fighting in

Korea, there was going to continue to be a national obligation on all able-bodied young men to serve in the armed forces.

In the absence of a planned, determined relationship between the federal government and higher education, the ROTC provided the only mechanism available to most colleges and universities to insure that they would participate in a broad program for the allocation of manpower to the armed services. The importance of such participation was, moreover, emphasized by the need of private institutions to maintain enrollments to assure income and the increasing tendency to raise tuitions to meet operating expenses. Although direct government subsidy was a possible solution to increased costs, more and more demands were being put on government, thereby increasing the difficulty of seeking public support and, in the minds of many educators, hardly lessening the risk that government support would lead to government control. As an alternative, most private colleges followed a policy of increasing tuition charges, aiming ultimately toward charges that would become commensurate with actual costs of education.[1]

Despite earlier pressures, the Army and Air Force ROTC students had not been required to enter active duty upon graduation. These services largely gained ROTC trained officers on active duty through the program of "Distinguished Military Graduates" initiated in 1948 in which a number of students were recommended for and voluntarily accepted commissions in the Regular Army and Air Force. After the Korean conflict began, the impetus toward required active duty was accelerated. Under the 1951 Act, ROTC students were initially placed in a special deferment category. Upon completing their sophomore year, however, Army and Air Force ROTC cadets, as well as students under the Navy's non-subsidized "contract" program, had to agree to serve on extended active duty for two years after being commissioned in the reserves. Those who did not sign such an agreement were dropped from the programs and became subject to draft as enlisted men. Since the

[1] See Richard H. Ostheimer, *Student Charges and Financing Higher Education*, New York, Columbia University Press, 1953, especially Chapter 1.

Universal Military Training and Service Act of 1951 also confirmed the acceptance of the principle of compulsory military training in peacetime, it was evident that this basic modification of the ROTC to an active duty program would be retained. Under the terms of the Act, every able-bodied young man was to be liable for military service for eight years, of which two were to be on active duty. It would have been a disavowal of the principle of equality of obligation if an ROTC deferment were allowed to act as an exemption from service under these conditions.

Revised requirements of an expanded Air Force, especially for air crews, also began to play an influential role in the conversion of the ROTC into an active duty program. Until 1951, only a small number of AFROTC graduates entered flight training and these did so only on a voluntary basis. Most AFROTC trained reserve officers were commissioned in "non-rated" or ground operations such as aircraft maintenance, finance, or procurement. Most pilots were trained, as before, largely through the aviation cadet program. This situation continued to prevail even at the time the Air Force increased the number of AFROTC units to 187, although it was hoped that about 10,000 of the annual target of 27,750 college-trained officers would elect and qualify for flight training. Within the next year, however, the Air Force planned to expand almost twofold to 143 wings, an expansion which required an equivalent increase in flight crews. In order to meet this new requirement without reversing the trend towards a higher educational level in its officer corps, the Air Force undertook a modification of its ROTC program. The mission of the AFROTC was essentially changed from the production of non-rated reserve officers to the production of active duty pilots and navigators, as well as non-rated officers who possessed skills especially needed by the service. In many ways, this change in mission was only a culmination of an original intention, a reflection of the increasing reliance on forces-in-being to meet the Air Force concept of modern warfare.

The acceptance of the principle of peacetime military service and the pressures of emerging Air Force requirements led in the spring of 1952 to assurances being given to all three military services by the Defense Department that ROTC graduates would be required to enter on active duty on commissioning. Plans and budgets were projected on this basis and the requirement was formalized in a directive issued that summer by Mrs. Anna Rosenberg, Assistant Secretary of Defense for Manpower and Personnel. Almost concurrently, both the Army and the Air Force replaced their specialized curricula with more general courses of study. The purpose was to train broadly based junior officers who, on entering active duty, could be assigned according to current procurement needs rather than specialized training.[2] In the case of the Air Force, the former specialized curriculum had been only a compromise, an attempt to train a reserve officer to a reasonable state of immediate use in a classified specialty. Otherwise, there was the danger that, if called up in an emergency, considerable time would have to be spent in preparing him for useful duty. With active duty now required, however, specialized training could be dropped as a basis for AFROTC courses, not only in order to develop a more flexible source of potential officers, but also to devote more effort during the college experience to urge ROTC students to volunteer for flight training after commissioning.

In the case of the naval ROTC the Korean conflict did not bring about any drastic changes. In marked contrast to the other services, the Navy chose not to expand the dimensions of the programs as a source of officers but rather to turn to its fast-production officer candidate schools if the need for active duty officers increased sharply. By 1950 and 1951, moreover, the Navy was commissioning the first full classes of "regular" NROTC graduates. These regular students, who were obligated to enter on active duty, were enrolled under the legislation passed in 1946 providing an officer procurement program for the Regular Navy in addition to the Naval Academy. It

[2] The Army inaugurated its General Military Science curriculum in 59 institutions in September 1952. The Air Force did not initiate its program until the next academic year. These programs are described in Chapter VII.

will be recalled that under its terms the Navy was authorized to pay the tuition and expenses for a pre-selected group of students, limited to 7,000, who were then obliged to complete a tour of active duty of predetermined length after graduation from college. At the end of this tour these young officers could choose to remain in the Regular Navy or change to reserve status and thus strengthen the Naval Reserves. The Navy, of course, also conducted its "contract" program, totaling 8,400, which originally required no active duty service on graduation, but only acceptance of a commission in the reserves.

After the outbreak of the conflict in Korea, NROTC contract students were obligated to serve on active duty for two years after commissioning in the reserves, while the tour of the "regulars" was extended from two to three years. But these changes were only extensions of existing policy and practice and, in the case of contract students, involved active duty for less than 2,000 reserve officers per year. No new NROTC units were established beyond the existing 52. By utilizing its OCS schools as an adjustable source of additional active duty officers as needed, the Navy retained its NROTC program as a relatively small, well-stabilized operation, as it still remains.

The situation with the Army and Air Force programs, as we have seen, was quite different. By 1953 these programs were greatly altered from what they had been prior to 1950. But by this time circumstances again had changed; they were not what had been anticipated when the programs were so extensively expanded. Although neither the Army nor the Air Force was going to approach the ROTC production targets that had been projected at the beginning of the Korean war, each service anticipated approximately 15,000 ROTC graduates who would be eligible for commissioning in June 1954, the first fruits of the Korean expansion. Yet even these less-than-projected results produced more ROTC trained officers for active duty than could be assigned. The Korean war did not spread into a more general one. Almost immediately upon entering office in 1953, the new Republican Administration engaged upon a determined program to bring national expenditures down to a conservatively reasonable level and, by a greater reliance on nuclear weapons and Air Force delivery capability, to cut back the active force levels of all three services. The Navy was able to absorb the effects of the cutback on its officer strength by adjusting the production rate of its officer candidate school, which had only a four months lead time; thus, the NROTC was not affected. But the Army and the Air Force could not shut off their ROTC machinery since students had entered and obligations had been incurred in 1950, 1951, and 1952 and the end products would automatically be appearing in 1954, 1955, and 1956.

The convergence of the two tendencies—the one to expand the ROTC programs of the Army and the Air Force and the other to utilize them for the production of active duty officers—precipitated an embarrassment of riches within the context of the evolving strategic doctrine. The Army paradoxically drew a number of advantages in the long run from a loss of students to the aggressive Air Force program between 1950 and 1953. In a number of the almost one hundred institutions in which both services had units, the Army enrolled only twenty-five percent or less of the total Army/Air Force ROTC student body in the academic year opening September 1951. At first the services sought to leave responsibility for a more evenly divided distribution to the local authorities. College administrators were, however, generally reluctant to make arbitrary assignments. They were especially reluctant to interfere with the free choice of the students to indicate the service of their preference, at least without clear guidance from the service departments. An arrangement was finally agreed upon in the summer of 1952 under which both services agreed to accept no more than sixty percent of the total ROTC enrollment (excluding naval students) on any one campus. Within the 60/40 ratio, local commandants, in conjunction with institutional authorities, were left free to work out procedures that would enable the maximum number of students to be accepted by the service of their first choice.

The Army was, also, ultimately saved by the fact that it

had not officially given up the earlier concept that a primary function of the ROTC was to produce reserve officers. It could, therefore, justify a substantial requirement for reserve officers not on active duty as well as those needed for a period of active service. Nevertheless, during 1954 and early 1955, for lack of vacant assignments, ROTC graduates had to be held back for months before being called to active duty. The Army was greatly criticized for these delays by educators and industrialists because young graduates were restricted in commencing civilian careers in the interim. Suggestions to bring these young men in for short training periods and then release them to the reserves were turned down at the Defense Department level, where the principles of the original Rosenberg directive were still supported. Finally, under the provisions of the Reserve Forces Act adopted in 1955 a solution was reached: Army ROTC graduates who could not be assigned for a full tour of duty of two years could be taken on for six months' training, conducted mainly in a specialized branch school, and then released with an obligation to continue training with the organized reserves. The Air Force, on the other hand, found no such solution for the surplus of non-flying officers produced through its expanded ROTC program. In comparison to the Army, it had no reserve requirement and its efforts to force students to fly by threatening to withhold commissions and to discontinue ROTC units somewhat arbitrarily encountered political opposition which the Department could not disregard. At the same time, its action in 1953 to force the retirement of older officers to make room for the anticipated flood of AFROTC graduates was a waste of trained manpower.

The gap between manpower policy and strategic requirements began to widen after 1955, not under budgetary pressures this time but under the more lasting impact of weapons development. It now became increasingly clear that technological advances had brought new weapons and techniques which could not be fully exploited by short-term personnel. The conversion of the ROTC from a reserve to an active duty program still did not satisfy these new requirements if most young ROTC officers chose to leave the armed services at the completion of their obligated tours of duty. The Air Force felt the effects of this dilemma earliest and most directly because of the size of its overexpansion and its limited reserve requirement. Under the increasing complexity of Air Force technology, it became more and more evident that young officers were of greatest value only after two or three years of intensive training. The wholesale exodus of ROTC trained officers after short-term service required a turnover and retraining of manpower that greatly weakened Air Force capabilities. The Air Force therefore began to seek ways to narrow its ROTC enrollment down to a lean core of highly motivated cadets, many of whom could be relied on to make their careers in the service. In 1957 it took a long step in this direction by drastically limiting the number of students in non-flying categories and by requiring that graduates in both the pilot and navigator categories agree to serve on active duty for five years after commissioning. For many young men, the decision to join the AFROTC now involves a decision as to whether or not to make the Air Force a life career.

The Navy is now also moving in this direction. The period of active duty for regular students who entered college in the autumn of 1957 and thereafter has been extended from three to four years. Moreover, the active duty obligation for both regular and contract students entering the naval flight program has been raised to three and a half years following a flight training period that lasts from sixteen to eighteen months. These moves are intended to have an effect on the retention rate of regular students, which has only recently begun to rise to a desirable level. By February 1958 only 125 of the 958 commissioned graduates of the first full Holloway Plan class, the class of 1950, remained on active duty, a figure of 13.2 percent. The retention figures for later classes has been somewhat higher, reaching 285 out of 1,384 commissioned graduates, or 21.2 percent, for the class of 1954.[3] The retention rate

[3] Hearings before a Subcommittee of the Committee on Appropriations, House of Representatives, 85th Congress, 2nd Session, *Department of the*

that the Navy presently hopes it can reach and hold is 25 to 30 percent. It is clear that the new active duty requirements in both the Air Force and Navy programs are only the first in a series of actions that are shaping the programs to the needs of the services for career officers.

Since the Korean conflict the Army has made increasing use of its Distinguished Military Graduate program to bring ROTC graduates into the regular service on what is expected to be a career basis. A high figure of 968 was reached in 1952, with 696 entering under the program in 1953, 375 in 1954, 516 in 1955, 525 in 1956, and 681 in 1957. The DMG program is, in fact, producing more young officers for the Regular Army than West Point. The Army has recently taken administrative steps to facilitate the retention of ROTC graduates, both among the DMG group and reserves. Its solution of six months tours of active duty for training to take care of the surplus, moreover, is, at best, a temporary measure of as yet untried worth and not readily applicable to the other services. There are even some Army planners who question the wisdom of such short tours. They point out that ROTC graduates spend all their time in basic branch training and no time in actually leading troops. Yet under future conditions of nuclear warfare, unusual initiative and responsibilities, including the command of atomic weapons, will be delegated to the officers of even small tactical units. Under the modernization and cutback on reserve units, moreover, there will be fewer opportunities for young officers to get the necessary leadership experience with reserve components.

The shift in the ROTC programs from the production of reserve officers to the production of active duty officers, and the

---

Navy Appropriations for 1959, pp. 172-177. The Bureau of Naval Personnel has pointed out that the retention rate is actually higher because of two factors: (1) in the case of the class of 1954 a number of regular NROTC graduates did not request retention on schedule but did so later on; and (2) since 1955, 127 officers who had been regular NROTC graduates in early classes but had not requested retention later reverted to regular from reserve status under the provisions of the Navy's Augmentation Program.

prospect of a further shift to the production of career officers, have raised a myriad of issues. They are issues, however, which are of a pattern with the questions raised for the nation by the prospective change from the citizen soldier to the professional soldier as the basis for national defense. The difficulties thus far encountered in adjusting the ROTC programs to meet new requirements do not necessarily lie in the ROTC concept *per se*, but are due in large part to the propensity towards mobilization planning for general war that has pervaded American military policy. The immediate consequences have been overexpanded Army and Air Force programs. Yet these consequences do not point to mistakes of the military departments alone. The services had to be prepared for large-scale expansion if the Korean conflict had broken out into a third world war. College and university administrators also contributed their share to the confusion and uncertainty that has most recently characterized the programs. Both the military establishment and the colleges and universities have to focus their sights onto the new objectives if there is any hope that they are to be met.

2. CHANGING OFFICER REQUIREMENTS AND THE SCOPE OF THE ROTC PROGRAMS

The overexpansion of the Army and Air Force programs after the outbreak of the Korean conflict has had almost paradoxical results. In the case of the Air Force particularly, it has now resulted in more junior officers than can be trained as pilots, but fewer experienced pilots for assignment to priority units like the Strategic Air Command. The primary difficulty has not stemmed basically from the expansion itself, but rather from the objectives behind the expansion. We have noted that, in both cases, the objective was to develop a reservoir of junior reserve officers in anticipation of an all-out mobilization arising out of a major war triggered off by the Korean conflict. It was not until 1953 and 1954 that Army and Air Force strategists began to adjust their organizations to the increasing requirements for a professional career service. By this time the dam-

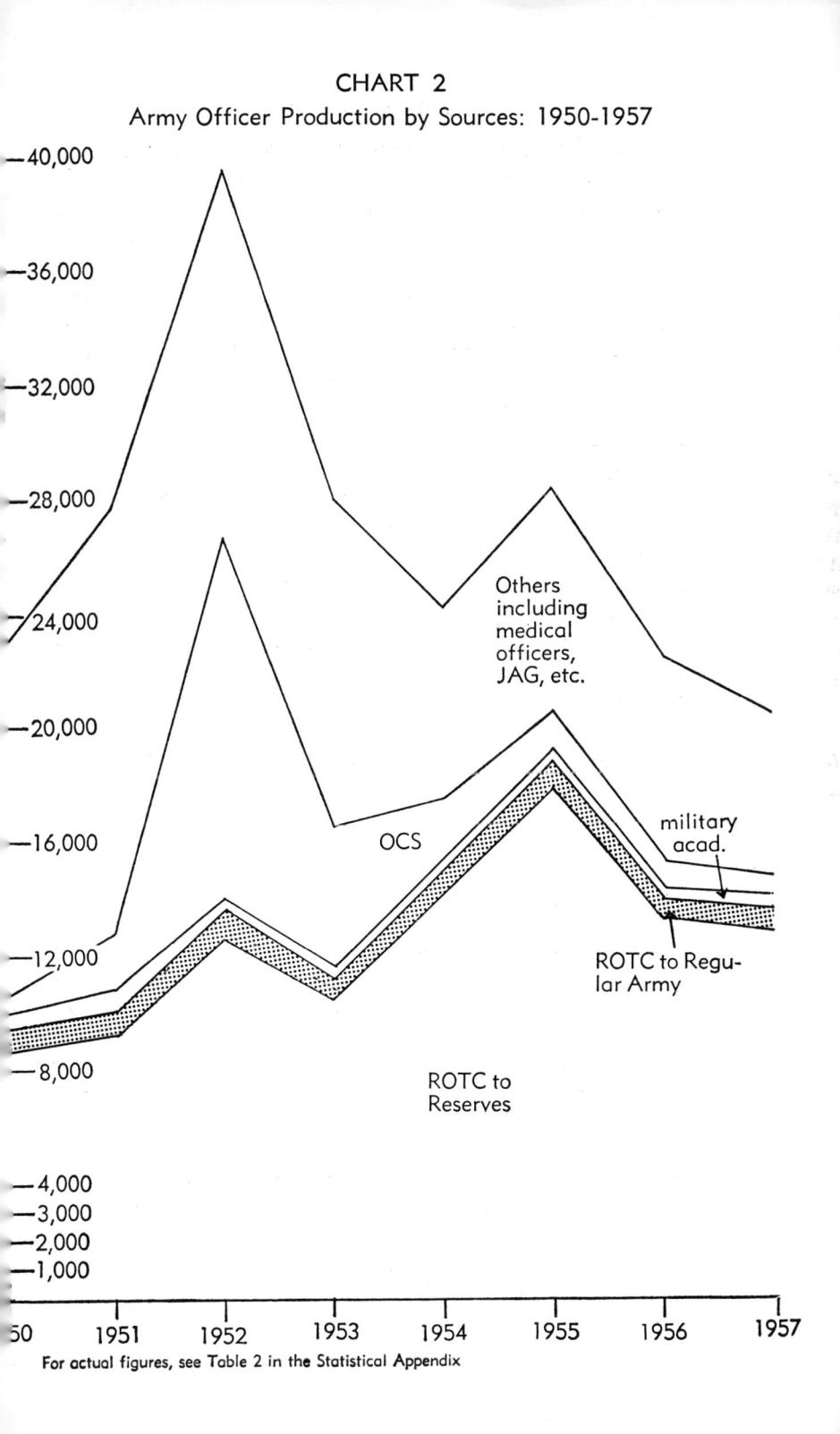

CHART 2
Army Officer Production by Sources: 1950-1957

For actual figures, see Table 2 in the Statistical Appendix

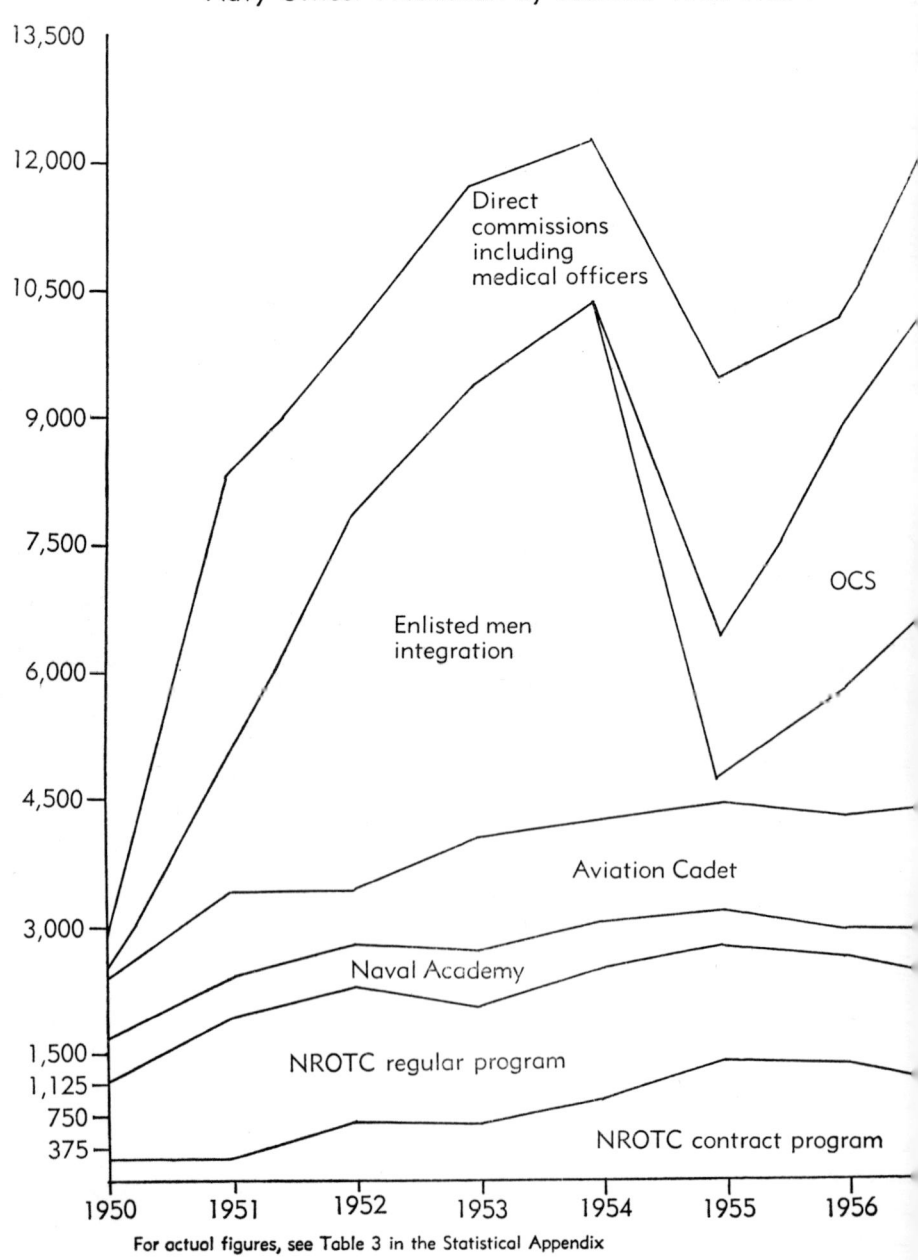

CHART 3
Navy Officer Production by Sources: 1950-1957

For actual figures, see Table 3 in the Statistical Appendix

CHART 4
Air Force Officer Production by Sources: 1953-1957

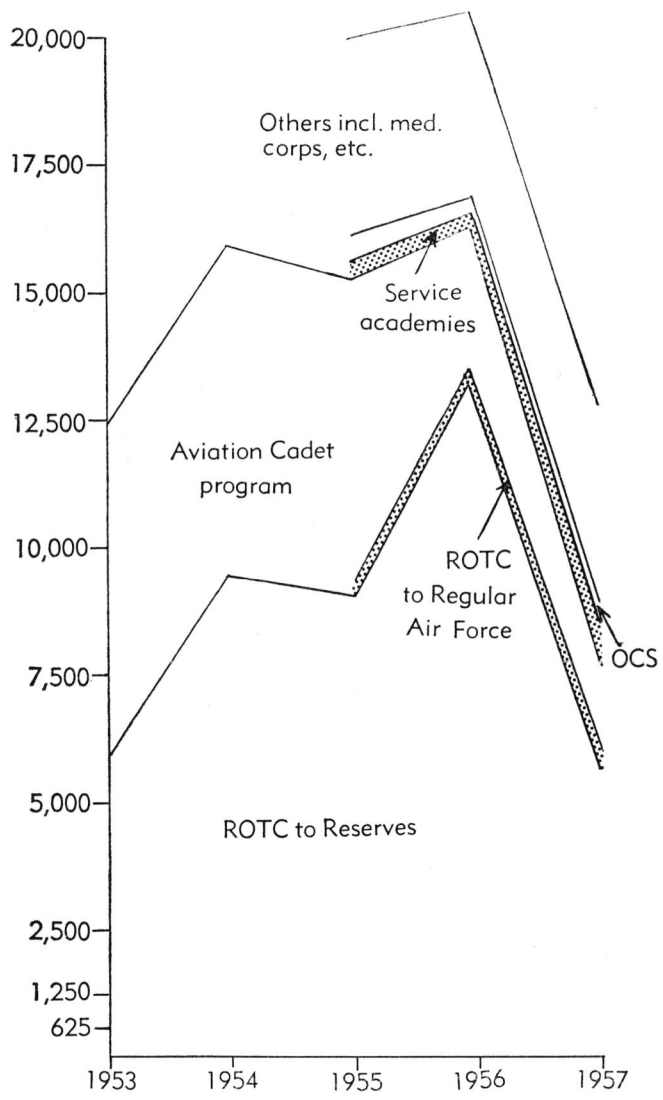

Others incl. med. corps, etc.

Service academies

Aviation Cadet program

ROTC to Regular Air Force

OCS

ROTC to Reserves

For actual figures, see Table 4 in the Statistical Appendix.
Figures were not available for the years 1950, 1951, and 1952.
Only partial figures were available for the years 1953 and 1954.

age was done insofar as the ROTC programs were concerned; for both services found that they had tied themselves down with strong commitments both to the students enrolled in the programs and to the institutions. The problem of surplus graduates could have been quickly resolved by appropriate personnel policies, but these involved breaking prior commitments to the students, and in many cases personal hardship as well. The pressure of public and Congressional opinion denies such freedom to the services. The Air Force did, in fact, withhold commissions from a number of non-rated AFROTC graduates in 1954 but was later forced to make arrangements for these men to become officers if they wished after they were on active duty.

The present situation, therefore, lies between two poor choices. On the one hand, there is the prospect of continuing surpluses from the programs despite the adjustment to more selective requirements. This remains possible because the number of participating institutions has not appreciably diminished since the Korean expansion and the total college population is continuing to rise. On the other hand, ROTC enrollments will drop off if future draft calls continue to decline or disappear altogether. Obligations such as the five years of active duty for AFROTC flight and navigation officer candidates will also tend to discourage enrollment. Should the total ROTC enrollment continue to decline while the institutional base remains as broad as it is, the result can only be smaller and, often, uneconomical units. The agreements between the services and the colleges and universities participating in their programs are clearly two-sided and cannot agreeably be discontinued without the mutual concurrence of both parties. The difficulties involved in adjusting the ROTC programs to the selective requirements of a professional officer corps have thus been increased by the reluctance of many institutions to give up ROTC or AFROTC units although they are deemed to be unproductive by the services.

The Army began to approach the problem of unproductive units in 1953 under the impending threat of budget restrictions.

In seeking to develop criteria for the retention of units in the program, it set upon a general rule-of-thumb of "100 in—25 out." This is to say, a college would be allowed to stay in the program if a minimum of 100 freshmen enrolled in the Army ROTC each year and a minimum of 25 graduates accepted commissions. The first year the college failed to meet these standards, it was to be placed on probation for one additional year, at the end of which it would be dropped if the input and output requirements were again not met. In the application of these regulations during the academic year 1953-1954, almost ten percent of the participating institutions failed to qualify by enrolling fewer than 100 freshmen.

The Army's formula, however, raised a number of complications. First, past enrollment figures also proved that in many of these institutions, fewer students dropped out of the program, once enrolled, than the general average. Second, the Army, by applying quantitative standards exclusively, was putting itself in the position of depriving itself of graduates from many institutions of high academic standing at a time when its personnel policies were being revised to attract and retain skilled and talented men in the Army. Third, despite their low initial enrollment, most of these institutions managed to produce the minimum number of commissioned graduates. It was made clear, moreover, that almost all schools wanted to retain their units. As a result, the minimum freshman enrollment of 100 was dropped as a standard for discontinuing an ROTC unit. The standard of 25 commissioned graduates was, however, retained. But this has not offered the Army a very effective method of paring its program down to the strong viable basis called for by its impending manpower demands. The Army continues to meet the problem of having more ROTC graduates than can be used in the active service by assigning them directly to reserve components after six months of active duty training. There is, however, a question how long this alternative will remain a legitimate function. Indeed, the Army indicated that it proposes to control the output of its ROTC program by setting quotas on the number of students who entered the advanced course in September 1958.

The Air Force's requirement of a five-year obligation serves as a method of cutting its program back, but it is acutely aware that this technique will eventually disclose how uneconomical the AFROTC program is so long as the institutional base is not progressively narrowed. The reluctance of the Air Force to take any positive action to discontinue units at the present time is mainly attributable to the sorry experiences of the past and to a recognition of the general instability of the AFROTC program since the Korean conflict. Only two years after greatly expanding its program in 1951 the Air Force was forced to admit that it had accepted too many colleges and enrolled too many students either in non-rated categories or with too little desire to fly. By 1955, the consequences of its hasty expansion had led it to consider cutting back the number of participating institutions. The Air Force therefore addressed a letter to the presidents of all institutions in which AFROTC units were located, advising them that it now had to consider seriously "the prudence of continuing the operation of units whose [freshman and sophomore] enrollments show limited numbers of potential flying training applicants. . . ."

This communication from the Air Force gained an almost unanimously hostile reception. The announcement in 1953 of the change in the objectives of the AFROTC program had already caused many college administrators to suspect that the Air Force might well begin to renege on the promises of fruitful collaboration meted out in 1951 and 1952. Indeed, these suspicions had seemed confirmed when the Air Force went so far as to deny commissions to non-flying AFROTC graduates in 1954. The logical explanation that the Air Force was now forced, for reasons of "sound management," to review the productivity of units against objectives that were different from those which had governed the program only three years earlier thus suffered from the prior existence of strained relationships. Despite these warning signals, the Air Force announced late in 1955 that more than twenty AFROTC units would be closed down. Moreover, this action was presumably being taken without first receiving the general agreement of the institutions that they had no quarrel with the decision. The fact of the matter was that many of the institutions disagreed and they promptly proceeded to voice their opposition to the Department of the Air Force directly and through the Congress. In consequence, Secretary Quarles promptly reversed the earlier ruling and announced that no unit would be closed unless the college desired it. In point of fact, nine AFROTC units, including those at Amherst, Columbia, Williams, and Yale, were closed on that basis. The general policy of not shutting units except with the expressed agreement of the college itself has continued to prevail.

The burden of initiative in closing down an AFROTC unit is thus being left up to the colleges and universities. With enrollments during the last two academic years having declined under the pressure of lowered draft calls and the new requirement of five years of active duty, the burden is moreover turning into a real problem. Many administrators are forced to ask themselves, in all honesty, if they are justified in keeping what seems to be an uneconomical enterprise on their campuses. It is of course questionable whether this is in fact a matter for which the colleges should bear primary responsibility. Nevertheless the private colleges which have accepted ROTC units since the Second World War generally solicited them as a measure that could be taken to maximize the continual flow of students in case of national emergency. Indeed, on the outbreak of the Korean conflict, college administrators were strong in urging that the ROTC programs be retained as the primary source of officers for the services instead of the OCS system. They accepted the expansion of the Army and Air Force programs as a hedge that would enable them to retain students even in the event of large-scale mobilization. Current military manpower requirements are, however, being shaped by new factors, new weapons, and new commitments for which a new concept of relationships between higher education and the armed services is needed. On the one hand, the colleges and universities need to demonstrate that they are prepared to accept the military profession as a proper field for which they can prepare young men. On the other, the military services need to indicate confidence in the capacity of civilian institutions to do so.

3. THE QUESTION OF FEDERAL PURPOSE IN THE ROTC

There are thus two essential steps that must be taken if the ROTC programs are to adjust effectively to meet the changing officer requirements of the armed services. First, the services themselves must clarify the objectives of the programs in the light of the changing nature of their officer requirements; second, the colleges and universities must begin to understand the changing nature of the military profession. These steps can, in turn, lead to a more rewarding relationship than presently exists. Such a relationship cannot be achieved, however, without positive direction from the national level. The diverse pattern of American higher education and the jealously guarded freedoms of institutional independence make central planning difficult, and also make it difficult for the services to know what the viewpoint of higher education is on any particular issue. Who represents higher education? The relationship of higher education to the armed services at the local level is nevertheless clearly conditioned by the direction and guidance that come from the national level. Local problems of jurisdiction, curriculum, credits, and academic time cannot be resolved within the framework of changing objectives unless these objectives are positively formulated at the national level and clearly transmitted for the guidance of the programs at the institutional level. Simple professions of mutual cooperation, no matter how sincere and necessary, are not enough.

Basic to all current issues involved in the ROTC programs, therefore, is the question whether the real federal purpose and the changing objectives of the programs are properly recognized by the national government and whether it is providing sustained and meaningful support for their achievement. One of the most persistent and practical issues is whether the federal government should provide financial support to colleges and universities for construction of armories, classrooms, offices, and other facilities used in ROTC instruction. For decades the land-grant institutions, which historically have been most closely identified with the ROTC programs, insisted that the federal government should share the costs of facilities and not force the colleges and universities to accept the complete burden. With the expansion of the programs after the Second World War and the rising costs of plant construction and maintenance, the question of financial aid for facilities has become more acute, particularly in the case of private institutions which must rely upon endowment funds, fees, and private giving to support capital expenditures. In its informal negotiations with colleges in 1945, the Navy went so far as to promise its support for legislation to meet such expenses and has continually insisted that any provisions be retroactive to cover the entire postwar period.[4] The Army, however, has had to oppose the retroactive clause or face the embarrassing and impossible charges of institutions that constructed armories and other training facilities for the ROTC prior to 1940.

The implications of the retroactive clause have been complicated by the periodic drives for economy against rising military expenditures and the feeling on the part of many officers and federal bureaucrats that ROTC facilities are a proper contribution of higher education to the national defense. They have suggested that the services are, in effect, sharing in the expenses of colleges and universities by providing instructors, texts, and other materials and equipment that contribute to the educational program, and that all of this is costly to the services, even though no direct financial payments are made to the institutions. They have also been reluctant to support financial aid

[4] Unfortunately some college and university administrators have interpreted the 1945 promise as one of financial aid rather than one of support for legislation authorizing such aid.

for facilities construction as long as the issue of unproductive units remains unsettled. While sympathetic to the position of college administrators, in a showdown they have preferred to use their funds for more pressing needs. Although numerous bills authorizing federal aid (the most recent providing contributions on a matching basis) have been introduced in the Congress, the Department of Defense endorsed none of them until 1958. The recent bill did not, however, pass review by the Budget Bureau. Of greatest concern, perhaps, is that nowhere was it considered against the changing role of the ROTC, but continued to be viewed almost exclusively as part of support for the reserve components. It consequently suffered from the low priority that reserve affairs presently hold in relation to the military budget.[5]

As the financial burdens upon institutions of higher education have increased, the unwillingness of the Department of Defense until recently to take an unequivocal stand on facilities legislation irked college and university administrators. Actually this attitude was part of a larger dissatisfaction with the general administration of the programs by the services. Part of this dissatisfaction stemmed from the instability of the Air Force program in recent years and from the difficulties involved in the shift of the Army program from being wholly a reserve program. It also stemmed from the perennial complaint of the land-grant and state institutions, and more recently from private institutions as well, that the services have often seen fit to ignore their responsibilities for the programs. Discontent with the situation has mounted as memories of the crisis thinking of the Korean war period, with its specter of depleted enrollments, have faded.

[5] A survey of ROTC facilities in 344 institutions in 1955 disclosed their total estimated value to be $192,973,757. See the Summary of Results of the ROTC Facilities Questionnaire in *The Educational Record*, July 1956, pp. 243-247. In 1957 the Department of Defense estimated that the federal government's share of the cost of new facilities, on a matching basis, as authorized in proposed legislation, would amount to approximately $100,000,000. Letter to Honorable Carl Vinson, Chairman, Committee on Armed Services, House of Representatives, from L. Niederlehner, for the General Counsel of the Department, July 31, 1957.

THEIR NATURE

During 1957 college and university administrators were irritated further by the manner in which the services responded to another issue. This concerned the value of the requirement of many institutions that all male students enroll in basic ROTC. The basic course is now required in almost two thirds of the Army and Air Force institutions at which units are located. These include all but two of the land-grant institutions, a majority of the state institutions, and slightly less than half of the private schools.[6] As the history of the ROTC has shown, it was the concept of war as a conflict between large citizen armies that gave the idea of compulsory military training practical meaning. But support of compulsory training has also stemmed from a feeling that all able-bodied males, particularly those who have had the opportunity of higher education in public institutions, have an obligation to prepare themselves for military service. Compulsory ROTC has been justified also, quite apart from its military significance, as a means of developing character, leadership, and self-discipline among students. This proposition is advanced in some private institutions, including church-affiliated schools.

With the changing nature of warfare and the requirement of the security interests of the nation for skilled manpower in fields other than military, the rationale of the first two of these arguments has lost much, if not all, of their validity. There remains the question whether character building among college students, no matter how praiseworthy, is a proper responsibility of the armed services. The land-grant institutions have continued, nevertheless, to regard their participation in the ROTC programs as part of their public service responsibilities and have generally had a more genuine identification with national defense than most private colleges and universities.

The question has arisen, however, whether compulsory military training during the first two years really contributes to the

[6] The Navy ROTC program does not participate in the compulsory dilemma because its quota, for regulars and contracts, is restricted by legislation to 15,400 at any one time. A land-grant student can, of course, fulfill the requirement of compulsory military training by joining the NROTC if a unit exists at his college.

officer production of the programs or whether it can be abolished without material damage to current objectives. As early as 1953, the Bureau of the Budget, acting exclusively from a financial viewpoint, had set numerical as well as financial ceilings which would have restricted the total number of freshmen that could be enrolled in the Army and the Air Force programs. The possible effect would have had policy repercussions, for it would have been necessary either to cut down the number of units or eliminate compulsory training. Under considerable pressure from the services as well as from the land-grant colleges, the Secretary of Defense determined that the budgetary and not the numerical ceilings were to govern. As a result, the storm passed, since the services found it possible to accept all freshmen in institutions requiring ROTC for two years and still meet expenses within available funds.[7]

In relating the compulsory issue to current program objectives, the main advantage of requiring all freshmen and sophomores to take ROTC is to widen the manpower pool from which students for the advanced course are selected. In point of fact, compulsory training offers the military departments two years in which to judge the performance and potential of the cadets and seek to persuade the best students to continue in the program. To this extent, therefore, compulsory ROTC offers a built-in method of achieving greater selectivity and would seem to be an important feature in meeting current requirements. There is, however, considerable difference of opinion on this point. On the other side of the coin, it is maintained that the idea of compulsion repels rather than attracts students towards the armed services and that the best kind of officer, especially one who is potentially a career man, will develop from young men who have volunteered for the ROTC either because they are genuinely interested or because they choose it as the most attractive alternative. Moreover, it is pointed out that the attrition rate in the compulsory institu-

[7] See, for example, the testimony of Major General Hugh M. Milton II before a subcommittee of the Committee on Appropriations, House of Representatives, 83rd Congress, 1st Session, *Department of the Army Appropriations for 1954*, pp. 438-441.

tions, both in the institutions themselves and particularly in the ROTC programs, is high, and that the services must handle a large number of disinterested freshmen and sophomores to procure a proportionately few officers.[8]

But, whatever the case, the increasing college enrollments which are predicted to jump from the present total of approximately three million students to between five and six million by 1970 are bound to present some awesome administrative problems insofar as compulsory ROTC is concerned.[9] A good percentage of the increased enrollment will undoubtedly be carried by the land-grant and state universities which presently comprise the majority of those institutions which require two years of military training.[10] Larger enrollments will, of course, mean an even broader selection base, but also a greater number of cadets in training who are not going ahead to accept commissions. Surely with the quantum jump in enrollments predicted there might well arrive a point of diminishing returns beyond which compulsory ROTC is no longer practical and certainly no longer necessary to meet modern military manpower requirements.

There is, nevertheless, a good deal of question as to who is going to take the first step in looking at the compulsory issue

[8] See the tables in the Appendix showing the number of officers commissioned by institution of origin for the years 1955-1957. A good deal of interesting data has been recently collected for the Army by a private research agency, on the attitudes of students in selected institutions, both public and private and with compulsory and voluntary programs. The findings in this study generally confirm our own observations as analyzed in this section. See *The College Student and the ROTC*, A Study of Eight Colleges, prepared for the Human Resources Research Office of the George Washington University by the Bureau of Social Science Research, Inc., Washington, D.C., September 1958.

[9] Projected enrollments by 1970 are based on the statistics developed in John D. Long, *Needed Expansion of Facilities for Higher Education—1958-1970*, American Council on Education, Washington, D.C., June 1958.

[10] Although a number of state universities that are not land-grant in origin and some private colleges also require compulsory ROTC, the arguments in favor of the compulsory feature are generally expressed by the well-organized American Association of Land-Grant Colleges and State Universities.

realistically against the shift in the primary purpose of the ROTC programs to the provision of career officers. It is agreed by all parties that the decision, under the original Land-Grant Act and all subsequent statutes and rulings, is one for the institution or state authorities and not a prerogative of the federal government. The Land-Grant Association, however, sought guidance in this area from the Department of Defense early in 1957 in asking for a policy statement "as to whether the continued requirement of basic ROTC by those institutions which maintain this requirement, is or is not valuable as a contribution to the national defense and security."[11] The implications of the question were generally two-fold. First, a considerable amount of pressure has been applied in recent years from both faculty and student levels to eliminate the burden of compulsory ROTC, especially in the light of added curriculum requirements. This pressure has not, as in the 1920's and 1930's, been a reflection of pacifist agitation. It has, on the one hand, been a genuine reaction to the impact of modern technology on warfare and the popular notion that greater firepower requires less manpower. At the same time, it has originated in an appreciation that the draft provides a sufficiently strong coercive factor to produce ROTC recruits so that compulsory military training becomes superfluous.

A second implication of this question was the growing dissatisfaction and sense of frustration with respect to the programs. It was closely tied in the minds of college administrators to the issue of federal support. Why, they asked, should we go to the large expense of constructing facilities for the ROTC if the services do not demonstrate clearly that the federal government firmly supports the programs? Can we be sure of any reasonable continuity or must we anticipate frequent alterations of policy with resulting inconvenience to our institutions and uncertainties and even broken promises to our students? Can we expect that the federal government will provide a fair

[11] Letter from President Troy Middleton, Chairman National Defense Committee, American Association of Land-Grant Colleges, to Secretary of Defense Wilson, January 28, 1957.

share of the costs of educational programs from which it derives direct benefit?

The question put to the Department of Defense by the Land-Grant Association on the compulsory issue involved, therefore, the whole concept of the ROTC, its role in the manpower planning of the services, and the relationship of the federal government to the colleges and universities. The response of the Department in May 1957 was, however, considerably less encompassing. It quite drily stated "that the question of compulsory basic ROTC is strictly a matter of institutional prerogative or State Legislature, and that no valid conclusions can be drawn as to the relative value of compulsory basic ROTC versus voluntary basic ROTC." The answer was generally based on an Army study which was attached and which, somewhat pedantically and narrowly, approached the whole problem from the legal and historical basis with little relationship to the changing manpower requirements of the service. A less thoughtful but more direct Air Force statement was also attached to the reply. In sum, the Air Force position was that compulsory ROTC contributes little to the "primary objective" of producing "officers to fill specific requirements of the active Air Force." Moreover, whatever its benefits in helping the Air Force educate "the largest number of students in air age citizenship," they are "difficult to measure." The Air Force therefore could not "justifiably support the continuance of" compulsory ROTC from the point of view of its own program and concluded that the issue "should continue to be the prerogative of the institution."[12]

The attempt of the Defense Department to avoid opening up the obviously troublesome problems concerning the Land-Grant Association did not, however, succeed. For the following October, a delegation representing the land-grant and state university groups brought the issues up before a meeting of the Armed Forces Policy Council in which the Secretary of Defense, the Secretaries of the three services, the Joint Chiefs of

[12] Texts in Circular Letter No. 18, American Association of Land-Grant Colleges and State Universities, June 28, 1957.

Staff, and their principal assistants were all present. The educators also had the advantage of having as their spokesman President John A. Hannah of Michigan State University who had served as Assistant Secretary of Defense for Manpower and Reserves in 1953 and 1954 and who had had to deal with the first repercussions of the post-Korean expansion of the Army and Air Force programs.

In his presentation, President Hannah centered his arguments on the immediate question of compulsory ROTC. But in reviewing the various concepts of future war and related military manpower needs, he challenged the military departments to undertake a complete reassessment of their ROTC programs. During the course of his arguments he suggested that the programs got into trouble when their objectives were changed from their original relationship to the reserve components. He also pointed out that even if future wars are wholly conceived as "push button affairs," it was his guess "that the operations of civil defense at home will, at least in the early stages of any future war, have to be assumed by the military . . . [and] it thus appears . . . important that the ROTC program be continued if for no other reason than as a dependable source of men able to establish and maintain order—for it will require men able to take and give orders to prevent chaos."[13]

In response to President Hannah's challenge, the Secretary of Defense and the three service secretaries avowed the importance of ROTC and their support of the programs. Indeed, in subsequently confirming the results of the meeting in writing, Undersecretary of Defense Quarles reversed the earlier response to the Land-Grant Association by clearly stating "that those colleges and universities which require all eligible students to pursue the basic courses make an additional and important contribution to our national security." More important, perhaps, he also announced that "we are initiating a compre-

[13] Quoted from brief of statement presented by President Hannah as reproduced by the American Association of Land-Grant Colleges and State Universities, the National Association of State Universities, and the State Universities Association.

hensive study of our entire program with the purpose of clarifying our objectives. . . ."[14]

This series of events offered the services the opportunity to relate the ROTC programs more completely and meaningfully to the manpower needs of modern military strategy and to define a more fruitful basis for collaboration with American higher education than presently exists. Unfortunately they did not take advantage of the opportunity. The study of the program was relegated to normal staff channels without the direction and guidance that this top level intervention should have stimulated. Moreover, the immediate purpose of the educators concerned with the compulsory issue was achieved. They received a statement of policy to support them in maintaining compulsory ROTC if they so wished. They, no less than the military staff, had no particular advantage to gain in pressing too vigorously for changes in the programs.[15]

A good many of the current issues involved in the ROTC programs cannot, however, be resolved without a sharper delineation of changing objectives than presently exists. To be sure, the problem is affected by its relation to the conflict over strategic doctrine, selective service, the role of reserves, the force levels of the services, and the priority of service demands, particularly on weapons development. Nevertheless the officer requirements of all three services can be determined in broad perspective, both in terms of quantity and quality. They clearly indicate the emergence of a military profession, more complex and important than the United States has ever known, a profession that must look more deliberately than before to civilian colleges and universities as a source of skill and talent.

The problem is a large one, certainly larger than the ROTC programs themselves. It goes to the heart of the relationship of

[14] Text in Circular Letter No. 8, American Association of Land-Grant Colleges and State Universities, March 17, 1958.
[15] The whole issue of federal purpose and support of the ROTC programs was raised again in the spring of 1958 by the action of the Navy in reducing the quota of NROTC regular students in certain private colleges and universities. This matter is discussed in some detail in the following chapter.

the federal government to higher education in America and to the need for a more clearly defined federal policy. In no other area is the federal need and purpose more clear and direct than in the provision of officers for the armed services. If agreed principles of federal support cannot be developed here, what hope is there in other areas, where the purpose of the federal government is less certain but the contributions of the nation's colleges and universities no less significant to the national welfare and security? It seems clear that the conversion of the ROTC programs as a source of professional officers cannot be undertaken in a vacuum. It must be related to the development of national policies for education and manpower.

CHAPTER V · THE ROTC AND NATIONAL POLICIES FOR EDUCATION AND MANPOWER

1. The Determination of National Manpower Requirements
2. The Quest for a National Policy in Education
3. The Special Problems of Military Manpower Requirements
4. The Administrative Organization of the ROTC Programs

THE ROTC programs have been operated to meet specific manpower requirements of the national government. We have suggested that these requirements are changing as the programs come to have increasing importance as a source of active duty and career officers. The American system of higher education has not been deliberately designed, however, to meet the manpower claims of the government. Its purposes are as diversified as the system itself. The ultimate goal of American higher education has been to create a variety of means and opportunities so that each young person can develop to his or her full intellectual potential. As such, the educational system is a clear reflection of American society. The greatest efforts in the last fifty years have been exerted toward widening the educational base by eliminating, through private and public action at every level, economic and social barriers to opportunity. The emphasis has always been on the individual, with an accompanying faith that the needs of society will be served, without deliberate direction and planning, by the development of individuals to their full capabilities.

1. THE DETERMINATION OF NATIONAL MANPOWER REQUIREMENTS

It cannot be said that there has ever been a national purpose to American higher education except insofar as the nation would be best served by a well-educated citizenry. The motivation to learn has never deliberately grown out of a concept of national service except in special cases such as the service academies. The reasons for learning, for taking advantage of the opportunities for higher education, have more often been related to the values held in highest esteem by American society at any given time, by what most people thought were the main reasons for going on to take academic work beyond secondary school. If these values coincided with the needs of the nation, so much the better; if they did not, who was to say what the national needs were?

The President's Commission on Higher Education, which looked at these relationships shortly after World War II, concluded that "American colleges and universities must envision a much larger role for higher education in the national life." Moreover, the members of the Commission were wise and courageous enough to agree that "the wider diffusion of more education . . . will not serve the purpose unless that education is better adapted to contemporary needs. . . ." The Commission was, in fact, on the verge of opening a Pandora's box of problems. Who defines the "contemporary needs"? Who decides whether or not they are being met? Who decides how education should "adapt" if we do get to the point where it is agreed that it is necessary to do so? What the Commission was approaching was a definition of the gap that often exists between national needs and individual desires. But when the Commission called for a "strong and dynamic national community, intertwining in harmony and unity of purpose an infinite variety of individual talents and careers. . . ," it did not answer how this harmony and unity were to be achieved. It only warned American colleges and universities that "they can no longer consider themselves merely the instrument for producing an intellectual elite; they must become the means by which every citizen, youth, and adult is enabled and encouraged to carry his education, formal and informal, as far as his native capacities permit."[1]

The idea of direct intervention by the federal government to establish and assure "unity of purpose" has, except in time of war, been repudiated. It has almost uncritically been accepted that the national government, no matter how democratically conceived and administered, cannot be trusted in matters that touch upon the individual's freedom of opportunity and movement in the field of education. In 1952, for example, the Commission on Financing Higher Education sponsored by the Association of American Universities concluded that higher education should not seek new programs of direct federal aid to help meet its financial problems because "the freedom of higher education would be lost." The Commission based its conclusions on a series of what it seemed to accept as inevitable deductions: that the "federal government is a powerful institution," that "power means control," that "diversity disappears as control emerges," and that "under control our hundreds of universities and colleges would follow the orders of one central institution."[2]

With this philosophy of education firmly entrenched in the American culture and this prophecy of the stultifying effect of direct federal participation generally accepted, the ROTC programs are clearly a major exception to all the rules. For the production of junior officers for the armed services has not, like the education of scientists, of engineers, of language and foreign

[1] *Higher Education for American Democracy*, A Report of the President's Commission on Higher Education, December 1947.

[2] *Nature and Needs of Higher Education*, The Report of the Commission on Financing Higher Education, Columbia University Press, 1952, pp. 157-164. The authority of the Commission to speak for American higher education is suggested by listing several of its members: Detlev W. Bronk, President, Johns Hopkins University; Paul H. Buck, Provost, Harvard University; Lee A. DuBridge, President, California Institute of Technology; Frederick A. Middlebush, President, University of Missouri; J. E. Wallace Sterling, President, Stanford University; and Henry M. Wriston, President, Brown University.

service specialists, been left almost entirely to the interplay of incentives and motives in the marketplace of careers. Taken in conjunction with the service academies, the ROTC remains the single federal program that deliberately operates to allocate a segment of American manpower resources to meet a specific national requirement. Most federal programs in higher education involve the purchase of services by the government. In the case of fellowships offered by the National Science Foundation, the Atomic Energy Commission, and the Public Health Service, the federal government does seek to increase the number of skilled scientists and medical technicians.[3] The fellowships are, however, granted for purposes of advanced work in a career-field which the recipient has already chosen. The ROTC programs, on the other hand, operate at the undergraduate level when the choice of a career is not clear and a good many factors—personal, educational, and social—enter into influencing the direction a young man might take. With the growing need for career officers rather than reserve or even temporary active duty officers, the historic circumstances which have put the programs on the college campus have thus placed the military profession in a special position from which to attract young men into the services.

2. THE QUEST FOR A NATIONAL POLICY IN EDUCATION

From time to time the notion has been pressed that the federal government should exert a more positive and general influence in the field of higher education in order to meet certain manpower requirements, particularly as those requirements relate to national security. It has been expressed in the comments of individuals and groups that have been charged with formulating recommendations on a number of separate

[3] For a summary of federal aid to students see Charles Quattlebaum, *Federal Aid to Students for Higher Education*, prepared for the Committee on Education and Labor, House of Representatives, 84th Congress, 2nd Session.

issues, all involving in one way or another the relationship of the government to higher education.

Among the several purposes involved in the original drafting of legislation covering educational opportunities for veterans of World War II, for example, was a concern that manpower shortages were bound to occur in important professions, important from the point of view of their relationship to the national security, as a result of the wartime absence of so many young men from institutions of higher education. Indeed the report of the committee under Brigadier General Frederick H. Osborn established by President Roosevelt during the war to study the problem of veterans' education included the statement that: "All our work has been based on one fundamental proposition, namely that the primary purpose of any educational arrangements which we may recommend should be to meet a national need growing out of the aggregate educational shortages which are being created by the war." Although there were other reasons for recommending educational benefits for veterans—troop morale during the war and veterans' readjustment after the war—the committee made it clear that "we have regarded any benefits which may be extended to individuals in the process as incidental."[4]

In suggesting a program that would meet its primary concern without neglecting the other purposes, the committee sought to meet the needs of both mass and selective education. It recommended that one year of education be offered to any service man or woman who had served six months or more in the armed forces. But it also recommended that financial assistance to enable veterans to pursue courses for an additional one, two, or three years be subject to certain conditions: first, "that completion of the courses they are taking will serve to meet recognized educational needs"; second, "that by superior performance on a competitive basis they have demonstrated

[4] The Preliminary Report of the Armed Forces Committee on Postwar Educational Opportunities for Service Personnel, July 30, 1943; reprinted in Hearings before the Committee on Education and Labor, U.S. Senate, 78th Congress, 1st Session, *The Servicemen's Education and Training Act of 1944.*

the likelihood that they will profit from these courses"; third, "that they continue to make satisfactory progress in the courses and to give promise of future usefulness."

Although approved by the President, the recommendations of the Osborn committee met stiff criticism, on the one side from members of the Congress who looked upon the proposals as a danger to individual liberties and states' rights and on the other from educators who saw them as a means for the government to encroach upon the prerogatives of educational institutions. Responding to this criticism, Congress adopted the broadest kind of educational bill possible. The GI bill was not used as a means of meeting anticipated national manpower requirements. Limitations on benefits were based neither on ability nor on professional or other quotas but only on length of military service and acceptance by an educational institution. The principle of free choice was maintained and those students who received benefits were under no obligation or even indirect pressure from the federal government to pursue particular courses of study that related to national purposes. Likewise, the question of the competence of an institution to provide the education the veteran wanted was left under the GI bill to the existing system of accreditation without the superimposition of federal standards. In sum, the programs of education for veterans left the educational system to operate without federal control or pressure, but reinvigorated it by the influx of several million students, a good percentage of whom might never have pursued courses in institutions of higher education if they had not had federal financial assistance.[5]

One of the areas in which future manpower shortages had been anticipated during the Second World War was scientific research. This occupied a good deal of attention in the report of postwar scientific research submitted to President Truman

[5] For a summary of the results of the GI bill, see *Readjustment Benefits: Education and Training, and Employment and Unemployment*, A Report on Veterans' Benefits by the President's Commission on Veterans' Pensions, Staff Report No. IX, Part B, House Committee Print No. 291, 84th Congress, 2nd Session, September 12, 1956.

in June 1945 by Dr. Vannevar Bush, director of the wartime Office of Scientific Research and Development.[6] Dr. Bush's report had been written in direct response to questions put to him in late 1944 by President Roosevelt. These generally involved the role of the government, both domestically and internationally, in research and development in the physical sciences. They specifically included the following query with regard to scientific education and manpower: "Can an effective program be proposed for discovering and developing scientific talent in American youth so that the continuing future of scientific research in this country may be assured on a level comparable to what has been done during the war?" By the time Dr. Bush's reply to these questions came up for debate before the Congress, the war had ended and the explosion of nuclear devices over Hiroshima and Nagasaki had announced to the world that a new era in scientific development had been opened.

The Bush report had centered around the establishment of a National Science Foundation and included a recommendation for a federal program of scholarships and fellowships for young men and women who showed promise in scientific fields. Specifically the report called for 6,000 four-year scholarships to be awarded each year and 300 three-year fellowships. The scholarships would be awarded by state committees of selection and the Fellows chosen by a national committee. It was also suggested that "all those who receive benefits under this plan, both Scholars and Fellows, should be enrolled in a National Science Reserve and be liable to call in the service of the Federal Government, in connection with scientific or technical work in time of war or other national emergency declared by Congress or proclaimed by the President." The Bush report thus recommended, within the field of science, the kind of federal relationship to higher education which the Congress had rejected in passing the GI bill. It was, nevertheless, to

[6] *Science: the Endless Frontier*, A Report to the President by Vannevar Bush, Director of the Office of Scientific Research and Development, July 1945.

a great degree similar to the approach taken in the Navy's regular ROTC program which was authorized by legislation passed during the following session. Under the Navy program, the federal government offered four years of college education to young men who indicated a desire to make their careers in the Navy, who passed a qualifying examination and were then selected by state committees, and who agreed to serve in the Navy for a specified period before deciding whether or not to request to stay in as regular officers or to revert to reserve status.

The basic recommendations of the Bush report were not, however, translated into public policy until 1950, by which time the American monopoly on nuclear weapons had been broken by the Soviet Union and the need for basic scientific research for military purposes became urgent. The five years of debate, of procrastination, of doubts and fears, were full of problems having to do with how a National Science Foundation should be administered and how its activities should be controlled. Yet essential to the debate was the honest difficulty involved in accepting the realization that science and, indeed, education had become instruments of national policy. For the United States had never had a policy on science or education and had never defined its national objectives or organized its national resources except on a temporary, emergency basis during periods of crisis.[7]

In the early debates on the Bush report, the opinion of most educators on the scholarship recommendations showed a clear consistency with the stand they had taken on the GI bill: that any federal scholarship program should be a general one and not restricted to any specific professions. The Bush report had demonstrated a sharp awareness of the problems involved in federal encouragement of scientific training while nothing was being done to further other professions. The report acknowledged that "since there never is enough ability at high levels

[7] See *Higher Education for American Democracy, op.cit.*; and *Science and Public Policy*, A Report to the President by the Chairman of the President's Scientific Research Board, August 1947.

to satisfy all the needs of our complex civilization for such ability, we would not seek to draw into science any more of it than science's proportionate share." Within this understanding, there were two features to the proposed scholarship program: first, it was not so large as to attract students who, given the opportunity, would pursue courses in non-scientific fields; second, it was, nevertheless, presented on the assumption that there was a national need to nurture basic scientific research which had to be met whether or not provisions were made to take care of other needs. This was, in fact, brought sharply into focus when, after the first A-bomb explosions, Dr. J. Robert Oppenheimer testified that "what happened during the war was not in any proper sense scientific work; it was the exploitation of skills, techniques, fundamental knowledge, and even to some extent of the human relations between scientists, all of which had been cultivated in the days of peace; an exploitation which has tended to impoverish our stocks rather than to increase them."[8]

The report of the President's Scientific Research Board in 1947 marked the continued need for young research scientists and the continued lack of progress since the release of the Bush report in 1945. Even more than the Bush report, the President's Board linked the need for students in the physical sciences to needs in other fields and to the principle of free choice in education. The work of the Board was, in fact, carried on simultaneously with the work of the President's Commission on Higher Education, with both groups relying greatly on the White House staff for assistance and comprising a two-pronged attack on the development of a national policy for science and education. Thus the Scientific Research Board warned that "it would be a serious mistake . . . to establish a scholarship or fellowship program in the physical and biological sciences alone." It also included in its report the firm conviction that "in normal times, freedom of choice must be allowed to operate

[8] Hearings before a Subcommittee of the Committee on Military Affairs, U.S. Senate, 79th Congress, 1st Session, *Hearings on Science Legislation*, Part 2, p. 300.

in education, as well as elsewhere, if we are to preserve our free institutions" and the assumption that "in free competition, the physical and biological sciences will get their share" of trained people.

It will be recalled that it was during this same period that pressures developed within the armed services for an extension of the subsidized undergraduate program then exclusively confined to the Navy's regular students.[9] This was a matter of particular concern to the Air Force, which was now emerging not only as a separate service but also as the key to a new strategic doctrine based on the deterrent force of airpower. The Air Force, moreover, needed more college-trained men. In a deliberate and aggressive move to raise the educational level of its officer corps and gain the skill and brainpower it needed, it began to campaign for the establishment of a separate Air Force Academy as well as a subsidized Air Force ROTC.

The opportunity for the Air Force to present its case for a subsidized ROTC program came in early 1948 when the Committee on Civilian Components was set up by Secretary of Defense Forrestal under the chairmanship of Gordon Gray to study the status of the reserve system. After studying the manpower requirements of the services, the Committee recommended, *inter alia*, that subsidized education be made available, along the lines of the Navy's regular program, to students under all three ROTC programs who were accepted as candidates for the regular service or for extended active duty as reserve officers. This recommendation together with those of the Commission on Higher Education and the Scientific Research Board were, in fact, translated into legislative proposals by the Truman Administration and presented to the Congress in 1950. Under direction of the President, the scholarship recommendations of the three bills were, moreover, interre-

[9] See Chapter III, Section 3, for a more detailed analysis of the service positions and the work of the Gray Committee on Civilian Components during this period. The situation is again discussed here only in relation to the development of a general policy on education and manpower.

lated to form a single policy. There thus evolved a theory of federal aid to education which provided that military and scientific manpower needs could be given special attention within a legislative program that also provided for a general scholarship fund. As coordinated by the Office of Education, the ROTC and science proposals were "aimed to serve primary categories of national defense needed by providing a steady and continuing supply of scientific and military leadership and manpower." The proposed student aid bill "would complete the picture by supplying noncategorical aid to students of outstanding ability for study in any field of their own choosing at any institution of higher education to which they gain admittance." Although the Korean conflict had broken out before the student aid and ROTC bills could be considered by the Congress, the point was made that "these legislative proposals have been weighed in the light of the nation's need for the 'long pull,' not as emergency measures to meet the Korean situation."[10]

In point of fact, measures that were taken to meet the Korean situation have until recently obscured the need for the scholarship and ROTC bills although they have only reinforced the need for a coordinated federal educational policy. The Congress did establish the National Science Foundation in 1950 but the Foundation's scholarship program had to be postponed. The nation's supply of trained scientists and science teachers had by then fallen so low that, within a limited budget, the Foundation had to give priority "to fellowships rather than scholarships, because the completion of graduate work will have the most immediate effects upon the national supply of trained manpower."[11] The Congress, moreover, passed legislation shortly after the Korean conflict broke out, extending educational benefits to veterans similar to those under the GI bill of World War II. Under the Korean bill, more than

[10] Buell G. Gallagher, "Correlation of Scholarship and ROTC Programs," in *Higher Education*, Vol. vii, No. 9, January 1, 1951.
[11] The First Annual Report of the National Science Foundation, 1950-1951, p. 17.

140,000 students were enrolled in institutions of higher education at the opening of the academic year 1953-1954 and over 285,000 in 1954-1955.[12] In addition, the Universal Military Training and Service Act of 1951 established a firm military obligation for able-bodied young men, thereby furnishing the incentive of draft deferment and service as officers for large numbers of college students to join ROTC units. Under these conditions, a military scholarship program extended to all three services was not essential even though the Air Force and now the Army, as well, supported the ROTC bill in order to raise their programs to a position of equal attractiveness to the Navy's regular plan. Through the interaction of the National Science Foundation fellowship program, veterans' educational benefits, and the acceptance of the principle of peacetime conscription, however, there did in fact emerge a relationship of the federal government to higher education which involved the provision of scientific and military manpower for national purposes alongside a general program of scholarship assistance based on traditional principles of decentralized control and individual choice.

A number of factors have developed more recently, however, which tend to disrupt this somewhat pragmatic approach. Most serious, perhaps, is the realization that the incentives in American society have not encouraged the number and, more important, the kind of young men needed in the scientific and military professions. This situation has been discussed particularly in relation to science, where the needs have been deemed to be a matter of national survival following the launching of the first earth satellites in October 1957 by the Soviet Union. As a step towards meeting the demand, the Eisenhower Administration recommended an expansion of the National Science Foundation fellowship program and a federal program of scholarships and student loans, under which awards would be made "in various fields of study" and "administered by state scholarship commissions or boards." Never-

[12] *Readjustment Benefits: Education and Training and Employment and Unemployment, op.cit.,* p. 98.

theless, it was emphasized that "preference would be given to students with good preparation in science and mathematics, thus assuring that many would pursue science and engineering courses in college." At the same time the Administration also recommended a system of grants to states to support testing and guidance programs in order to identify talented young people and offer them special counsel in choosing and preparing for their careers.[13] Other programs submitted to the Congress for consideration were larger than the Administration bill. But they all emphasized, to varying degrees, education in mathematics and the physical sciences. This emphasis was retained in the final bill which included a fellowship program but eliminated the scholarship provision, putting all undergraduate student aid on a loan basis. Provision was, however, made for forgiving loans for those who later entered the teaching profession.

In presenting its program, the Eisenhower Administration clearly sought to avoid any action which would lead to federal control over education coming in through the back door of federal aid. Indeed, the philosophy of government which has characterized the Administration has emphasized the decentralization of public welfare activities to the states and local communities. It has most pertinently been reflected in the 1957 report of the President's Committee on Education Beyond the High School which recommended that federal aid to higher education should be carried out "only by methods which strengthen state and local effort and responsibility. . . ."[14] Nevertheless, the citing of students who are proficient in mathematics and science for preferential treatment is just as clearly a coercive element in the program as if the federal government were to establish a scholarship fund for science students only and administer it in rigid conformity to this pur-

[13] See the memorandum on aid to education from the Secretary of Health, Education and Welfare to the President in the *New York Times*, December 31, 1957; also the President's Education Message to Congress in *New York Times*, January 28, 1958.
[14] The President's Committee on Education Beyond the High School, Second Report to the President, July 1957, p. 24.

pose. What in fact is being done is that the federal government has identified fields in which there are, in the words of the Osborn Committee in 1943, "educational shortages," and is, through direct action, proceeding to set into operation a program to make up the deficiency. This means, in effect, that faith is not enough, that widening the educational base may not result in meeting national manpower needs, that a gap can, in fact, exist between national needs and individual desires no matter how patriotic a people may be. When this happens the issue must be faced. Does it become a legitimate and indeed essential function of the federal government, in the interests of national security, to recognize the gap and act to close it?

3. THE SPECIAL PROBLEMS OF MILITARY MANPOWER REQUIREMENTS

There is a dangerously wide gap between professional officer requirements and readily available talent. Unfortunately there is too little enthusiasm among American college students for a life of service to the community or the nation. Few students enter civilian institutions clearly motivated towards careers in the public service. This attitude is particularly forceful when applied to the military profession. A military career falls low in the scale of values not only among students, but among their parents, their teachers, and their friends, who continue to think in terms of the experiences of the Second World War, or even earlier. For most students, the ROTC is, at best, an alternative and relatively more satisfactory method of fulfilling one's service than doing so in the enlisted ranks, but not a means of starting on a career.[15]

[15] See Robin M. Williams, Jr., Edward A. Suchman, and Rose K. Goldson, "Reactions of College Students to Manpower Policies and the Military Service Prospect," in *The Educational Record*, April 1953, pp. 101-107; also Robert E. Iffert, *Retention and Withdrawal of College Students*, Bulletin 1958, No. 1, Office of Education, 1957, Chapter 4, Reasons for Going to College, p. 21. Data on student motivation continues to be inadequate. It is one of the measures which must be perfected to develop a sensible manpower policy. Some work in this area is being done by the Committee on Personality Development in Youth appointed by the Social

NATIONAL POLICIES

The concept of the ROTC as an alternative form of military service is not, however, adequate to enable the programs to meet the requirements for career officers. This will prove even more so if there is any serious modification of the present selective service system which results in weakening the compulsion of military duty. The officer procurement base which is now widened by the threat of the draft might be narrowed to a dangerous point of low returns. A good deal is currently being done to keep young officers in the services: increased pay, increased opportunities for advancement on the basis of technical competency, and increased benefits to ease the disruptive effects of normal family life which a military career often requires. All these will certainly be for nought if young men of promise and talent do not, in the first instance, enter the armed services. It may not, however, be feasible or reasonable to continue to force large numbers of them through the armed forces in the hope a few will be attracted to a military career if the more fundamental purposes of selective service begin to lose their validity.

These thoughts give rise, of course, to the possibility of a program of subsidized education such as that proposed by the Committee on Civilian Components in 1948. The proposed legislation which would have extended the scholarship and allowance benefits of the Navy plan to the other services has been dormant, however, since 1953. As presented to both the 82nd and 83rd Congresses, the bill included provisions for the procurement of reserve and temporary active duty, as well as career officers, through the ROTC. First, it would have authorized a program under which students would have only received a small monthly allowance and been obliged to accept a reserve commission and duty with a reserve unit for a specified period. It would also have authorized two kinds of subsidized programs under which students would have received tuition and allowances for four undergraduate years. One subsidized program

---

Science Research Council in October 1957; see *Items*, SSRC, New York, September 1958, p. 27.

was designed to produce reserve officers who would enter on extended active duty with the regular forces before being assigned to a reserve unit; the second was designed to produce career officers and would have obliged the students to enter on active duty on the same basis as graduates of the service academies. With these three programs, the services would have been free to utilize whatever combination was necessary to meet their projected officer requirements.

The ROTC bill ran into a series of complications. First, there was never complete agreement from the three services on the provisions. The Navy was understandably insistent that no action be taken that would reduce the benefits it could already offer under its own program on the basis of the 1946 legislation. It particularly opposed the recommendation of the Bureau of the Budget, to which both the Army and Air Force gave their agreement, to limit tuition payments to $600 per year. Any such restriction would either have prevented the Navy from continuing its program at a number of major private colleges and universities or required NROTC regular students to begin to pay part of the tuition themselves. This problem was not so acute in the case of the Army and Air Force whose programs were, in terms of numbers of enrolled students, principally situated in state and land-grant universities. These two services were, therefore, willing to accept the limitation on tuition on the assumption that it reduced the total cost and made the bill more palatable to the Congress. Second, the Navy objected to the elimination of military status for ROTC cadets. Under its regular program, the Navy appoints NROTC students as midshipmen when they enter college. They are, in this capacity, subject to greater service control than Army and Air Force cadets, although the circumstances of civilian colleges do not permit anything like the control the Navy holds over midshipmen at the Naval Academy. The extension of military status to the students in all three programs, however, would have presented problems that the much smaller Navy program does not encounter. The greater number of students under military discipline, the greater the possibility of seeming to superimpose military standards over the regulations of civilian institutions and inciting the opposition of educators who supported the purposes of the bill but who were not ready to risk any loss of institutional prerogatives.

While the lack of service agreement made it difficult to present a strong position to the Congress, the bill would have had little chance of passing under the best of circumstances. There seemed little reason for increasing ROTC benefits when, in 1953 and 1954, both the Army and the Air Force found themselves with greater numbers of ROTC graduates entering on active duty than they could effectively assign. At the same time, the disappointing retention rate of young naval officers who had entered through the regular NROTC program in 1950 and 1951 began to cause doubt in the minds of some as to the validity of trying to produce career officers through a subsidized ROTC program.[16] This latter argument, moreover, gained greater support after 1953 and 1954. Not only did the Navy program continue to produce less than desired results but Air Force experience indicated that proportionately more pilots trained through the aviation cadet program choose to stay in the service after their first tour of obligated service than the more highly educated products of the AFROTC.[17] The problems of constant turnover in the officer ranks are not, however, just the result of having depended on the ROTC programs so heavily. The rate of resignations from young graduates of the service academies has also been alarmingly high. More fundamentally the problems reflect the gap between the national sense of values and the requirements of national security

[16] See Hearings before a Subcommittee of the Committee on Appropriations, House of Representatives, 85th Congress, 2nd Session, *Department of the Navy Appropriations for 1959*, pp. 172-177.

[17] See Hearings before a Subcommittee of the Committee on Appropriations, House of Representatives, 85th Congress, 1st Session, *Department of the Air Force Appropriations for 1958*, pp. 469-471. For example: "In the case of pilots obtained through the aviation cadet program, 34 percent intend to stay in the Air Force, 31 percent are undecided, and 35 percent intend to separate. On the other hand, of the pilots obtained through the AFROTC only 12 percent intend to remain in the Air Force, 28 percent are undecided, and 60 percent plan to leave the Air Force."

and have led to measures being taken through increased pay and incentives to make a military career more rewarding to young men of talent.

In 1958 the changing nature of the officer corps and the increasing concern with its qualitative aspects gave new life to the idea of extending the subsidized features of the Navy regular program. This move was most active in the technical branches of the Army. The Ordnance Corps, for example, proposed a subsidized program to meet the serious shortage of well-qualified young officers it now faces. It recognized that it must look to civilian education for technically qualified men and that to secure them it must meet the competition of other manpower claimants.[18] The Ordnance proposal coincided with the needs of the Army generally and thus was redrafted in the Office of the Deputy Chief of Staff for Personnel to apply to the entire Army, on the model of the Navy's regular program. It was expected to present the plan to the Congress as soon as approved within the Executive branch.

What the ROTC programs represent is a means of allocating a portion of the talent of the nation to meet military requirements. The relationship of military requirements to other national manpower requirements is, therefore, of considerable importance. As the idea takes shape that it is possible and indeed necessary to think in terms of national manpower requirements and to consider positive forms of government action to insure that essential requirements are met, the prior presence and acceptance of the ROTC programs on college campuses have put the armed services in a special position: they are already in direct contact with the major sources of educated manpower. The implications of this special position are presently most obvious in the case of the Navy's regular program. In one university from which data is available, for example, NROTC regular students made higher intelligence test scores,

[18] *The Army Ordnance Scholarship Plan*, Department of the Army, Office of the Chief of Ordnance, February 18, 1958. The Ordnance Corps indicated that it was more than one third short of its authorized regular officer strength.

on the average, than students getting bachelors' degrees in any field of study.[19] The conclusion, in this limited situation, is that the Navy's preferential position permitted it to make prior claim on the most promising young men available. Any future consideration of extending the provisions of the Navy's program to all three services will certainly have to take account of the effect on other national manpower requirements.

The relationship of military requirements to other national manpower requirements is, however, changing as the nature of the military requirements themselves change to the need for a stable career service. In the past, it was the concept of short-term military service that caused a turnover in the civilian labor market as it did in the armed forces. This was particularly striking in the case of young engineers entering the services through the ROTC in 1953, 1954, and 1955. In an era of increasing technology young engineers make extremely attractive officer candidates, but they were also in great demand by industry in these years of an expanding economy. The ROTC programs were therefore of grave concern to the engineering profession for they were the instruments through which the armed forces had won prior claim on what was feared might rise to sixty percent of the engineering graduates in any one year. The problem was not only that these young men would be temporarily lost to industry. It was also that many might not be fully and properly utilized as engineers during their tours of duty. It was therefore possible that they would return with their skills dulled and, in some cases, their desire to be engineers so far gone that they might be lost to the profession completely.[20] The impending crisis in engineers

[19] The university is the University of Texas. See Dael Wolfle, *America's Resources of Specialized Talent*, New York, Harper and Bros., 1954, pp. 260-261. Our field studies suggest that this condition prevails at other institutions.

[20] For a statement of the views of the Engineering Manpower Commission of the Engineers Joint Council, see Carey H. Brown, "The Problem of Scientific and Engineering Manpower," in *Toward Unity in Educational Policy*, American Council on Education Studies, Series I, Reports of Committees and Conferences, No. 55, July 1953, pp. 113-118.

did not in fact arise. It was probably averted by a combination of two factors: the establishment of the alternative of six months' active duty for training under the 1955 Act, particularly for Army ROTC graduates; and a decreasing civilian demand for engineers from the high in 1953 and 1954. The close relationship between military and civilian manpower requirements is still valid, however. An unstable military manpower situation will have repercussions on the civilian economy. From this point of view, whatever is done to improve and strengthen the career military service will benefit the civilian economy by avoiding a turnover of manpower to meet national defense requirements.

This does not eliminate the competition between the military services and the civilian economy. Indeed, the competition is intensified. It is a competition for quality, however, and operates most fiercely at the source of educated manpower, in the colleges and universities of the nation. It therefore gives rise to two basic questions: first, should the armed services continue to have a special position, with or without scholarships, on college campuses? second, what form should this special position take? The second question is discussed in the following chapter on curricula and instruction and presupposes an affirmative answer to the first. This presupposition requires an explanation at this point.

The need of the armed services for a steady flow of college graduates into the officer corps has been established in the introductory chapter of this book. The professionalization of the officer corps, the impact of technology on the instruments of the military profession, and the increased and more varied responsibility of officers—all these support a program for bringing well-educated men from civilian colleges and universities into the armed services. Could this need be met if the services did not run special programs on the campuses? This question can be answered in several ways, depending on what assumptions are made on the future of the draft. Given the picture of future military manpower planning that has already been discussed, it would seem sensible to assume that even if draft legislation is retained after 1959, future draft calls will be low. This, in turn, assumes, of course, the long-range, relative success of the military pay bill and other steps that have been taken to retain men of ability in the armed services.

Under these circumstances, the commissioning of college graduates will depend on the voluntary desire of young men to become officers. But, as already emphasized, the rising demands of society for professional and specialized talent, taken against the low regard in which the military profession is still held, place the armed services in a stringent competitive situation. Under the operations of our relatively free society, the ultimate determining factor in the selection of a career by young men of ability and talent is the attractiveness of the job. In this situation, the security of the nation demands that some special provision be made to encourage such young men to enter the professional military service. This cannot be left to the free choice of the open market. What the services need most of all is some sort of mechanism by which they can attract to a military career the kind of broadly as well as technically educated young men suggested in the introductory chapter. This means, to use a term frequently employed by officers concerned with these matters, an opportunity "to do a selling job" on the campus. This is the principal, yet commonly unspoken justification, of the ROTC programs. It involves a chance to maintain representatives of the services on the campuses in frequent contact with students, in a position to explain the nature of military responsibilities and opportunities, to screen the best of the candidates, and to provide the rudiments of military training. These needs are no less real within the operation of a subsidized program, which only opens the door to a career but does not convince young men of talent that they should enter it beyond any obligated service. The record of the Navy regular program to date would seem to suggest that this is so.

After much debate and delay, the Air Force in November 1958 announced an officer procurement program that will permit college men to enter the service without enrollment in the AFROTC at all. This does not mean that the Air Force now feels it can "sell" itself without having AFROTC units. The program is described as a small direct commissioning program, limited to 300 for the first year, "to meet fluctuating active duty officer requirements which cannot be predicted sufficiently early to be met by Air Force ROTC." The Air Force has emphasized, moreover, that this program will not replace AFROTC, which will remain "the primary source of commissioned officers." It is supplementary rather than alternative to the ROTC to meet needs which are not met from established sources, through a short lead time program. To a great extent, the response of college graduates to this new program might well depend on their indirect exposure to and second-hand knowledge of ROTC activities on their own and other campuses.

Yet for all this, the programs must operate intelligently on the campuses if they are to do a good job of "selling." Their mere presence hardly insures success. Beyond the purposes of the services, they must also operate in such a manner as to minimize conflicts with other essential manpower needs of society. In the absence—if not impossibility—of clearly defined national needs and policies in other areas, this is never easy and simple. It depends upon the careful correlation of military programs to the broad purposes of higher education, on the one hand, and to the broad responsibilities of the federal government, on the other.

4. THE ADMINISTRATIVE ORGANIZATION OF THE ROTC PROGRAMS

Unfortunately, the correlation of the ROTC programs to the broad problems of education and manpower suffers from the separateness of administrative arrangements and the lack of effective coordination between the services themselves and between the military departments and higher education. It seems at times as though there is a tacit agreement among the departments to minimize any interference with each other's

NATIONAL POLICIES

programs and to resist together any interference from outside parties, official or unofficial. Each service administers its program in accordance with the peculiarities of its own organizational setup and self-asserted objectives. Changes, often even those with broad implications, are usually the result of service decisions based on service needs and determination.

As with other of its educational activities, administrative direction of the Army ROTC is scattered among several agencies at different levels. Overall policy guidance is provided by the Assistant Secretary for Manpower, Personnel, and Reserve Forces, the Deputy Chiefs of Staff for Military Operations and Personnel, and the Assistant Chief of Staff for Reserve Components. Within the Department of the Army in the Pentagon much of the staff work for these offices is provided by the Office of the Chief of Army Reserve and ROTC Affairs. Operational direction and administration, including the design of the curriculum, rests with the headquarters of the Commanding General of the Continental Army Command (CONARC) and specifically with the Deputy for Reserve Components, although some of this authority is delegated to the headquarters of the commanding generals of the six numbered armies within the United States.

In the Navy, NROTC is treated administratively as a part of the overall training function. The Bureau of Naval Personnel is the organization most directly concerned. The training division, in this bureau, has supervisory authority over the NROTC. This division also directs training activities for enlisted personnel and has some administrative authority with respect to the Naval Academy, the Naval Postgraduate School, and the Naval War College as well. Policy guidance is provided by the Office of the Chief of Naval Operations and by the Assistant Secretary for Personnel and Reserve Forces.

The Air Force presents still another pattern of administrative supervision. With its establishment as a separate service, the Air Force had a rare opportunity to start from scratch in erecting an administrative structure for its officer education program. As early as 1946 the AAF had turned away from the relatively decentralized control of the Army and Navy and had established a single, unified organization, which it called the Air University. The Air Force, moreover, in implementing plans for officer education, recognized a distinction between the education and training functions by placing them in separate organizations. The latter are the operational responsibility of the Air Training Command and the Continental Air Command. In 1953 administrative supervision of the AFROTC was transferred from the Continental Air Command, which is responsible for the Air Force reserves, to the Air University, within which a separate AFROTC headquarters was established.

As now established, the Air University is one of the important commands of the Air Force, and Headquarters AFROTC is one of its constituent units, of which others include the Air Command and Staff College, the Air War College, and the Air Force Institute of Technology. Policy decisions concerning AFROTC, as with the Army and Navy programs, are made in Washington by the Air Staff and principally by the offices concerned with personnel and training in the Office of the Deputy Chief of Staff for Personnel, notably the Office of the Director of Personnel Procurement and Training. Within this latter office ROTC affairs are handled by a Professional Education Division. Policy guidance is given by the Assistant Secretary for Manpower, Personnel, and Reserve Forces.

In sum, both the Navy and the Air Force, unlike the Army, have associated administrative supervision and operation of their ROTC programs with other officer procurement and educational functions. The Army, on the other hand, has retained the connection with reserve forces although, as with the other two services, it has come increasingly to look upon the ROTC as a procurement source for active duty and long-term career officers.

The existence of three separate administrative arrangements is more than just confusing. They are practical obstacles to the establishment of a method whereby ROTC problems might be dealt with in terms of their broader ramifications. College administrators are almost certain that any inquiry they address through organized channels will be answered from the particular viewpoint of the individual service with little regard to the other services or to broader federal issues, let alone their educational implications. They thus pursue pressure-group methods as the only way to press their point. To a certain extent national educational associations provide a formal mechanism for this work. More effective perhaps is the appeal to members of the Congress and to political appointees in the Executive Branch, often addressed as distinguished alumni or trustees. Such methods are classical safety valves in the American political system and have great value in dramatizing and highlighting inadequacies in the programs. In the absence of a strong organized system of review and coordination, they subject the ROTC programs to an *ad hoc* kind of crisis analysis which is often inconclusive and generally inadequate to meet long-range needs.

A recent case may well serve as an illustration of the problems involved in ROTC coordination. In April 1958 the Chief of Naval Personnel suddenly notified fifteen institutions, almost all of them private, that the number of regular NROTC students annually entered in each in the coming academic year would be reduced. In previous years, each institution in the program had received the same number of regular students— ranging from 31 to 35. It was now explained that, since the inauguration of the regular program, there had been an average increase of $500 per year in charges in institutions in the high tuition category. By decreasing quotas in these institutions for reasons of "economical management," and correspondingly increasing quotas in others, the Navy would be able to enroll 1,800 incoming NROTC regulars instead of the 1,600 that would be possible if equal quotas were retained for all institutions. When the heads of the private institutions protested this action, the Navy added that the retention rate of graduates from the high tuition institutions was generally lower than the overall mean. In the case of the few public institutions in which quotas were decreased, the sole reason offered was a lower than average retention rate among its graduates.

The Navy's action erred in two ways. First, it tended to penalize the regular NROTC program for the low retention rate among graduates when the reasons for personnel turnover in the service are infinitely more complex. In so doing, it cut down the influx of young men from many private institutions in which the standard of admission and quality of instruction are high. This was done without regard to the reasons why young men of talent and ability have, in recent years, been more likely to accept a position in the civilian economy than to make their careers in the armed forces. It disregarded completely, moreover, an argument Navy spokesmen themselves have often expressed: the value to the Navy of the flow of these men into the reserves and the support that they can give to the Navy as they rise to positions of responsibility in the business and professional communities, quite apart from their availability for recall to duty in time of crisis.

Aside from any contradictions to its own need for superior talent, the Navy's action was clearly at variance with the trend of federal educational policy. This has tended to encourage more realistic tuition charges by private institutions in order to avert a situation that might require large-scale federal aid to higher education and disturb its pattern of diversity and independence. It has been set forth in the 1957 report of the President's Committee on Education Beyond the High School which states, *inter alia*, the following: "The Committee recommends that charges to students in public institutions in general be increased no faster than the pace of family discretionary income; *that charges to students in private institutions in general be gradually increased in order at least to maintain the proportion of total costs paid by students*; and that programs of student assistance be stepped up to support increases in tuition and other charges."[21]

This unilateral action was deeply resented by representatives

[21] The President's Committee on Education Beyond the High School, *op.cit.*, p. 90. (Italics added.)

of the institutions involved who protested directly to the Navy, to the educational associations, to the Congress, to the Defense Department, and even to the White House.[22] In fairness, the Navy made no pretense in judging whether or not it had acted in accordance with federal policy. It had acted according to Navy policy as seen through the eyes of its own staff, concerned with the Navy's own problems. It was not concerned with the broader question of the relation of the federal government to higher education.[23] For all intents and purposes, the Navy and the educators who protested the Navy's action were talking at cross purposes. More serious, perhaps, was that nowhere was there available a strong system of review and coordination through which these two points of view could have been funneled. This situation exists despite the fact that for many colleges and universities the ROTC programs represent their major, if not sole, connection with the operations of the federal government, and service policy, for them, represents federal policy.

Outside the defense establishment, two means of review and coordination are available, although they are far removed from ROTC problems *per se* and, in practice, are not extensively used. One of them is through the Executive Office of the President. Also, a department or sub-unit of the executive branch may be authorized by specific presidential directive to serve in this capacity. An example of coordination through this means was the work of the Office of Education in 1949

[22] On the other hand, the executive secretary of the American Association of Land-Grant Colleges and State Universities states that the tuition charges of an institution are not a suitable measure of what the federal government ought to pay for the educational services that it receives since these charges do not represent actual cost. He proposes, therefore, a formula based on actual cost for services that would provide a fair return to all. Letter of R. I. Thackrey to authors, July 17, 1958.

[23] The comments of an officer of the Bureau of Naval Personnel in this matter may be of interest: "The mission of the NROTC . . . is *NOT* to finance higher education, *BUT* to educate and train future naval officers. . . . Those colleges which look upon the Regular NROTC Program as a means of financial assistance, most assuredly have overlooked the fundamental mission of the Regular NROTC Program and the essential purpose for which it was inaugurated."

and 1950 in relating the proposed ROTC bill to the plans for student aid and National Science Foundation scholarships.[24] A second general mechanism exists in the Congress, particularly through the appropriations procedure. A request to the Congress for funds for the construction of ROTC facilities, for example, would undoubtedly precipitate a review of the relationship of this request to the government's policy on grants and loans to higher education for other capital construction. Both these mechanisms, however, are generally geared to operating after a policy decision has been made within the defense establishment. Again using the facilities bill as an example, the Congress has refused to hold hearings on this bill for several years until there was an agreed position coming out of the Defense Department which offered a reasonable chance that the bill could pass. Otherwise the legislators, under pressure from colleges and universities in their districts to favor the bill, might have been forced into an embarrassing position of opposition. The Executive Office of the President, particularly through the Bureau of the Budget, and the Congress can stimulate a policy decision in the Defense Department through criticism that the present ROTC programs are not properly coordinated with governmental policy. But, unless the President directed otherwise, the responsibility for developing a policy to meet the criticism would rest with the Defense Department.

The weakness of the Defense Department in achieving coordination of the three ROTC programs is therefore of considerable consequence. Basically, the weakness has stemmed from the distance that separates the general manpower policies adopted at the highest departmental levels and the actual operations of the ROTC programs. These are the exclusive concern of the military departments and, within the departments, the military as opposed to the civilian staff. On the one hand, the military staff will more often than not resolve problems that arise in the course of operating the ROTC programs within their own narrow interpretation of overall policy with-

[24] This is described in Section 2 of this chapter.

out referring them higher. On the other hand, proposed changes in policy referred to the military staff for comment are usually tested there for consistency with current policy and procedure rather than against future requirements. There is no doubt that the military, as opposed to the civilian attitude, is more resistant to change, an attitude which stems from the well-established military principle that the training of personnel is a prerogative of military command. It also has roots in the concept of combat responsibility which precludes taking action when assured results are not maximized.

These comments open many questions. Are the military departments, from the point of view of their organization, governing attitudes, and receptivity to creative ideas, well equipped to adapt the defense establishment to changing requirements? Is there any way of determining when it may well be in the long-term interests of the national security to overrule the unanimous opinion of the military departments? Is the Secretary of Defense equipped to judge when this might be so and to act effectively when he does? These questions are applicable to any number of vital national security problems. Indeed this heightens their relevancy to the problems of the ROTC programs.

Unfortunately, the only formal consultative machinery which was available to the Secretary of Defense for dealing with the ROTC programs, did not operate effectively and, in fact, failed to operate at all for a period of several years. This was the Joint Advisory Panel on ROTC Affairs.[25] The panel was a subunit of the Reserve Forces Policy Board and reported to it. The parent body had its origins in the Committee on Civilian Components, established as a temporary study group in 1948 but subsequently maintained on a permanent basis, changed

[25] Department of Defense Instruction No. 5120.5, Subject: *Joint Advisory Panel on ROTC Affairs Charter*, dated January 13, 1956. The Panel was formally dissolved under a DOD memorandum of May 1, 1958, which eliminated all but a specified number of committees (including the Reserve Forces Policy Board). It was subsequently reconstituted in November, 1958. This development is discussed below.

in title, and set up on a statutory basis under the Armed Forces Reserve Act of 1952. It is the Board that is specifically designated as the responsible agency of the Department of Defense for interdepartmental program coordination on ROTC affairs.[26] The ROTC thus has been considered within the traditional context of the reserve forces. Given its primary function of strengthening the reserve components, however, the Board contains institutional barriers to the conversion of the ROTC from a reserve to an active duty and career program. There is clearly a question whether its interests are not now too narrow to be consistent with the changing role of the ROTC programs.

The panel, nevertheless, offered a means for a variety of views to be expressed on the programs and the possibility of looking at the ROTC from a broad perspective. It was made up of civilian educators named by the major educational associations and, in the later years, the superintendents of the service academies. A good deal of the vigor of the panel depended, of course, on the individuals chosen by the associations. Too often, perhaps, the educators on the panel were chosen for their ability to represent the particular interests of the group they represented rather than their own broad understanding of manpower and particularly military manpower problems. Or else they themselves were reserve officers, active in reserve affairs and automatically tagged for appointive posts on committees having to do with ROTC because of its historical connection with the reserves. Nevertheless the procedures under which the panel operated inhibited the effectiveness of many of the able educators who were, at various times, appointed to its membership. With no fixed meeting schedule, the panel was subject to call by its chairman, an educator chosen by the chairman of the Reserve Forces Policy Board. From its first meeting in September 1950, the panel met a total of nine times. After the first two meetings, there was normally an interval of about a year between sessions. The last meeting of the panel was held in October 1956. From then, it was

[26] Department of Defense Directive No. 1215.3, Subject: *Reserve Forces*, dated July 18, 1951.

NATIONAL POLICIES

dormant until it finally drifted into dissolution in July 1958 before being reconstituted on a new basis several months later.[27]

The infrequent meetings of the panel, its changing and uneven membership, and the general policy of the services not to refer any matter to the panel unless ordered to do so, considerably weakened its possible role in achieving more coordination between the programs of the three services and between the programs and the education and manpower policies of the federal government. Under its charter the panel did not, however, have to wait until a matter of concern was referred to it for consideration. Among its responsibilities, it was charged "to maintain a periodic review of the ROTC programs of the Military Departments." What reviews were carried out by the panel consisted of little more than perfunctory recitations of the status of the programs by representatives of the services. Frequently members of the panel raised penetrating questions during the course of meetings, questions about the status of ROTC graduates in the service as compared to academy men, or about the utilization of specially trained ROTC graduates on active duty. Most of the time little more was done than to refer these questions to the military departments and circulate the service-oriented responses, usually justifying the status quo, as attachments to the official report of the meeting.

The services themselves frequently failed to use the oppor-

[27] This discussion is primarily based on a review of the official reports of the meetings of the Joint Advisory Panel on ROTC Affairs. The educational associations represented on the panel just prior to its reconstitution in November 1958 were the following: Association of American Colleges, American Association of Land-Grant Colleges and State Universities, Association of Military Colleges and Schools, Association of Naval ROTC Colleges, National Association of State Universities, and Association of Urban Universities. Representatives of the services were included as non-voting members. Actually this membership had included other groups prior to 1956: the American Council on Education, Western College Association, Middle States Association of Colleges and Secondary Schools, Northwest Association of Colleges and Secondary Schools, New England Association of Colleges and Secondary Schools, North Central Association of Colleges and Secondary Schools, and Southern Association of Colleges. It was at the time these educational associations were eliminated from panel membership that the superintendents of the service academies were added.

161

tunities offered by the panel to ease their relations with the colleges and universities on matters of disagreement. In its meeting of September 1953, for example, the panel discussed the problems involved in the overexpansion of the AFROTC. The panel made it clear that there were dangers in "the proposal to reduce current officer output by unilateral reduction in the number of established Air Force ROTC units." The panel made a point of advising the Air Force that it was important to fulfill the commitments upon which it had originally engaged and be completely honest and straightforward with the students. Despite what was in fact good advice, the Air Force proceeded to withhold commissions from a number of AFROTC graduates in 1954 and to inform a number of institutions in 1955 that it was withdrawing its AFROTC units. Both actions subsequently had to be rectified, but only after they had succeeded in severely damaging the confidence of college and university administrators in the Air Force, damage which has yet to be fully repaired. Similarly there was not even a gesture on the part of the Navy to bring before the panel the problem of increased tuition for regular students discussed above.

The relationship of the Joint Panel to the Reserve Forces Policy Board was certainly too narrow a base from which to look at the ROTC. Any change will have to tug hard at the umbilical cord which continues to tie the programs to the reserves, particularly in the Army. Unfortunately, changes already made have not even attempted to do this. In the autumn of 1958, the Joint Panel was reconstituted, again as a subsidiary of the Board. The major alteration has been in the composition of the panel. The military departments are no longer represented and other members are named in their individual capacities although selected to be representative of the interests of the various educational associations. The thinking behind these changes has been dual: first, the military departments can be called in for advice at any time and need not be directly represented, a move which is consistent with the recent policy of streamlining defense administration by cutting down the number of interdepartmental committees; second, individual advisors, chosen for their experience in the field and not primarily for their affiliation, will be more qualified and freer to devote themselves to the problems facing the panel without feeling obliged to defend the group they represent. These changes may well result in a more aggressive advisory group. Nevertheless, a question arises whether the changes have been basic enough to break the bonds with the reserves, or indeed to help to solve a more serious problem: the impotence of the Defense Department in bringing pressure to bear on the military departments in matters of manpower and personnel. Indeed, during the 1958 hearings on the reorganization of the Department of Defense, Secretary McElroy made a point of emphasizing to the House Armed Services Committee that "the tremendous responsibility for recruiting, training, equipping, and supporting the component elements of the unified commands as well as all forces not included in unified commands will rest with the individual military departments."[28] In line with this thinking, the reconstituted panel provides only for a means of communication between higher education and the civilian level of the Department of Defense. It leaves it up to each military department to establish an advisory relationship of its own with the colleges and universities without a definite tie-in between the different advisory groups.

It has already been observed that recruiting and training are functions which the military departments, and particularly the military staff within the departments, jealously guard. This was forcibly demonstrated in 1955 when all three services unanimously opposed a plan prepared by the Defense Department to make the ROTC programs more attractive to students specializing in engineering, science, and languages. The plan was principally developed on the initiative of Assistant Secretary Carter Burgess, Donald Quarles, then in charge of research and development activities at the Defense level, and the

[28] Hearings before the Armed Services Committee, House of Representatives, 85th Congress, 2nd Session, *Reorganization of the Department of Defense*, p. 5,976.

Director of the Office of Defense Mobilization, Arthur Flemming. In essence, it called for about 6,000 ROTC students to be chosen at selected institutions during their freshman year for specialized training in areas of military need, particularly. These students would devote academic time usually given to regular ROTC courses to advanced work in their fields of specialization. In lieu of summer camps or cruises, they would be assigned to on-the-job specialized training with service units and on entering active duty after commissioning would be sent to posts where their specialized training could be continued and fully utilized.[29]

The opposition of the services varied, but in each case it was based on a narrow conception of officer requirements. The Army pointed out that there was no existing legal authority to undertake such a program and that it would entail certain administrative complexities. But beyond these, it asserted that the plan was diametrically opposed to the concept of the recently inaugurated General Military Science program and did not in fact meet the real reason for the loss of science and engineering majors: the requirement of active duty for all ROTC graduates. The Navy explained that the plan did not meet its requirement that an officer should serve in a line billet for several years before taking postgraduate work and subsequently filling a specialized position. The Air Force, finally, opposed the specialized personnel plan because of the possible adverse repercussions it might have on its drive for flying officers. In the wake of the frequent and abrupt changes in its own manpower planning between 1950 and 1955, the Air Force argued that what was now especially needed in its program was "stability" and that "further modification, unsupported by firm military requirements" would tend to weaken the confidence of institutions of higher education in the AFROTC.

In the face of this opposition, the Defense Department

[29] This plan was discussed before the Eighth Meeting of the Joint Advisory Panel on ROTC Affairs on 12 September 1955; see report dated November 7, 1955, together with attached comments of the three departments.

dropped the plan entirely. Taken against the increasingly obvious specialized needs of the services, their action in shutting themselves off from a source of great potential skill leaves much to be desired.

The Secretary of Defense nevertheless still retains broad policy powers and responsibilities in this, and other fields, which the reorganization legislation passed in 1958 strengthened rather than weakened. He cannot delegate these to the Assistant Secretary for Manpower, Personnel, and Reserves, who, like other Assistant Secretaries, is a staff advisor to the Secretary, has no command authority of his own, and cannot issue orders to the secretaries of the military departments except on implicit instructions from the Secretary. The responsibility for raising the ROTC programs out of the uninspiring hands in which they have too long rested is his. Two facilities are available to him for assistance: the advisory function of the Assistant Secretary for Manpower, Personnel, and Reserves, and consultative machinery such as the Joint Panel. Much of the help he receives from the latter and possibly from the former, as well, will depend on the direction he gives to such consultative machinery. This is a problem to which we shall return in the final chapter.

The problems of military manpower and national policies in education and human resources are not simple; indeed, they are frighteningly difficult. To capture their relation to each other is even more troublesome. Nevertheless the ROTC programs offer a focus through which this can be accomplished. It would be a defeat of more fundamental purposes if the officer requirements of the armed services were to be met through the subordination of the sources of educated manpower to the needs of the federal government. Yet there has to be an alternative to totally centralized control, on one side, and the dangerous weakness of irresponsible diversity, on the other. Is American pragmatism up to the task of creating a national policy in education and manpower without the loss of freedom that comes from pluralism? The ROTC programs present an area of national concern in which this question has to be answered.

CHAPTER VI · THE ROTC ON THE COLLEGE CAMPUS

1. Indoctrination and Centralized Control
2. An Outline of the ROTC Curricula
3. The Quality of Instruction
4. The Issues of Credit and Academic Time

UP TO THIS POINT, this study has been concerned with external issues of the ROTC programs beyond the college campus. In Chapter I we emphasized the importance of forces-in-being, the changing and diminished role of reserve forces, and particularly the need of the armed forces for highly qualified career and long-term officers. We pointed out that these officers must possess more than the traditional and essential soldierly qualities of leadership and devotion. Many of them must also be technically skilled in a wide variety of specialties, and all must possess a broad intellectual background. In Chapter V we concluded that the military services need some sort of mechanism on the campuses of civilian colleges and universities to attract the kind of talented men that they require and to motivate them toward a military career. The present chapter is thus devoted to this dimension of the ROTC programs, to their actual operation on the college and university campus.

1. INDOCTRINATION AND CENTRALIZED CONTROL

The ROTC programs now occupy a considerable portion of the attention of the student and likewise make a sizeable impact upon college life. During the interwar years this was not usually the case. ROTC courses, at least at the basic level, occupied a place in the minds of the students similar to that of required physical education. Usually these courses did not carry academic credit and were merely added to the regular college program. Advanced courses, although providing some credit, did not constitute much of a burden upon the student and did not interfere with his regular studies. Since the student was preparing only for a reserve commission with no anticipation of immediate active duty, there was no sense of urgency about ROTC training. During this period the number of institutions with ROTC units was limited and the enrollments in the advanced course relatively low, so that the total impingement upon higher education was minimal.

This is no longer the situation. Quantitatively the programs are much larger, affecting more and a wider variety of institutions and more students in each of them. Qualitatively, the attempt has been made to extend and improve the content, to introduce material of educational value rather than mere training. At the same time the ROTC programs have become of greater and more immediate importance to both the military services and to institutions of higher education—to the former as the principal source of active duty and regular officers, and to the latter as a substantial operation on the campus, as a contribution to the security of the nation, and also, in many cases at least, as supposed insurance against loss of male enrollment in the event of increased draft calls or more serious national emergency.

The increased importance and impact of the ROTC programs make it more than ever necessary to understand the two main characteristics that distinguish them from the regular educational activities. The first of these stems from the absolute core of the military profession itself, the feature that distinguishes it from all other professions. This is what Harold Lasswell identifies as the "management of violence."[1] It is the essence of the military profession; it must be understood by every

[1] Lasswell employed this term in his pioneering study, *World Politics and Personal Insecurity*, New York, Whittlesey House, 1935.

officer. It involves the ability to organize firepower, to order men into position, to respond instantly and automatically to known stimuli that announce danger. Because of this unique quality of the military profession, military men question the general education that has been developed as a base for the further professional education of doctors, lawyers, and engineers as a proper base for development in their own profession. This is why they insist that any system of officer training at civilian institutions, to be effective, must include a substantial portion of unadulterated military instruction.[2]

The special behavioral pattern which distinguishes the military from other professions is achieved at the service academies through a rigorous program of self-denial, of almost monastic existence, of obedience to ritual from which there is no recourse and no doubting. The result is a strong moral code which, to a military or naval officer, is the backbone of his service. It is a code, moreover, which is best recognized, acknowledged, and accepted early in a young officer's career. It is for this reason that the undergraduate experience is deemed to be so important, for it is during this period that deliberate influences can be used to develop the student's acceptance of the code. The whole atmosphere of West Point and Annapolis, and now also of the new Air Force Academy—not only the classroom instruction, but the living, eating, working, and playing—are used to build this essential behavioral pattern.

The pattern of behavior at most civilian institutions is quite different. Except in certain church-supported colleges there appears to be little reverence for "constituted authority," little inclination to seek out "austerity," traits used to characterize life at the academies. Indeed, a recent examination of values among college students has suggested a serious inclination in the opposite direction. According to this study, most students seem to "respect sincerity, honesty, loyalty, as proper standards of conduct for decent people." But their respect is less than

[2] For an analysis of the military profession, see Samuel P. Huntington, *The Soldier and the State*, Belknap Press of Harvard University Press, 1957, Chapter 1.

absolute. They themselves do not "feel personally bound to unbending consistency in observing the code, especially when a lapse is socially sanctioned," and, unfortunately, lapses are frequently sanctioned.[3]

The implications of this contrast in standards, if accepted at face value, can be serious from the point of view of the military services. It means that ROTC graduates entering the officer ranks might tend to weaken the moral code of the services and remain unsure links in a chain of command that is built on the principle of maximizing predictability. Actually, such a conclusion is based upon superficial appearances. It gives the present-day youth less than his due. He is, in fact, a highly adaptable fellow. Put to the test, he shrugs off his apparent casualness and irresponsibility and adjusts himself to the demands of the new environment. He behaves the way he does as an undergraduate because this is the normative pattern of values on the campus. When he finds himself in a different kind of situation, he has a knack of behaving in the expected manner. This is characteristic of a society with a high degree of social mobility. There is, however, a lack of calculated sureness about this ability to adapt which disturbs the military. They seek a response that has been practiced and that can be depended on because it has been demonstrated.

The method used by the services to develop traits of character that are consistent with their moral code is indoctrination. The process of indoctrination is usually indirect. In courses like military or naval history, it consists of studying a problem from a specialized point of view with little or no acknowledgment or weight given to other perspectives. In exercises like drill or repetitive learning, it seeks to develop habits of instantaneous response without questioning or reasoning. In its method and in its purpose, indoctrination is alien to the best ideals and objectives in American higher education. The presence of military programs on civilian college campuses therefore raises important problems of compatibility.

[3] Philip E. Jacob, *Changing Values in College*, New York, Harper and Brothers, 1957. For a summary of findings, see pp. 1-11.

CURRENT ISSUES

It is this dimension, then, that offers a problem when civilian educational institutions are utilized as sources of officer personnel. The deliberate insertion of influences into the process of civilian education to develop acceptance of the military code of ethics has to be handled with care. The military code must not be allowed to dominate but neither must its inner strength be allowed to be seriously weakened by the inherent characteristics of a civilian institution of higher education. Given the nature of present-day undergraduates, this is not as difficult a matter as the statement of the problem would suggest if all other things were equal. The difference between the attitudes of undergraduates and the precepts of military life are more apparent than real. Accordingly, military personnel responsible for the ROTC programs can afford to be less doctrinaire about this matter than many of them are willing to be. A less tense approach will be more likely to secure desired results. Yet a good deal of the tension on the part of the military and of fears on the part of the educators are rooted in misconceptions of each other's objectives and of the changing objectives of the programs themselves. Until these objectives are clarified, progress will be made only where circumstances bring together somewhat unusual and understanding men on both sides of the equation. Unfortunately, this happens all too infrequently.

There is another aspect of this matter that undoubtedly causes the services to regard the problem of indoctrination with such sensitivity. It is of special concern on campuses where there are ROTC programs of more than one service. In these situations, indoctrination not only separates the military services from higher education but also separates the services from each other. It is employed as a first step in converting the potential officer to a particular service-oriented view of the nature of warfare, and of the roles of the three services in the defense of the nation. Nowhere else is this made more clear perhaps than in the continual opposition of all three services to a common ROTC curriculum, especially during the first two years. Proposals for a common ROTC curriculum have originated from educators and from a number of study groups, usually dominated by civilians, since the Second World War. The matter most recently came up for discussion in 1953.[4] At the time the Navy took the position that its program was different from those of the other services in that it "produces an officer who, upon graduation, is fit for immediate service at sea." The Navy therefore argued "against any further limitation of instructional time in professional naval subjects which would prove fatal to the concept of providing the Fleet with officers ready for duty at sea." While its opposition was based on the requirements of technical training, the Navy also pointed out that "the first two years of a young man's college life are impressionable ones, of which use is now made to present a maximum of indoctrination in the principles of naval leadership." If a common curriculum were adopted "this most intangible, but in some ways most vital phase of instruction would suffer irretrievably with a resultant depreciation of morale of officers commissioned from the NROTC program."

There were also elements of indoctrination involved in the arguments of the Air Force and the Army. The Air Force emphasized that "motivation for flying is a basic objective of AFROTC training" and "this cannot be accomplished in a common course." The Army pointed out that "the instructional time available requires a high degree of specialization" in order to prepare "the new officer for constructive active duty service out of his two year tour." Nevertheless, "the most serious obstacle to an effective multi-service course lies largely outside of the subject matter itself" in the traditions, customs, and history of the services. "On the whole these do not appear formally in the curriculum," but "they may be the most important element in it," "they permeate every hour of instruc-

[4] The following résumé of service positions is based on comments submitted to the Joint Advisory Panel on ROTC Affairs in June 1953 and appended to the Report of the Fifth Meeting of the Panel held on 2-3 September 1953 (report dated 16 November 1953). The position of the services remains essentially unchanged. See also Commission on Organization of the Executive Branch, *Task Force Report on National Security Organization,* January 1949, pp. 17-18; and proposal of President John Hannah of Michigan State University, for a common two-year basic course, *New York Times,* May 11, 1953.

tion," "they are the most powerful influence in motivating the student towards the high ideals desired in the Army officer."

Given the problem of motivation, there is a certain validity in suggesting that orientation in the doctrine of a single service is a more direct and meaningful way to impress upon students the values and rewards of a career as an officer than any more general concept of national service. This is not to say that the inter-service issue is not a serious one, but rather to suggest that solutions lie in the reorganization of the military establishment and not, for the present at least, in the ROTC programs. Nevertheless, it may be well to emphasize that even if the services come to a point of agreeing to common ROTC courses, the problem of indoctrination would still exist. It is rooted in that most special of activities with which the military deal—violence—and has no counterpart in other professions for which colleges and universities are called upon to prepare young men.

The element of violence is also behind the second characteristic that distinguishes the ROTC programs from other functions of higher education. This is the element of centralized federal control. One of the features of modern military organization is the monopoly of the instruments of violence by the state. In terms of military organization in the United States, this means that the armed forces, as agencies of the federal government, are the sole prospective employer of the talent produced by the ROTC programs. Moreover, they, again as agencies of the federal government, hold a virtually complete control over the technical knowledge and data involved in the military profession. These factors, reinforced by the military principle that the training of military personnel is a prerogative of military command, create the need for federal participation in any program to produce military and naval officers. They explain, if they do not justify, why the armed services come directly onto the campus and offer instruction themselves, in courses that they prescribe and operate.

The centralized control of the ROTC programs has made them a bone of contention on most college campuses. This feature violates the autonomy which institutions of higher education cherish. Each of the military services enforces, with relatively few exceptions, a standardized uniform curriculum. They tend to regard all students and institutions in the same mold and provide little flexibility in the construction of the curriculum. To a certain extent this centralization and rigidity are an integral part of the training in discipline and obedience which is at the core of military education. To a greater degree, it is characteristic of all military training and education in which the standardized curriculum is the accepted norm.[5] This approach is in sharp conflict with, for example, a guiding principle in the accreditation policy of the Engineers Council for Professional Development, which underscores the importance of avoiding "rigid standards as a basis for accrediting, in order to prevent standardization and ossification of engineering education and to encourage well-planned experimentation." In contrast, a proposal by Harvard University in 1955 to adjust the Army ROTC program to take better advantage of the kind of education the university had to offer was turned down by the Department of the Army on the argument, *inter alia*, that any modification had to be thought of in terms of its eventual extension to other institutions.

The issue of centralized control is symbolized in the dual status of the ROTC unit on each campus. The unit is at the same time a detachment of its parent service, subject to all of the requirements and regulations of that service operating down through the chain of command, and a department of the college and university, nominally at least, subject to all of the regulations and practices of the institution. The officers assigned to the unit are under military discipline and control, yet they are expected to have faculty status. The courses of instruction are prescribed by higher headquarters, yet presumably are

[5] See Masland and Radway, *Soldiers and Scholars, op.cit.* Certain portions of this work, particularly Chapter 12 dealing with *ROTC and Other Undergraduate Education*, pp. 250-271, have been used in describing the curricula of the ROTC programs. The discussion of the service academies in this chapter is also based on the analysis in *Soldiers and Scholars*, particularly Chapter 10.

subject to the procedural arrangements that regulate all other courses in the institution. Each party in this arrangement must accommodate itself to the other. The services must adjust to the local calendar and schedule of classes and abide by certain local practices. The institutions must accept the fiction that they have complete control over the appointment of all faculty members and all courses of instruction.

These problems are aggravated when units of two or three services maintain ROTC programs on the same campus. The units are administered separately. In the case of the Army, unit commandants report directly to the commanding generals of the numbered armies on program matters and through the military districts for budgetary and logistical support, reporting to central headquarters only on special problems. Navy commandants report directly to the Division of Education and Training in the Bureau of Naval Personnel although, as in the case of Army commanders, they receive support through the local naval districts. Similarly Air Force units are all directly under the operational jurisdiction of AFROTC Headquarters at Air University.

On the campus itself, the commanders, who enjoy faculty status, coordinate their activities in accordance with local arrangements.[6] Rarely do they exert their prerogatives as faculty members except where their programs are directly involved. In general, their contacts with the faculty and administration are made through a civilian coordinator appointed by the president of the institution for this special purpose. In some cases two or three service units are grouped into one military department with the senior officer designated as chairman. More often the commandants are designated as coequal chairmen of their respective service departments with their activities coordinated by the president's appointee. None of the local arrangements, however, alters the separate organizations which the services staff on each campus, the separate channels of communication which they use, the separate regulations

[6] Interservice cooperation is still generally governed by the Statement of Joint Policies adopted in 1949. See Chapter III, pp. 92-93.

under which they operate, the separate courses of instruction which they maintain, and the separate objectives which they seek to achieve. Perhaps most important of all, none of these arrangements alters the fact that the ultimate source of authority on all but minor issues continues to rest with the military departments even though practical accommodations are sometimes made to meet special situations.

The ROTC units thus resemble foreign embassies within otherwise sovereign territories. This again, as with indoctrination, creates an anomalous situation. It also creates a danger, for it offers opportunity for centralized control over the actual educational process, a danger which can be avoided in the field of science, for example, where there are a variety of professional outlets and the individual institution has its own faculty and laboratories. A federal program may be needed to stimulate interest in teaching science or to provide grants or low-interest, long-term loans to build facilities, but in these cases the federal government does not prescribe the curriculum and supply the instructors and textbooks, as in the ROTC.

Yet in this situation, as with indoctrination, reasonable arrangements are possible if the issues are clarified and the situation is looked at realistically. For their part, the services need to recognize and adapt to the multitude of variations inherent in the pluralistic pattern of American higher education. They should provide more flexibility to take advantage of the particular strengths of each institution. This means less preoccupation with the standard, prescribed curriculum. College administrators and teachers, likewise, should be more realistic. To some extent, there is a good deal of naïveté in contending that an institution is completely free to set its own rules and standards. There are constant pressures from professional associations, such as the Engineers Council for Professional Development and the American Medical Association, which operate through a variety of means, including influence upon graduate schools and state licensing boards, toward establishing standards in their areas of special interest. Likewise a system of accreditation, operating through six regional accrediting associations, has developed as a means of enforcing minimum standards and protecting the public from fly-by-night schools. What is of special interest in both of these cases, however, is the practice of relying on the standards of private voluntary groups in which the institutions themselves usually play a part, rather than upon the imposition of relatively rigid programs by agencies of the federal government.[7] In the case of the ROTC programs, similar encouragement of institutional initiative and flexibility would reduce the risks of centralized control. What is perhaps of greater importance, it would undoubtedly strengthen the programs themselves.

2. AN OUTLINE OF THE ROTC CURRICULA

These special characteristics of the ROTC programs—indoctrination and centralized control—condition their operations on the campus. It is well to keep them in mind in examining these operations which consist roughly of two elements. One of these is conducted for the most part outside the classroom. This includes weekly drill and laboratory periods, during which the uniform is worn and the situation is clearly a military one rather than the usual campus instructor-student relationship. In all of the programs, time is given to instruction in such matters as military courtesy and customs, wearing the uniform, handling weapons, commands and orders, and the exercise of leadership. The purpose here is to teach the student to act like an officer when he assumes his first duties. He must know how to handle himself with superiors, equals, and subordinates, and he must be able to assume responsibilities within a military organization. Students are organized into cadet corps or battalions of midshipmen under the leadership of student officers. Advanced students are given considerable responsibility in

[7] For a description of the work of the Engineers Council for Professional Development, see the 25th Annual Report of the Council for the year ending September 30, 1957, pp. 33-35. For an interesting discussion on accreditation, see Fred O. Pinkham, "The Accreditation Problem," in *Higher Education Under Stress, The Annals,* of the American Academy of Political and Social Science, Vol. 301, September 1955.

the training of freshmen and sophomores. A variety of devices, including honor societies, drill and rifle teams, visits to military installations, and special ceremonial occasions, are used to stimulate *esprit de corps.*

The ROTC programs also include summer camps and cruises. Regular NROTC students are required to complete two summer cruises and one shore-based summer training program in aviation or amphibious warfare. Contract NROTC students take only one summer cruise following the junior year. The Army and Air Force programs require attendance at one summer camp, also following junior year. Since 1956 the Air Force and the Army have both been operating flight-training programs under legislation passed by the Congress. The Air Force looks upon flight training as a key element in motivating students towards flying and also eliminating, at an early stage, those not fit as pilots. The Army is using it in conjunction with the growing build-up of its own tactical aviation corps. Under the program, the services may provide thirty-five hours of light plane flight instruction for cadets in the advanced course, usually leading to a private license. In institutions where flight training is not yet available, the Air Force conducts a more modest flight orientation program under which cadets are taken out on one or more flights each year in order to give them the experience of flying and to see how they react. All of these efforts, of a practical, laboratory nature, add up to a considerable amount of time. All are designed to reinforce ROTC classroom instruction, that is, to expose the young college student to the military way of life and its code of behavior, to accustom him to a military organization and its weapons and equipment, and to get him ready for his first duty as a junior officer. These are objectives that cannot be accomplished in a normal undergraduate experience.

The second element of the ROTC program consists of classroom instruction, usually for academic credit. This is also expected to provide military training and indoctrination and to prepare the junior officer for duty. In recent years, however, the services have shown increasing interest in the educational value of the ROTC courses as well. The curricula of the programs of the three services reflect in some ways the curricula of the respective service academies. The Army and the Air Force have generally adopted programs of study designed to produce junior officers who have a varied knowledge of military subjects but who are not equipped to fill a post until they have pursued more intensive courses of technical training after commissioning. The Navy, on the other hand, seeks to produce a junior officer who is immediately available for shipboard duty on being commissioned. There is, however, reason for suggesting that the Navy practice is not too different from that of the other services. While ROTC-trained ensigns may be sent to a billet on a ship within weeks of graduation, their duties for the next several months will, in fact, constitute a kind of on-the-job training. Moreover, naval aviation candidates receive flight training for an even longer period. In any case, it would not seem unfair to say that the ROTC-trained officer of all three services needs a period of postgraduate training, whether in formal schools or on-the-job, in order to be reasonably competent from a professsional point of view. (It should hastily be noted that the same is true of the academy-trained junior officer.) This situation is bound to continue and to become more widespread as weapons become more complicated and dangerous, as the responsibilities of military leadership become more complex, and as the early period of postgraduate training becomes just the cornerstone of a professional career.

Army ROTC

Traditionally, the Army ROTC units were branch-affiliated; that is, they prepared candidates for reserve commissions in one of the separate branches of the Army. Often the branch was related to the special interests of the college or university. The schools of technology, for example, had engineering, ordnance, or signal corps units. Since the Korean war, however, the Army has converted to a general type of ROTC curriculum.

The change to the general curriculum, commencing in 1952-1953, was something of a revolution for the Army, for it marked the first fundamental adjustment in its ROTC curriculum since the inception of the program in 1916. It also was the result of a reassessment of the Army's program which began before the outbreak of the conflict in Korea in partial response to the competition first from the Navy and then from the expanding Air Force program for the most talented and best-qualified students. The impetus to review and convert the Army's course of study was given certain momentum by the criticism of the curricula of all three service programs by the Service Academy Board in 1949.[8] The Board had suggested that more attention be given to principles rather than to the application of techniques. It recommended that "the ROTC curricula should be revised to provide the prospective ROTC graduates with a broad general education." The pressure for change was also exerted from another direction beginning early in 1950. Under a new training concept developed by General Mark Clark on assuming command of Army Field Forces (now known as the Continental Army Command), the Army began to revise its training program so that every officer and soldier would be prepared for combat duty.[9]

Shortly after the outbreak of the Korean conflict, the further advantages of a general ROTC curriculum began to come into sharper focus. With the expansion of Army ROTC, the "branch material" program produced a number of serious difficulties in the orderly procurement of officers. The output of officers by branches was determined not by the Army's requirements but by the random establishment of branch units in colleges and universities across the country. Moreover, there were relatively few combat arms units (Infantry, Armor, Artillery) and it was in these branches that more officers were needed. Under a "branch immaterial" program, assignments could be gov-

[8] See the Final Report of the Military Education Panel to the Service Academy Board, Appendix I, A Report and Recommendation to the Secretary of Defense by the Service Academy Board, January 1950. For more on the Service Academy Board, see Chapter III, pp. 93-95.

[9] This discussion is, to some extent, based on a study entitled *Branch General ROTC Program*, prepared by G-3 on 26 December 1950 and distributed to other units for comment, DA Br. file 326.6, DRB, TAGO.

erned both by service need and individual aptitude. A change to a general curriculum thus offered the Army the opportunity to appeal to the students on a wider basis, to meet a frequent criticism of its manpower procurement system, and to relate its officer procurement system to changing officer requirements, while accomplishing its primary objective of training all ROTC officers in the techniques of combat leadership.

In the late spring of 1952 the Army presented a revised ROTC curriculum for review to a joint civilian and military committee called together by the Executive for Reserve and ROTC Affairs.[10] As presented, the revision resembled an infantry training camp course. With the help of the committee, however, the Army managed to develop a General Military Science curriculum that, it was hoped, would meet its officer requirements, as well as the major criticisms leveled against the ROTC courses and instruction by responsible college authorities. A key part of the new curriculum was a freshman military history course "which," it was said by one civilian member of the committee, "stresses the history of the Army and leadership as inspirational and integrating factors to add meaning to the large amount of detailed factual information presented in the course."[11] Beyond this, the GMS curriculum contains most of the elements of the former infantry branch curriculum, although better integrated than it was formerly and brought up-to-date to include instruction in new weapons and the tactics of the pentomic unit. The freshman year covers individual weapons and marksmanship in addition to military

[10] The Executive for Reserve and ROTC Affairs was then Major General Hugh M. Milton II, USAR, who later became Assistant Secretary of the Army for Manpower, Personnel, and Reserve Forces, and then Undersecretary of the department. The civilian educators on the committee were: Dr. Edward V. Gant, Assistant Professor of Civil Engineering, University of Connecticut; Dr. George C. S. Brown, President, Claremont Men's College; the Reverend Robert W. Woodward, Assistant Professor of Philosophy, University of Notre Dame; Mr. R. S. Johnson, Registrar, University of Florida; and Dean Harry G. Owen of Rutgers University.

[11] See Tentative General Military Science Curriculum, AGAO-3 (M) 352.11 (4 August 1952) G-3, Office of the Adjutant General, Department of the Army, 11 August 1952.

history, while the sophomore year includes instruction in crew-served weapons and map and aerial photograph reading. During the first year of the advanced course, there is a decided emphasis on leadership, with instruction in leadership principles, military teaching, and small unit tactics and communications. Finally, in his senior year the cadet is eased toward his service experience by instruction in staff procedures and operations, personnel management, logistics, and Army administration and military justice.

The GMS curriculum was introduced on an experimental basis in some fifty-odd institutions in 1952-1953. This experience was judged successful and all colleges and universities with Army units were invited to consider the change to GMS. At the present time almost ninety percent have done so. The conversion to the new curriculum has not, however, been wholly accepted even within the Army. The technical branches, and especially the Corps of Engineers, have resisted the change because of its emphasis on combat preparation rather than on a technical training and branch affiliation. They feel that graduates of GMS units are not adequately prepared for branch duty. In 1958 one review board proposed to the Department of the Army, *inter alia*, that it study a return to a branch material curriculum in each ROTC unit. Among some engineering colleges and a limited number of other institutions, the branch material curriculum has been retained, not particularly because it contains more technical courses that seem to fit in with the educational pattern of the institutions, but primarily because these institutions consider there is greater assurance that graduates will be assigned to the technical branches where the skills they acquired in their academic courses will be more fully utilized.

The GMS offers a total program of study which seeks to avoid the piecemeal, somewhat unrelated approach in the former branch curricula. It deals almost exclusively with military subjects. There are only two blocks of instruction which attempt to relate this essentially military training to considerations external to the armed forces. The first of these is the

CURRENT ISSUES

CHART 5
Army ROTC General Military Science Curriculum

FIRST YEAR—90 HOURS

Intro.	Individual weapons and marksmanship	American military history	Leadership, drill, and command
5	25	30	30

SECOND YEAR—90 HOURS

Map and aerial photograph reading	The role of the Army	Crew served weapons and gunnery	Leadership, drill, and command
20	10	30	30

THIRD YEAR—150 HOURS

Leadership	Military teaching principles	Branches of the Army	Small unit tactics and communications	Pre. camp	Leadership, drill, and command
10	20	30	55	5	30

FOURTH YEAR—150 HOURS

Operations	Logistics	Army administration and military justice	Service orientation	Leadership, drill, and command
50	20	30	20	30

30-hour freshman course in American military history, to which reference has been made. The second is a 10-hour unit in the sophomore year dealing with the role of the United States in world affairs. The latter is the only subject area in which most colleges and universities provide instruction themselves; some also offer courses in military history. In other words, the Army curriculum does not include courses or materials that duplicate instruction normally provided in regular academic departments. The question which is applied to the Army's courses is whether they are of collegiate standard at all.

The Army, moreover, makes no attempt to prescribe the courses that a student selects outside the ROTC program. An officer candidate may major in any subject that he wishes. The GMS curriculum, in fact, encourages a wide range of choice. The technical branch material curricula, on the other hand, tend to attract students in related courses of study in science or engineering, but even here the Army does not prescribe course selections and students majoring in other fields that are not relevant to the branch represented by the ROTC unit are permitted to enroll.

Navy ROTC

The Navy curriculum is similar to that of the Army in that it concentrates on the service itself—on its weapons, its mission, organization, and operations—and upon the responsibilities of the junior officer. Even more than the Army, the Navy uses history as a means of stimulating the interest of the beginning student in the service. Indeed the greater part of the freshman year is devoted to American naval history, from colonial times to the present. The rest of the freshman year is spent on such matters as naval courtesy and customs, discipline, the place of the Navy in the national security structure, and the missions and functions of the various ships, aircraft, and operational units of the Navy.

The second-year course is devoted to a study of naval weapons, including ballistics, ordnance, fire-control equipment, radar, and anti-submarine and amphibious warfare. Beginning in 1959, the Navy has compressed this instruction into half a year in order to permit inclusion of a civilian course in basic psychology in the time gained. This change has been made within the purposes of the Navy's new "leadership" program in the hope that a better understanding of human motivation among the officer corps will lead to better leadership and higher morale. During the junior year, the NROTC student takes instruction in naval engineering and damage control and in navigation. Finally, during the senior year, the prospective young officer has courses in naval operations and administration that contain instruction in aspects of the naval service to which he is likely to be exposed soon after his commissioning: standing watch, fleet communications, shipboard administration, and the exercise of leadership, among others.[12] In seeking to prepare the NROTC trained officer for immediate line duty at sea, the curriculum is thus more concerned with actual techniques of the service than the general program of the Army. Although, as has already been observed, the young ensign is far from completely competent, he has at least been taught to act like an officer in situations involving superiors and, also, enlisted personnel; he is acquainted with the weapons and equipment that he must handle; and he knows the special jargon of his service. This, the Navy argues, is the essential minimum required by the peculiar circumstances of shipboard duty where contacts are intimate and where, especially on smaller ships, duties assigned must be performed effectively.

The practice of prescribing more technical instruction than the other services derives from the same basic principle that underlies the program at Annapolis. The objective is to train the "immediately employable ensign." An attempt is made to crowd into the tight curriculum and the summer cruises the information and skills that the young officer will need when

[12] Students in the NROTC program who are candidates for commissions in the Marine Corps take a separate sequence of courses in the junior and senior years, conducted by a Marine officer. Marine officers also serve as commanding officers of NROTC units.

THE COLLEGE CAMPUS

he takes up his duties. Actually, as we have observed, almost all ensigns receive further training before assuming responsible positions, a large portion of them at flight school, others on shipboard as part of their initial assignment.

The concern with the "immediately employable ensign" is only one side of the picture, however. The Holloway Board appears to have envisaged the NROTC program as a part of a broad educational experience upon which to build a career. Included in its original report to the Secretary of the Navy in 1945 was the recommendation to "limit the requirements of the naval science subjects in NROTC colleges as necessary to insure that the student will attain an acceptable breadth of fundamental knowledge." Taken with the recommendation "to revise the academic curriculum of the Naval Academy to give a stronger emphasis to basic and general education," it suggests the Board's conviction that a broad undergraduate education is the fundamental underpinning for a naval career. Those essentially naval courses which the student pursues were undoubtedly considered important, but there is in the Board's report a sense of warning that these courses should not be a detailed résumé of naval material and techniques, but should contribute to the student's understanding of the role of the Navy and to his feel for naval operations.[13]

Nevertheless, the Navy leaves almost entirely to the student himself, through the courses he selects, the provision of a broad educational foundation, even though it pays more attention to these selections than do the other services. It requires students to complete mathematics through trigonometry either in high school or college, and to achieve proficiency in written and oral expression, as determined by the institution attended. Regulars must also complete one year of college physics by the end of sophomore year. The Navy permits contract students to select any course of study leading to the baccalaureate degree but excludes regulars from medical, dental, veterinary,

[13] Report from Holloway Board to Secretary of the Navy, *Study of proper form, system and method of education of United States Naval Officers of the Postwar United States Navy*, Part I, September 1945.

CURRENT ISSUES

CHART 6
Navy ROTC Standard Curriculum

FIRST YEAR—120 HOURS

Intro.	Def. org.	Navy organization	Naval history	Laboratory and drill
9	3	18	60	30

SECOND YEAR—120 HOURS*

Weapons and Gunnery	Radar	CIC	Air ops.	Anti sub. ops.	Amphib.	Guided missiles & spec. weapons	Laboratory and drill
44	5	4	3	8	4	22	30

* Beginning the academic year 1958-1959, naval instruction will be cut down to a total of 45 hours to provide time for an academic course in Psychology.

THIRD YEAR—120 HOURS

Naval machinery	Nuclear power	Ship stability	Navigation	Laboratory and drill
30	7	8	45	30

FOURTH YEAR—120 HOURS

Ship operations	Fleet operations	Shipboard administration	Military justice	Leadership morale, and personnel	Laboratory and drill
30	15	15	15	15	30

pharmacology, and theological study. Nor may a regular NROTC student major in music or art. Otherwise he is free to study as he wishes beyond the Navy requirements. It is suggested that all naval students include in their electives a second year of physical science, a course in personnel management and administration, two years of a foreign language, and a course in public speaking. At one time there was a feeling within the Navy that the NROTC program should include instruction in "foundations of national power" and during the Second World War the Navy pioneered such a course, conducted experimentally at Princeton by Professor Harold Sprout and subsequently at a number of other institutions. Now it is suggested that naval students take a comparable course which may be offered by the academic departments. The only course remaining in the prescribed curriculum not of a technical nature or dealing directly with naval operations and administration is the first-year course in naval history. But, as suggested above, this is not the kind of history course normally offered in a college history department.

In many ways the Navy's ROTC curriculum reflects the Navy's philosophy of sticking close to its own knitting and walking a straight line to a definite purpose. Nevertheless the clear objective of "an immediately employable ensign" may not always be consistent with the more general purpose stated by the Holloway Board of insuring that "the student will attain an acceptable breadth of fundamental knowledge." In effect, the problem is in trying to find a proper balance between the two. It is of greatest importance to understand that the relationship is not a static one. The present balance was primarily developed immediately after the Second World War. There have been great changes in the Navy since then and more seem likely, particularly in the areas of nuclear propulsion and guided missiles. The real question which has to be directed to the present NROTC curriculum, and indeed to those of all three services, is whether the balance between technical training and pre-professional education is fitted to the future educational needs of the officers corps.

CURRENT ISSUES

Air Force ROTC

Like the Army, the Air Force has since 1953 conducted a general course of study. Its "generalized" curriculum reflected the change in the primary objective of the AFROTC from a source of non-rated (i.e., non-flying) reserve officers, partially trained in a ground crew specialty and available in time of emergency, to a principal source of active-duty and career officers in the flight and navigation categories and in certain essential ground operations. The curriculum includes less technical study than either that of the Army or the Navy. It is essentially a pre-professional undergraduate program, a first stage followed by an intensive flight or navigation training during which the young officer attains the technical skill for his career in the Air Force.

Thus the approach of the Air Force is considerably different from that of the Army and the Navy. The latter offer programs consisting almost entirely of material related directly to their respective services. They rely upon the college or university to fill out the educational experience of the future officer, providing a minimum of guidance in the course of study that he selects. The Air Force curriculum planners, on the other hand, were anxious not only to motivate students toward flight training and an Air Force career, but to assure that they would receive instruction in certain non-technical subjects deemed significant for professional growth and development. In part this approach reflected the sensitivity of the Air Force to the lower educational level of its officer corps (a situation resulting from rapid expansion during the Second World War) and its impulse to secure more officers, particularly rated career officers, from among college graduates to improve this condition. But even apart from this, the designers of the AFROTC curriculum at the Air University were not willing to leave entirely to chance the kind of education that their students would receive. They felt compelled to include instruction in areas normally found in the usual college curriculum. In total classroom hours these courses amount to almost forty percent of the time allocated to AFROTC. They were included to provide

THE COLLEGE CAMPUS

what the Air Force believes to be the minimum background for "well-rounded junior grade officers who possess high growth potential."[14]

As originally conceived and promoted, the AFROTC program also had another purpose: to provide "air age citizenship education." It was generally conceded that more than half of the students enrolled in basic ROTC, especially in institutions where ROTC is compulsory for the first two years, would drop out before the junior year. The basic program, it was hoped, would not only serve to stimulate the best students to stay in the program but at the same time would establish a base of citizen support for the Air Force among students who discontinued their training. It was somewhat ambitiously considered that the Air Force had an opportunity to indoctrinate a large share of the male population of the country in understanding the air age, and to stimulate continuing support for the Air Force among the citizenry. While the other services have also looked upon their ROTC programs as a means to a similar end, they have not attempted to achieve this result by such conscious design.

As planned in 1953, the basic courses during the freshman and sophomore years were generally non-technical and were grouped under the broad heading of "air age citizenship education." During the first year the course covered an introduction to the program itself and to the principles of aviation, a study of the fundamentals of global geography, a discussion of international tensions and security organizations, and a discussion of the military instrument of national security. During the second year it dealt with the problems of a career in the Air Force, the moral and spiritual foundations of leadership, and an introductory discussion of aerial warfare which led to instruction in targets, weapons, aircraft, bases, and operations. As a total entity, the basic course sought to give the students an appreciation of the role of air power and an acquaintance

[14] Air Science 1, Volume 1, *Introduction to AFROTC*, Air University, Montgomery, Alabama, 1953. This objective is frequently found in Air Force publications and testimony on the AFROTC.

CURRENT ISSUES

CHART 7
Air Force ROTC Generalized Curriculum

FIRST YEAR (THROUGH 1957-1958)–90 HOURS

Intro.	Introduction to aviation	Global geography	Internat'l tensions and security organiz.	Military instrument of nat'l security	Leadership laboratory
4	16	10	15	15	30

FIRST YEAR (BEGINNING 1958-1959)–90 HOURS

1. Introduction to Air Force ROTC 2. Elements and potentials of airpower 3. Air vehicles and principles of flight 4. Military instruments of national security 5. Prof. opportunities in the U.S. Air Force	Leadership laboratory
Total of 60	30

SECOND YEAR (THROUGH 1958-1959)–90 HOURS

Career in the USAF	Aerial warfare — Targets and weapons	Aircraft	Bases	Air operations	Leadership laboratory
7	23	10	6	14	30

SECOND YEAR (BEGINNING 1959-1960)–90 HOURS

1. Evolution of aerial warfare from study of traditional warfare through the Korean War 2. Elements of aerial warfare—targets, weapons, aircraft & missiles, and bases and facilities 3. Operations in peacetime and in combat	Leadership laboratory
Total of 60	30

190

CHART 7
Air Force ROTC Generalized Curriculum
(Continued)

RD YEAR (THROUGH 1958-1959)—150 HOURS

Staff & base operations	Creative problem solving	Communicating in the Air Force	Instructing in the Air Force	Military justice system	Navigation	Weather	Camp prep.	Leadership laboratory
13	20	25	10	15	15	15	5	30

RD YEAR (BEGINNING 1959-1960)—150 HOURS

Introduction to advanced AFROTC Leadership and mission Communication Problem solving	5. Decision making 6. Leadership and management seminar 7. The military justice system 8. Preparation for summer training	Leadership laboratory
	Total of 120	30

RTH YEAR (THROUGH 1959-1960)—150 HOURS

Leadership and management	Mil. aviat. & evolution of warfare	Military aspects of world political geography	Briefing for service	PAS	Leadership laboratory
40	15	45	10	5	30

RTH YEAR (BEGINNING 1960-1961)—150 HOURS

1. Weather and navigation 2. Introduction to international relations 3. Military aspects of world political geography 4. The Air Force officer	Leadership laboratory
Total of 120	30

with Air Force weapons and operations. The heavy concentration of subjects deliberately designed to influence the students in favor of the Air Force way of looking at the world gave the program, even more than in the case of the other two services, an emphasis on indoctrination.

Those students who entered the advanced course had, by then, agreed to accept a commission in the Air Force if it was tendered on their graduation. The subjects covered in the last two years were, therefore, generally geared to an understanding of the role of an officer, his duties, responsibilities, and place in the Air Force, rather than to a broad look at the role of the Air Force itself. During the junior year the course covered command and staff concepts, creative problem solving, communications channels and skills, principles and techniques of learning and teaching, military law, courts, and boards, weather, air navigation, functions of the Air Force base, and preparation for summer training; during the senior year, leadership and management, military aspects of world political geography, foundations of national power, military aviation and the evolution of warfare, career guidance, and a final briefing on service in the Air Force prior to commissioning.

The Air Force in 1958 announced an adjustment in the AFROTC curriculum which shifts but does not change a number of courses.[15] The adjustment, effective September 1958, will take four years to become fully operative. Students already enrolled will continue under the current curriculum. Although the Air Force has declared that the new adjustment to the curriculum is "not a basic change," it has the effect of downgrading considerably the objective of air age citizenship during the basic course and placing greater emphasis on narrower Air Force subjects. The courses in global geography and international tensions will be transferred to the senior year and integrated with similar subjects already offered there. Similarly, courses "involving socio-psychological principles of leadership and communications" are being grouped together

[15] Air Force ROTC Letter No. 54-3, *Air Force ROTC Curriculum Adjustment*, Headquarters Air Force ROTC, Maxwell Air Force Base, 15 January 1958.

during the junior year. The first years will be spent on the technical subjects, with the more academic courses in international relations and geography being offered to advanced students, most of whom will have already accepted the long active-duty obligation required of flight and navigation candidates. The adjustment to the AFROTC curriculum is clearly an attempt to adapt it to the changing objectives of the program for career officers without any fundamental change of content.

This summary of ROTC developments in recent years suggests the extent to which the services have attempted to improve their programs, particularly the classroom phase. Important questions of educational policy and principle have been raised, including the validity and value of program content, the quality of instruction, the compatibility of the courses with the educational program of the college or university, and the adequacy of the entire effort in terms of the objective of gaining capable active duty and regular officers.

With respect to the laboratory element of the ROTC programs—that part conducted outside the formal classroom—it is clear that it is not education; rather, it is indoctrination and training. Yet if the premise is accepted that the armed services must maintain ongoing activities on the campuses to attract well-qualified and motivated young men, activities of this kind are essential. It may be argued that the conduct of practical military training activities is not compatible with the fundamental purposes of an institution of higher learning. In theory, this may well be so. As a matter of fact, many activities are accepted on the campuses of American colleges and universities in violation of this principle. Even if it is contended that the conduct of ROTC activities is no more inconsistent with the purposes of higher education than organized intercollegiate football, it needs to be recognized that, unlike football, ROTC activities are required by an important national purpose. What is essential is that the purpose of non-classroom, laboratory-type military training be understood and related to the changing objectives of the programs. Only then is there real justification for suggesting that some or all of these activities be taken off the campus entirely. This is a subject to which we shall return in the concluding chapter.

Turning to classroom instruction, for the moment, we find that the nature of the problem is somewhat different. It is here that the services ask for regular academic time and course credit, as well as faculty status for ROTC instructors. The issue of compatibility is thus more acute. Classroom instruction that involves indoctrination and training has worried some educational administrators and many more faculty members.[16] Is it a vital deviation from principle? If it is, it is certainly not a deviation from practice. Some institutions that parade as educational centers are little more than vocational trade schools. Others accept such affairs in addition to their central purposes. Still others openly teach rigid ethical systems. By and large American education has adjusted to this situation in a pragmatic way without diminution of its essential strength, as it has adapted to the variety of demands made upon it by society. Under these circumstances the necessities of national security, which require that the services be represented on the campus, can be accepted by higher education without great shock. Here again the problem is essentially one of finding a balance between military requirements and education. The military profession itself calls for a very large element of the latter. Again, what is essential is a better understanding of the educational preparation needed by the officers of the future, given the changing nature of the military profession.

To a very great degree, the military have responded to criticism of the ROTC curricula in one of three ways: by patching up the courses to meet specified points; in some cases by inviting civilian educators to teach the courses themselves; by standing on the unique qualities of the military profession and insisting that the civilian critics did not understand what was required and thus had no basis to comment. Such

[16] See, for example, *The Impact of An ROTC Program On A Liberal Arts College: A Case Study At Colgate University*, Hamilton, New York, 1954, particularly Chapter I.

tactics do not disturb the *status quo*; they merely tinker with it and have the advantage of seeming to be flexible within the limits of military requirements. But do they not really camouflage the basic issue? Have the ROTC curricula been geared to meet the future educational needs of the officer corps? Criticism is not valid, even if it comes from educators, if it is not developed with this objective in mind. We shall try to answer this basic question in the concluding chapter after we have first made clear what problems are involved with regard to the issues of quality of instruction and academic credit.

3. THE QUALITY OF INSTRUCTION

The ROTC programs are often criticized for the way they are taught rather than for what they teach, and much of this dissatisfaction stems from the performance of the military instructors. The services have been provoked to pointing out that a fair share of an officer's career is, in fact, devoted to teaching and that teaching is built into the very business of commanding men. What is, of course, being discussed in these cases is training, not teaching as it is understood and practiced in most institutions of higher education. The problem of inadequate instruction does not arise as frequently in courses in weapons, in military map reading, or in navigation. The problem that does arise is whether or not training in these areas is compatible with the intellectual level of the college or university. The question of inadequate instruction arises more often in courses in military or naval history, in international relations, or in political geography, courses in which indoctrination is an issue and in which it makes a distinct difference in the instructor's approach and in the student's reaction.

The attempt of the Air Force to provide instruction in various non-technical academic fields has raised the most serious questioning of the quality of ROTC instruction. This endeavor has imposed a heavy burden upon the limited personnel resources of the Air Force. Officers have been called upon to teach courses in geography, international relations, and personnel relations for which they have usually had little or no previous preparation or experience. As a consequence, the courses much too frequently have not been well taught. They have not only failed to provide the kind of educational preparation that is an Air Force goal but have produced disrespect for the service in the minds of many students. The effect has been just the opposite of that desired. The Air Force itself has recognized this situation. The recent shift of instruction in political geography and international tensions from the freshman to the senior year was motivated in part by a desire to remove these subjects from the high enrollment basic course, with its large staffing requirements, to the relatively low enrollment advanced program, in which fewer instructors are needed. It is felt that it will be possible to provide competent instructors for these courses in satisfactory numbers. At the same time, the Air Force recently has encouraged civilian instruction in these areas wherever possible.

The official position of all three services holds that assignment to an ROTC unit is an important mark in an officer's career. Where the contribution of the ROTC programs to the officer corps is understood and appreciated, this is undoubtedly true. Too often, however, the ROTC has been looked at as a "graveyard." In a good many cases assignment as a professor of military, naval, or air science is the last active-duty post for an officer. It can be a rewarding experience. But the program can also suffer from a lack of initiative and imagination which might well spring from the frustration of an officer who is being forced to withdraw from his chosen profession, while he still has many active years of living to look forward to. This need not, of course, be so. An officer with long service brings with him not only a full knowledge of the techniques of his service but a deep love for its traditions, a long experience of responsible leadership in war and in peace, the benefits of advanced training in the educational systems of the services themselves, and the unquestioning example of a man who has devoted his life to his country. However standardized and centralized the ROTC programs may be, the services are most aware of the influence of the military instructors, especially unit commandants, on the programs, on the students, and on the relations of the services with American higher education. It would therefore seem sensible to consider retaining on duty senior officers who have demonstrated outstanding ability as ROTC commandants even though they otherwise reach retirement age.

In principle, each institution has the right to turn down any officer nominated for assignment to the ROTC unit. In practice, the president or dean of faculty will not usually pose any objection if the unit commandant approves the nomination of junior officers to his staff. The approval of the commandant himself, however, is a matter of concern to the college authorities. A frequent complaint of many institutions is that the circumstances of nomination, the amount of information made available, the short time given for making a decision, the difficulties often involved in arranging a personal interview—all prevent an objective appraisal of whether the officer's qualifications equip him to be a member of the faculty. More often than not, the only check the institution has on the nominee's record is the opinion of the outgoing commandant who may, during the short course of his tenure, have earned the respect and confidence of the college authorities. If, however, he has not earned their respect, they have no one to look to for guidance and are forced into the unrewarding practice of having to pursue the matter through official channels. In any case, the college usually has to accept evaluations on the qualifications of commandants and of the members of his staff as taken from the special point of view of the services themselves, from their qualifications as officers rather than as teachers, with little or no consideration being given to the fundamental difference between military training and academic education.

All three services hold instructors' orientation courses for officers prior to assignment to ROTC units, the Navy conducting its course at Northwestern University, the Air Force at the Air University, Maxwell Air Force Base, and the Army at the various Army headquarters. These orientation courses are, however, essentially procedural in nature. The Navy course, for example, includes instruction in administrative and educational procedures, educational psychology, and speech. The emphasis is entirely on how to present the subjects and not on the substance of the courses. To the extent that the curriculum concentrates on service techniques, it should, of course, be true that experienced officers need no instruction themselves. But where the curriculum goes beyond the technical, the course will be taught from the bias of the officer's own indoctrinated viewpoint so long as he bases his teaching on little more than the prepared manuals which each service provides for his guidance. In courses in military and naval history and in international relations, therefore, the problem of indoctrination is in fact made more serious by the poor background and preparation most officers have in these fields.

The Army sought to attack this problem, with the help of the Ohio State University, by organizing a two-week course in military history for officer instructors in ROTC units.[17] The magnitude of the task involved in raising the teaching of military history in Army ROTC units is somewhat underscored by an analysis of the officers who attended the course in 1957. Of 131 officers, 17 had never taken a college course in history, 71 had had from one to three college history courses "of one sort or another," and 37 had taken four or more courses. Except in a small number of cases, moreover, the officers indicated little prior interest in reading and owning books in military history.

Ohio State also sought to deal with this same problem in the AFROTC program. In 1957 it proposed, and the Air Force accepted, a short course in which Air Force ROTC officers could "be taught content or subject matter rather than methodology."[18] Forty AFROTC instructors consequently attended a

[17] The Army Military History course was part of a program made possible by the bequest of the late Colonel Ralph D. Mershon for the purpose of encouraging work in the field of military education. The Army course was held in 1956 and 1957; final reports of the Director, Colonel T. N. Dupuy, to the Commanding General, Continental Army Command, and to the President, the Ohio State University, are dated 10 October 1956 and 9 September 1957.

[18] See *Report of the Ohio State University - Air Force ROTC Instructor*

series of lectures and workshop sessions at Ohio State for about three weeks during the summer of 1957. As a result of their experience, the staff conducting the summer program reported that it continued to adhere "to its original view that the average AFROTC instructor in non-military courses is seriously lacking in the minimum content knowledge for teaching these courses. . . ."

The conclusion of the Ohio State staff is consistent with the general deductions to be made from the background of the group attending the Army history course. Both experiences tend to raise a serious question as to the real effect a short summer course can have. In most instances the best that can be hoped for is that the officer instructor will be stimulated by contact with the subject matter and with historians and political scientists to begin to read and to study in history and politics. Unfortunately the contribution which his interest can make to his teaching is largely mitigated by the short-term assignment that is a general rule for ROTC instructors in all three services. By the time the instructor begins to grasp and really understand the non-technical subjects he will, more often than not, be transferred, with little chance that he will ever again be assigned to an ROTC unit. Until he has a full grasp of the subject, he will be forced, by the workload with which he is usually burdened if for no other reason, to rely on the service-prepared texts and his own indoctrination for guidance in his teaching. Ideally, if the ROTC curricula are to include non-military subjects, instructors should be given a year or two of graduate study in civilian institutions prior to assignment to ROTC units, as is the practice for officers assigned to the social sciences at West Point and the Air Force Academy.

The quality of instruction is seriously affected by the texts and other teaching materials provided. In the technical areas these are of the training manual type, descriptive rather than analytical. While they are adequate for the purpose, they, like the courses for which they are designed, are not of general

---

Training Program, 29 July to 16 August 1957, Columbus, Ohio. This program was also made possible by the Mershon Fund.

college caliber. The text used in the Army military history course since 1956, which was prepared by professional historians in the Office of the Chief of Military History, is a very considerable improvement over the manual formerly issued. Portions of it are excellent, but unfortunately it was deliberately underwritten almost at the high school level and does not excite the interest of the superior college student.[19] A more substantial volume is employed in the NROTC naval history course, prepared by civilian members of the Department of History faculty at Annapolis and used also at that institution.[20] These volumes emphasize the combat operations of their respective services rather than their relationship to national policies.

Because of the large amount of non-military instruction in the AFROTC generalized curriculum, provision of text materials for this program presented a problem. Headquarters AFROTC chose to prepare a complete set of manuals. In the non-military areas, at least, the very large and costly effort could have been more profitably spent in the selection of textbook and other materials available from commercial publishers. The manuals, characteristically, are full of details and written below the college level. Two large volumes of readings were prepared for the senior course in military aspects of world political geography, drawing heavily on published materials, much of it from standard college texts in geography and international relations. While this is a worthwhile collection of some excellent material, it was quickly dated and is of uneven quality, overloaded with factual information, and lacking in systematic conceptual analysis.[21]

All three ROTC programs also make considerable use of training films, maps, and other visual aids. Unfortunately some

[19] Department of the Army ROTC Manual 145-20, *American Military History 1607-1953*, Washington, July 1956, 510 pages.
[20] E. B. Potter, editor, *The United States and World Sea Power*, Englewood Cliffs, Prentice-Hall, Inc., 1955, 963 pages.
[21] Air Science 4, Volume III, Books 1 and 2, *Military Aspects of World Political Geography*, Air University, Montgomery, 1954, 950 pages. At this writing an entirely new text is being prepared. More than half of the chapters have been written by civilian teachers of geography, on a contract basis.

of this material is designed for the basic training level and is not geared to a high intelligence mean. Some of it, on the other hand, is well done and facilitates instruction. There is always the temptation of the inexperienced teacher, however, to use these devices as a crutch to support an ineffective performance.

Some ROTC commanding officers, particularly in the Army and Air Force programs, recognizing the inexperience of their own staffs in teaching history, geography, or international relations, have sought the cooperation of civilian faculty members. In other situations the initiative has come from within the host institution. The assistance has taken various forms, extending from an occasional lecture to full responsibility for a block of instruction.

These arrangements, which are worked out within the framework of the ROTC curriculum, are the exception rather than the general rule. There are limiting factors at work both within the college or university itself and within the military service. Usually assistance is provided by the civilian instructor as a matter of good will rather than as a concern of his administrative supervisor for improved teaching in the ROTC program. If this comes as an added burden to his regular teaching schedule, he is reluctant to accept it on a continuing basis. His administrative superior is likewise reluctant to incur the increased cost of providing added personnel to assume full responsibility for the effort.

There are, moreover, limitations on civilian instruction in the minds of the military authorities that come from the very reasons why these non-military courses are included in the ROTC curricula. They have been included not only as a means of broadening the interest of students in national security affairs. They have, to a greater degree, been included to interest students in the particular military service. While civilian instruction and the substitution of academic for standardized ROTC courses might seem to pave the way for civilian education to live with the military programs, there is serious doubt among the military that civilian education is equipped to integrate the ROTC curricula into its own courses of study to a meaningful degree, or that it is in the interests of the objectives of the ROTC programs, as viewed by the services, to do so. An ROTC course is an exercise in developing the attitudes and habits of being in the Army, the Navy, or the Air Force. It is this dimension that military men insist is missing and will always be missing in civilian education. While all three services have accepted civilian instruction in certain ROTC courses such as military history and geopolitics at some institutions, they have not, except in very special cases, wanted to weaken the impact of military instruction that comes from the presence and authority of an officer in uniform. This attitude continues to bar increased utilization of civilian instructors. It does little, however, to solve the problem of poor military instruction.

4. THE ISSUES OF CREDIT AND ACADEMIC TIME

All of the current problems of the ROTC programs on the campuses come to a focus on the credit issue. Most military men take the view that the really meaningful way the colleges and universities can show their readiness to accept responsibility for the preparation of officers is to offer full academic credit for ROTC classroom instruction. This, they say, would be action and not just words. They resent the idea that the programs be conducted entirely outside the classroom, feeling that this relegates ROTC to second-rate status. At the same time, they seek the status of other departments through the recognition that academic credit for ROTC courses carries.

In dealing with the credit issue, the military run into the frustrating reality of the decentralization of authority in American higher education. Although the colleges and universities have gone so far as to accept, without real institutional approval the curricula imposed from outside, they have retained the right to determine whether or not full credit toward graduation should be given for these courses. As a result, ROTC courses are an overload on students in many institutions either because they do not receive full credit or because the degree requirements in certain programs are so extensive that ROTC courses must be elected as extras.

This situation is a most acute problem in schools of technology, where required courses have become so numerous that adjustments to the normal four-year span are being made and five-year programs are being developed. Most recently, certain recommendations of the American Society for Engineering Education (ASEE) have led, in many institutions, to a reduction of credit allowed for ROTC toward the first degree in engineering.[22] These recommendations were made following a study undertaken during the years 1952-1955 by the Society's Committee on Evaluation of Engineering Education. In its report, the committee came to the conclusion that "the major differences in course objectives, course organization, and qualification of instructors are valid reasons why the ROTC courses generally cannot contribute in a major way to the professional and liberal education of an engineer as do other courses in the curricula." The committee went so far as to suggest that "ideally, no substitution of ROTC credit should be allowed either for engineering courses or for those in the humanities and social studies." They urged, however, "as a practical matter" that if an institution allows a substitution of the last two years of ROTC for humanistic and social studies, credit for the ROTC courses "should not exceed one quarter of the total credit allotted to this area."

Even this "practical" solution has, however, been discouraged by the report of the Humanistic-Social Research Project of the ASEE.[23] Serious reservations were recorded about the substitution of ROTC courses for courses in the social sciences: the poor quality of instruction in ROTC classes; the fact that ROTC "classes are seldom conducted in an atmosphere encouraging to the free exchange of ideas"; the fact that "the

[22] For a comprehensive discussion of this matter, see the memorandum dated July 5, 1957 addressed to colleges and universities with ROTC units by the Executive Secretary of the National Commission on Accrediting, Washington, D.C., on the subject, *Academic Credit for ROTC Courses Elected by Engineering Students.*

[23] *General Education in Engineering*, A Report of the Humanistic-Social Research Project, the American Society for Engineering Education, 1956.

rigid control exercised by military authority over subject matter and examinations is out of the hands of the academic faculty." The suggestion was, therefore, made that "as a matter of long-range policy it would be better if the trend were reversed, and the military were asked to substitute, where it is appropriate, academic credit earned in regularly scheduled collegiate courses for some of its requirements."

To a certain extent, the credit problem has been brought about by the apparent differences between the basic objectives of the services and the engineering profession. The services are primarily concerned with producing a potential officer and have set down the courses of instruction they consider necessary to do so. The engineering profession has not taken it upon itself, through the American Society for Engineering Education or the Engineers Council for Professional Development, to impose or introduce its own standards for military and naval officers. Its interest lies in producing competent engineers who, it is true, may also become officers. Of primary concern, however, is their engineering education which, under the progress and scope of technology and the growing appreciation of a broad, liberal background for work in all the professions, leaves little room for training in the professional attributes of the services. In this situation, the training the services believe is necessary for officers is placed in question by being relegated to a low priority in the student's total undergraduate experience. What is being suggested is that a graduate of an American engineering college can become a competent officer with less military or naval education than the ROTC curricula presently contain. It is, moreover, frankly typical of the problems the armed services run into in looking to civilian colleges and universities for young officers. Unlike the academy system, two sets of standards are actually operating in the ROTC programs.

The fact of the matter is that the problem of two standards accurately reflects the true nature of the military profession. It not only encompasses other professions within it but it also has distinctive qualities of its own. An officer is not simply a soldier, a sailor, or an airman. He also needs to be well-schooled in a technical specialty and well-equipped with a general education that will permit him to grow intellectually and professionally. How can he learn to be an officer and provide for his future professional development at the same time? Is a balanced program possible that can provide both? The answer lies in an examination of the changing educational requirements of the military profession and of the related responsibilities of higher education. We undertake this task in the following final chapter.

PART FOUR

THE FUTURE OF THE ROTC

CHAPTER VII · PRINCIPLES AND PROPOSALS

1. The Military Profession and Higher Education
2. The ROTC Curricula
3. Motivation toward a Military Career
4. The Issue of Federal Purpose and Support

THE success of American pragmatism stems in considerable measure from the ability of American society to evoke change and to adjust flexibly to that change, retaining its essential qualities yet creating new arrangements to meet new demands. The evolutionary process is an uneven one, however. Not infrequently some time passes before there emerges a recognition that certain institutional arrangements, designed for an earlier purpose, must be revised to satisfy new objectives for which they have come to be used, or that one feature of the national life must be brought into a new relationship with other features upon which it has a bearing, but which have moved forward at a different pace, or in a different direction.

The Reserve Officers Training Corps programs of the three services are now in this situation. On the surface they appear to be working reasonably well. The services, while displeased with certain of the program features, are generally satisfied with the way they are working. They have no plans for significant alterations. College and university administrators display a similar attitude. They too grumble about uncertainties and inconveniences, but are anxious to retain the services on their campuses and suggest no fundamental changes in the present relationship. Thus the ROTC programs appear to present no

THE FUTURE

serious problem. It would seem that they can be continued with only minor adjustments as time goes on.

These surface manifestations are deceptive, however. Basic changes are at work both within the armed forces and higher education and external to both that are subjecting the ROTC programs to strain. Examination of these factors, moreover, suggests that the programs may no longer be consistent with the broader purposes of the armed forces and of higher education. We do not wish to suggest that the ROTC programs call for an entirely new and strikingly different formula by which all of their shortcomings, inconsistencies, and sources of friction would be eliminated. The quality of a free society dictates that adjustments to meet new and critical needs conform to established values and patterns of behavior, preserving the pluralistic qualities of society, avoiding rigid, formalistic solutions, and nourishing the autonomy and the dignity of the individual. This is certainly the case with respect to the relationship of higher education to the requirements of national defense. Within these limits the time has come to jettison a good deal of the historical baggage that has encumbered the thinking about the ROTC programs and to make a fresh approach to their operation. This is essential if inconsistencies and contradictions are to be minimized and if the human resources of the nation are to be utilized effectively for the highest national purposes.

1. THE MILITARY PROFESSION AND HIGHER EDUCATION

The first and perhaps most significant conclusion that may be drawn from this inquiry is that the objectives for which the Army, Navy, and Air Force programs are maintained need to be clarified in the light of the degree of professionalization of the armed forces that now prevails. The change in the character of the military services is a reflection of even broader alterations in their size, composition, and nature, stemming from their response to rapid and revolutionary advances in weapons technology, accelerated progress in the art of warfare, and threatening world conditions. These circumstances have underscored the importance of highly competent and effectively equipped professional military forces and have diminished the role of reserve forces. The traditional concept of a citizen army and the various programs that are associated with this concept are no longer valid. Even when it is granted that the manner and scope of the strategic application of armed forces are uncertain, ranging through the full spectrum of possibilities from all-out massive retaliation at one extreme to the limited use of small forces for limited objectives, it is clear that the conventional employment of mass armies no longer makes sense. The need is for stable, highly mobile forces-in-being, trained for a variety of functions and operations and equipped with weapons of increasing firepower. Such forces need more career and long-term, non-regular officers of the highest caliber and dedication. Increasingly these professional officers must have both a broadly based educational background and specialized and intensive advanced preparation. This analysis leads to the conclusion that present arrangements for the procurement of officer personnel must be evaluated primarily in terms of their contribution to the newer objective, that is, to the production of potential career and long-term officers, and only secondarily in terms of the production of reserve officers.

This situation changes the fundamental position of the ROTC programs on the campus. When they were designed primarily to produce reserve officers, the element of competition with other professions and vocations was minimal. A student did not look upon his military service as excluding his chosen field; it was an obligation to be assumed only in time of emergency. If more professional officers are to be recruited, however, military service will itself be the chosen field. In this situation the competitive factor will, of course, be significant. Throughout this book we have emphasized the growing needs of American society for highly trained manpower. This need has been doubling every decade and probably is increasing at a faster rate at the present time. Long-range estimates indicate that demand will exceed supply by an increasing margin in the future.

It is in this situation that the armed services must come to the colleges and universities for a considerable portion of their professional as well as reserve officers. But, as we pointed out in Chapter v, present trends suggest that the recruitment of college men into the officer corps will depend more and more upon voluntary choice. Under these circumstances, as we added there, the services must have some sort of mechanism to place them in a special position to attract able young men. On the surface, present arrangements appear to be acceptable. The services find themselves on some three hundred campuses, including those of the largest and best-known institutions. In two thirds of the schools all male students are required to enroll in basic ROTC. Yet we conclude that this position is not satisfactory and that it will become less favorable unless remedial action is taken.

Quantitatively ROTC output looks all right. Ideally the Army would favor a larger output of ROTC graduates for the reserve forces, but present production rates are actually adequate for the level of reserves permitted by budgetary and manning provisions. Otherwise the ROTC programs are producing adequate numbers of officers for both the active duty and the reserve requirements of all services at present force levels.

Qualitatively the situation is different. The ROTC programs are not contributing adequately to the strong professional officer base required for the forces-in-being. Almost all of the testimony that we have obtained has confirmed that the ROTC product makes excellent officer material. But too few of these men elect to remain in the military. The services are not securing their share of talent for long-term and career duty, particularly in certain specialized categories. This is demonstrated by the relatively high attrition rates of ROTC-produced officers, including NROTC "regulars" and AFROTC pilots. In the stiff competition with other career opportunities, the services are not doing as well as the present and projected security requirements of the nation demand. The ROTC programs alone are not to blame for this situation. Resignations among graduates of the service academies are also too numerous for comfort. Moreover, the principal issue is the attractiveness of a military career and not the sources of entrants into that career. This is a direct reflection of the values placed by American society upon the military profession.

This turn of events points to the need for a redefinition of values and incentives with respect to higher education and utilization of talent to meet the needs of society. The need of the armed forces for a share of this talent is plain. Equally obvious now is the fact that national security depends not only upon the readiness of the military services but upon the entire productive and creative fabric of our national life, upon scientists, technologists, industrialists, and leaders in the professions. The pressing and constantly rising need of the nation for highly skilled talent in all professional and technical areas, brought about by this situation, would seem to point to the necessity of a clearly defined national policy for education, one which would identify requirements, allocate priorities, and provide for the development of educational and training facilities to assure the matching of supply and demand. Yet, as our analysis in Chapter v indicated, there is no such national policy, nor is one likely. We are convinced, moreover, that such a policy would be undesirable. Let us explain.

We do not share the fears of those who cry with alarm whenever any kind of federal aid or direction to education is suggested. To these people we would point out that we already have a good deal of both, without unsatisfactory or potentially dangerous results. On the other hand, we do believe that from a practical standpoint our highly diversified and pluralistic system of higher education can work most effectively and creatively if a high level of decentralization and individualism is maintained. Such a system is more likely to keep ends and means in balance while at the same time maintaining institutional autonomy and avoiding the dangers of gross miscalculation of requirements.[1]

[1] In this connection note, for example, the difficulties that beset the

THE FUTURE

The answer is not a comprehensive national policy for education, with all the parts dovetailing into a precisely calculated totality. Nor should it go to the other extreme, a directionless hit-or-miss series of responses to separate problems, isolated and unrelated attempts to meet needs as they appear. Rather, the situation calls for something in between. First, the requirements of our society for higher education and skilled manpower in the professional and specialized areas must be kept continually under investigation. As a nation we have much to learn about these matters. The idea of national manpower and education policies is relatively new to us. We still have a great deal to learn about such matters as the measurement of needs and resources, the factors that motivate choice of profession or vocation, the impact of both federal and private fellowship programs, and so forth. Communication among responsible individuals and agencies both in and out of government must be open and effective, so that a wider and deeper area of mutual understanding of the issues involved can take shape. Within such a context separate plans and programs can be evaluated or formulated, minimizing contradictions and inconsistencies.

Since coercive elements in this approach would be minimal, its success would depend upon the development of a system of values and incentives that would promote the flow of individuals into educational programs and professional and occupational areas of rising demand. First, this requires a commitment to higher education of a very high order on the part of the nation as a whole. It is significant that the reports of professional educators and others who recently have visited the Soviet Union have testified to the "total commitment" of that nation in this respect—the "almost universal belief . . . in the value of higher education, and the [willingness] to pay the

---

Soviet Union in attempting to match manpower supply and demand. See "Manpower Chaos Plagues Moscow," *New York Times*, June 12, 1958.

very high costs that are involved in money, in plant, in human effort."[2] Certainly our society demands no less.

Second, this approach requires a greater awareness of the needs of our society for professional and specialized talent and a willingness to reward this talent appropriately. This means that the incentives for entering and remaining in certain professions must be increased, particularly in science, teaching, the arts, *and the military profession*. It means also the conscious manipulation of schemes devised to attract people of high potential into these areas, such as fellowship and scholarship programs, draft deferments, and military pay plans, to name but a few.

Responsibility for achieving a proper relationship of higher education to the needs of society rests with individuals and agencies of the federal government and with leaders in higher education, but leadership must come ultimately from the former. In Chapter v we raised the question whether, when a gap developed between national needs and individual desires, it was a legitimate and essential function of the federal government, in the interests of national security, to recognize the gap and act to close it. We conclude that this *is* both legitimate and essential. While representatives of colleges and universities must share the initiative in stimulating critical reexamination and generating new ideas and proposals, only the federal government is in a position to crystallize wide response to such initiative and to translate consensus into action. Particularly is this so with respect to the ROTC programs, for here the federal government's responsibility is clear. These programs are maintained to meet certain specific needs of agencies of the federal government, the armed forces.

Accordingly, the time is overdue for the federal government to clarify the essential federal purpose of the ROTC programs and to provide continuing, meaningful support. Certainly the procurement of well-prepared personnel for the professional military service is a responsibility of the federal government.

[2] Report of the U.S. Commissioner of Education, L. G. Derthick, *New York Times*, June 14, 1958; Report of Chancellor E. H. Litchfield and others, *ibid.*, July 14, 1958.

THE FUTURE

This is clearly acknowledged in the operation of the service academies. Yet the colleges and universities are producing more regulars than the academies, quite apart from the output of reserve officers. Even so, in the administrative arrangements employed, and in its handling of such issues as facilities legislation and the compulsory requirement, among many others, the federal government has not demonstrated a similar acknowledgment of the fundamental federal purpose involved in the operation of the ROTC programs. Such an acknowledgment should be reflected in the attitude and manner in which officials of the services and of other agencies of the government approach the operation of the programs. Decisions at all levels should be made in terms of the bearing of the matter at hand upon the essential federal responsibility. Actions by one service should no longer rest only on the needs and interests of that service, but should involve consideration of the impact of such action upon the programs of the other services, and, indeed, upon the policies of the entire federal government in the areas of manpower and education. The narrow, service-oriented action of the Navy in reducing the quotas for NROTC regulars at certain institutions cited in Chapter v is an example of the sort of thing that must be avoided.

2. THE ROTC CURRICULA

Our analysis in Chapter vi has led us to the conclusion that the curricula of all three services are not adjusted to the increasingly important needs for long-term and career officers. They are not consistent with the two objectives which the services should pursue in developing an on-campus program: motivation for service and pre-professional preparation for a career.

What are the essential points to be taken into consideration in developing an on-campus program that will best meet these objectives? The first of these points, it seems to us, is recognition that the relationship of undergraduate collegiate education to preparation for the military profession has reached a phase in its development similar to the relationship of such education to medicine, law, engineering, and other professions. In many respects the ROTC programs, coupled with the regular courses selected by the student from the offerings of the college or university, constitute pre-professional undergraduate preparation for the technical education and training of a military career, just as undergraduate courses provide preparation for graduate study and practice of medicine, law, and engineering. One essential difference remains, however, and this stems from the need to motivate toward a military career.

Trends in the educational preparation for other fields, therefore, offer a useful means of analysis of the ROTC curricula. Such preparation in its earliest phase took the form of an apprenticeship, that is, "living in" with a clergyman or physician, "reading law" with a practicing attorney. Subsequently came the establishment of theological, medical, and law schools, and eventually these required an undergraduate degree as a prerequisite for admission. As more and more specialized occupational groups developed in American society, educational programs were provided, in such fields as engineering, agriculture, education, nursing, and journalism. These were at both the undergraduate and the graduate level. Generally these programs were devoted to the techniques and practices of the profession or vocation; they did little more than regularize the instruction of the apprenticeship and bring it into the classroom.[3]

Although such instruction has become more elaborate and formal, the emphasis in many cases has remained upon the skills and techniques of the craft. There is nothing inherently wrong with this, if the concern is merely preparation for the job at the lowest level. It is clearly inadequate, however, for preparation for advancement to higher and broader levels of responsibility where the skills of the technician are increasingly less useful and the ability to relate to other factors and to manage large affairs becomes increasingly important. Accordingly, professional education is tending to give greater attention to principles and general theory. This trend is not yet far

[3] John S. Brubacher and Willis Rudy, *Higher Education in Transition, An American History: 1636-1956*, New York, Harper and Bros., 1958, Chapter 10.

advanced. It has moved farther in some fields more than in others, and at some schools more than at others.

Dr. Earl J. McGrath, executive officer of the Institute of Higher Education at Columbia University, has proposed, after an investigation of these trends, several general propositions that should apply in the design of a professional educational program.[4] First, instruction in basic technical subjects should be strictly limited to that which is essential for initial employment. It should not include information needed for future demands of the profession. Second, specialized instruction within the professional field should be left to the postgraduate period, either in a graduate school or on the job, as in the training programs conducted by various industrial organizations. Third, even such specialized instruction as is provided should deal with broad general principles rather than with factual details and technical processes of limited application. The professional curriculum should concentrate on these principles and upon key ideas and concepts, in the development of a corpus of general knowledge relevant to the profession. Fourth, the program should attempt to cultivate in the student the attitude that his education is only beginning, so that he will make an increasing effort to continue his education on an informal basis and to cultivate intellectual curiosity.

These principles are pertinent to the undergraduate phase of preparation for the military profession. They are already reflected in curricular developments at the service academies, especially at the Military and Air Force Academies. They are also relevant to the ROTC programs, particularly since these programs have become significant sources of regular and longer term active duty officers. As indicated earlier, the educational experience of ROTC undergraduates constitutes the

[4] Dr. McGrath's propositions are based upon observations of educational programs in eight fields (agriculture, business administration, education, engineering, journalism, music, nursing, pharmacy), conducted as part of a larger study of education for the professions. We are grateful to him for a memorandum on this matter prepared for our use. Of interest, also, is Dr. McGrath's article, "Are Liberal Arts Colleges Becoming Professional Schools?" 1958, Institute of Higher Education, Teachers College, Columbia University; see also *New York Times*, August 31, 1958.

pre-professional education of military officers in somewhat the same way that the liberal arts curriculum provides the pre-professional education of lawyers and doctors. Unlike the law and medical schools, however, the armed services conduct part of the undergraduate instruction themselves after having planned, without institutional participation, prescribed courses. Examination of the curricula of the ROTC programs of each of the services within the frame of reference of these principles of pre-professional education suggests that changes are called for. We turn first to Army ROTC.

Army ROTC

We observed in Chapter VI that the Army curriculum is perhaps less pretentious than those of the other services. It does not include courses or materials that duplicate instruction normally found among college courses available to the student by election. Both the General Military Science curriculum, which is now followed in almost ninety percent of all Army units, and the several branch curricula, are concerned with what is essentially military training. This does not include information needed beyond the period of initial duty. The value of this classroom instruction appears to be of limited utility to the Army, however. It comes in small doses spread over a period of four years, is concerned too much with details that are easily forgotten, and too frequently fails to challenge the imagination of the superior student, or even, in many cases, of the average student.

One of the most interesting twists that we have observed is the enthusiasm for summer camp shown by the same ROTC students who call the ROTC classes during the academic year "Mickey Mouse" or "gut" courses. The better the student is, the more likely he is to be highly motivated by a challenging program expertly presented. Military courses offered by officers in academic surroundings are not challenging even if they are well taught. But military courses taught by officers in military surroundings are both and the response of students is good. Part of the answer to the objective of motivation is a lengthened summer camp and possibly a second camp, and correspondingly less classroom attention to military subjects during the academic year. Such an arrangement would also permit greater concentration on pre-professional preparation for a military career. This can be done in ROTC designed courses that get away from a "nuts and bolts" approach to the subject matter and emphasize key military issues and concepts, and through greater use of the student's time in appropriate academic courses available on an elective basis. In this connection, it should be emphasized that all Army officers, Military Academy graduates as well as ROTC products, receive specialized military training in the branch basic course that they attend immediately after being commissioned. This course in fact repeats almost all of the technical military training now included in the ROTC curriculum. Officers who remain in the service, moreover, attend Army schools at regular intervals well beyond mid-career.[5]

Two proposed modifications to the Army ROTC curriculum and alterations that have actually been inaugurated at several institutions indicate the kinds of changes that might well be made. In recent years two separate recommendations have been made to include all technical ROTC instruction in summer camp work and to accept academic courses offered by the colleges in fields such as American history, mathematics, and physics in lieu of most of the present ROTC courses. To a certain extent, such a plan is similar to the Platoon Leaders Program run by the Marine Corps which depends on concentrated training during two summer camp periods of six weeks' duration each to give the college-educated officer a firm basis for troop leadership. Both recommendations, however, have thus far been turned down by the Department of the Army and would, undoubtedly, have been turned down by the other services as well. The first was the product of a special faculty committee set up at Harvard University in 1953 to review the

[5] General Willard G. Wyman, former commander of the Continental Army Command, has suggested that a newly commissioned officer be sent to an advanced school for professional training like that given in other professions such as medicine. *Army Times*, August 16, 1958.

PRINCIPLES AND PROPOSALS

Army's program at the time the University was asked to accept the GMS curriculum. Reporting in 1954, the committee recommended a modified form of the GMS curriculum which organized the course on a three-year basis, transferred much of the technical training to an extended summer camp of nine weeks, and provided for joint civilian-military instruction where feasible.[6] The Army, nevertheless, continually rejected Harvard's offer to undertake the modified program on an experimental basis. The crux of the Army's argument was that the Harvard plan would not be adopted because it could not be standardized. In so arguing the Army did, in fact, recognize the special facilities and teaching talent which a university like Harvard has. It also succeeded in preventing its own program from taking advantage of these same assets.

A similar plan was more recently drawn up at First Army Headquarters, New York, early in 1957. This was presented at a conference on Military Training and the College Man that was concerned with ROTC in institutions where initial enrollments on a voluntary basis were low but where most students who started stayed in the program. This situation has been found to be true in many private schools, particularly. It was felt that a major factor keeping more students from enrolling was the time requirement when taken on top of a full academic program, especially in the scientific and engineering fields. First Army Headquarters therefore developed the broad outline of a new ROTC curriculum that called for most of the military instruction during two summer camp sessions and in the senior year just prior to commissioning. Under the plan, no military instruction would be offered during the freshman year, which would be used as a time for recruitment and selection, and very little instruction would be offered during the sophomore and junior years.[7] The First Army plan has, however, received little support at higher levels. One practical objection that has been offered is the higher training costs

---

[6] Draft #3, *A Proposal for a Modification of the Army ROTC Program*, Harvard University (1955?) (Mimeographed).

[7] First United States Army ROTC Conference, *Military Training and the College Man*, Appendix A: New Program, 24 January 1957.

THE FUTURE

involved in a second summer camp, costs which are presently difficult to meet because of the budget cutback on reserve affairs. Such an objection does not, however, take into consideration the fact that the ROTC is no longer a reserve program and that it should not be treated as such for budgetary purposes. A program that is producing as many career officers as the ROTC should be looked at from a broader perspective than as a program within the scope of the reserve components.

In spite of these setbacks, Harvard University was permitted in 1956 to go forward with a more modest adjustment of the four-year standard curriculum. This provided for inclusion of two regular offerings of the university, one a history of civil-military relations, presented by the Department of History as one of its regular offerings, and the second on government and defense, presented by the Department of Government.[8] These were substituted for portions of the more technical instruction. The courses may be applied, moreover, for concentration credit in the same manner as other departmental courses and may be applied toward the degree requirement. This arrangement therefore increases the electives available to the student for other purposes. At Yale University, likewise, courses taught in the history and geography departments have been substituted for the basic military science courses. These are: in the first year, the emergence of America as a world military power, and the History of the United States since 1865; in the second year, field and map study, and the geographical and political bases of national power.

Princeton University has also inaugurated changes in the standard curriculum, which at Princeton leads to a commission in the artillery. In 1952 it introduced a course on the history of military affairs in western society since the eighteenth century. Perfected by an academic staff that has pioneered in the study of military history, this course has been organized and taught in the best tradition of intellectual inquiry. The

[8] In 1958, when the government and defense course was discontinued, the ROTC student was permitted to elect one of several other appropriate courses in the Department of Government.

Army substituted this course for its own military history course. The course was also accepted by the Air Force in lieu of a portion of its program and, briefly, as an extra course, by the Navy.[9] As a regular offering of the university, the course was open to any student.

Subsequently in 1957 Princeton worked out a rather extensive modification of the Army curriculum. All but three of the eight one-semester courses of the ROTC program are university courses, offered by regular departments of instruction. In the freshman year the student takes a two-semester introductory physics course designed for Army ROTC students. This provides a sound grounding in physics with special additional material on topics of particular value to a future Army officer. In his second year he elects a course in psychological aspects of group organization and operations and the history of military affairs course. If he goes on to advanced ROTC he takes two military science courses in the junior year and one military science and one university course in the senior year. For the latter he may take either of two offerings of the economics and politics departments, the economics of national security and military strategy and national security policy, respectively. Thus military training as such is limited to the afternoon drill and laboratory periods, the three military science courses, and the summer camp. Full degree credit is given for the military courses. Those responsible for this new program at Princeton believe that it will afford men preparing for officer candidacy "a sound grounding in the fundamental disciplines upon which military technology, policy, and operations are based."[10]

Navy ROTC

In Chapter vi we observed that the Navy curriculum is similar to that of the Army in that it concentrates on the service

[9] The Princeton staff prepared a comprehensive book of readings for this course. See Gordon B. Turner, *A History of Military Affairs in Western Society Since the Eighteenth Century*, New York, Harcourt, Brace & Co., 1953, 776 pages.
[10] *New York Times*, May 19, 1957. For details of the Princeton ROTC program, see *Official Register of Princeton University*, the Undergraduate Catalogue Issue for 1958-1959, pp. 268-271.

itself, but that, much more than does the Army, it emphasizes the techniques of the service. It is in this respect that the Navy curriculum deviates most sharply from the principles of professional education that we set down earlier. It deals with "factual details and technical processes of limited application" rather than "key ideas and concepts." This tendency basically stems from the Navy's determination to produce an "immediately employable ensign."

We also observed in Chapter vi the possible conflict between this objective and the counsel of the Holloway Board in 1945 that the undergraduate student, both NROTC and Academy, "attain an acceptable breadth of fundamental knowledge." Controversy, of course, reigns over what is the measure of "acceptable." The Navy already goes far in setting up a measure in prescribing civilian courses in mathematics and physics for NROTC students and suggesting what kinds of courses they elect in other fields. But certainly more could be achieved in this direction by following the pattern of the new Army ROTC curriculum at Princeton, that is, substituting courses in the physical sciences and engineering for instruction in the technical naval fields such as weapons and naval machinery, and a course in one of the social sciences for naval history. To a certain extent the Navy recognized the contribution civilian education can make to its specified needs when it recently substituted an academic course in basic psychology for instruction in weapons in order to strengthen the midshipman's preparation for leadership responsibilities.

An example of what might be done at other institutions is, in fact, provided by an NROTC curriculum introduced at Massachusetts Institute of Technology in the fall of 1956. For some time the Navy had been anxious to establish a unit at MIT, but MIT was reluctant to accept the Navy's standard curriculum. It was, however, interested in a Navy program that could meet the professional interests both of the Institute and of the students themselves. The Navy saw this as an opportunity to secure technically trained officers for special duties in connection with the changeover to nuclear propulsion in

PRINCIPLES AND PROPOSALS

naval vessels and the increased use of electronically controlled missiles. Accordingly it proposed a special curriculum in which NROTC courses are limited to the freshman and senior years. These are first-year courses on naval orientation and the history of seapower, and a senior course on naval industrial management and leadership. The latter is a special course prepared for the MIT program in collaboration with the Institute's School of Industrial Management. During the sophomore and junior years, the students devote all of their academic time to courses of the Institute, although they do meet with NROTC staff officers once a week to participate in lectures on guided missiles and nuclear propulsion. These meetings are primarily a means of keeping in contact with the Navy and less a course in substantive learning. Students in this program are enrolled in the contract category and thus participate in only a single summer cruise following junior year, during which their practical instruction is confined to engineering subjects. To encourage them in their specialties, the Navy plans to offer temporary employment to MIT contract students at various naval industrial or base installations during the other summer periods. Finally, graduates of the program will be offered commissions as engineering duty officers in the Naval Reserve and will be ordered to duty in engineering or research positions both afloat and ashore for a period of two years active duty.[11] Whether many will then seek to transfer to the Regular Navy will undoubtedly depend on their service experience.

The Navy has been quick to point out that the MIT unit was established as a pilot project and that there are no present plans to extend the same kind of program to other institutions. Any extension would, from the Navy's point of view, have to be limited to those primarily technological institutions where faculty and facilities are available for laying a solid groundwork for dealing with nuclear propulsion and guided missiles. This is consistent with the preciseness and stability which has always characterized the Navy's program. The MIT program

[11] *The Massachusetts Institute of Technology Bulletin*, General Catalogue Issue, Cambridge, July 1958, pp. 41-42.

THE FUTURE

is not the result of the application of any educational concept of pre-professional preparation but of the demands of Navy manpower requirements. It is perhaps of more than just passing interest that the two are here in harmony.

No fundamental break with the concept of the "immediately employable ensign" is possible until there is a complete understanding, at all levels, of the changing nature of naval operations. Even staunch old-line officers admit that the best NROTC, and, for that matter, Academy, graduate is generally useless for the first several months of duty on board a battleship, let alone a smaller ship where his mistakes cannot be so well hidden. If this is so, what will be the case when the full impact of nuclear propulsion, now only in its infancy, and other technological advances, have had their effect on naval operations?

The fact of the matter is the officers of the future Navy are going to have to be knowledgeable about these advanced scientific and engineering fields whether or not they are immediately assigned as engineering specialists. Courses in naval machinery and operations will have little real meaning unless the young officer has had a good grounding in mathematics, physics, and engineering science. In other words, the increasing complexity of the instruments of naval warfare make a broad pre-professional education essential to an officer's preparation. As difficult as it may be for Navy men to accept, shipboard learning, and the preparation for shipboard learning, may no longer be the most important element in a midshipman's training.

Air Force ROTC

The generalized curriculum of the AFROTC presents a different problem. By design the Air Force has attempted to reduce technical material and to include non-technical courses judged to be necessary to assure a well-rounded educational background for career development. In doing so, it introduced into its own curriculum areas of instruction that fall within such academic disciplines as geography, political science, history, psychology, education, and speech. It has also acknowledged an avowed objective of educating the college youth of the nation for "air age citizenship." Thus the issue is less—as with the Army and Navy—the overloading of classroom time with technical, military training that can better be handled in summer camp or on the job. The issue is, rather, the attempt of the Air Force to offer instruction in non-military subjects and to indulge in air age citizenship.

Actually the objective of air age citizenship has been sharply criticized within the Air Force itself in recent years. No longer is the program justified on this basis. To a large extent, the criticism was touched off by a report of the Inspector General of the Air Force dated July 1, 1956, which found that an intensive training program was required after an AFROTC trained officer was commissioned because the AFROTC program itself failed to provide him with a good grounding in military fundamentals and the principles of military leadership. Quite candidly the report questioned the necessity and indeed the propriety of the Air Force's indulging in a broad program of educating the general citizenry and suggested that the program be brought down to first things first: the provision of rated officers for the career service. Whether the AFROTC should be primarily an educative program or a narrow officer procurement program was, in fact, a reflection of the conflict and differences within the Air Force itself, differences of concept between the AFROTC staff at the Air University, Maxwell Air Force Base, and those in charge of procurement and training at Air Force Headquarters.

In response to critics who question the attempt of the AFROTC curriculum to provide a background in non-technical subjects, Air Force officers have replied that it cannot be certain that colleges will offer courses in the areas that the Air Force deems necessary. They have made this point particularly with respect to the instruction in geography. They also declare that courses in such areas as international relations, political geography, and the psychology of leadership require a special Air Force "twist" to emphasize the special implications of the subject matter for future officers and to motivate them toward an Air Force career.

There is, of course, some question whether the difficulties of motivating the AFROTC student can be solved through manipulation of the curriculum. Indeed, the introduction of flight instruction and the extension of the postgraduate obligation limit the contribution of the curriculum to this objective. It mainly provides an introduction to the Air Force on the basis of which the student will, among other influences, make his decision whether or not to enter the advanced course and accept the obligations involved. Yet even at this, it is fully expected that flight instruction will eliminate as well as attract students to flying careers by detecting, at an early stage, those who fail pilot training.[12] Indeed, flight instruction offers the Air Force the best incentive and the best test for good flying officers. The attributes which the Air Force would like to find in a young officer once his desire and ability to fly are confirmed, can, moreover, probably be best attained by full concentration on his academic studies. There is bound to be a certain receptivity in a young man, who has chosen to assume considerable obligations, to suggestions as to what academic courses would best equip him for his Air Force career. In so definitely putting its ROTC program on a professional-career basis, the Air Force might do well to consider the approach taken by the leading civilian professional graduate schools and associations which do not impose a system of courses on the student, but recommend a pattern of study from among the courses already offered in colleges and universities.

A memorandum of the commandant of Headquarters AFROTC sent to the commanding officers of all units in May 1958 opens the way for just such an approach. As such, it represents a very substantial step forward, unless it is narrowly interpreted at the staff level. In this communication and in a

[12] See testimony of Brigadier General (now Major General) R. H. Carmichael, Director of Personnel Procurement and Training, U.S. Air Force, before a Subcommittee of the Committee on Armed Services, U.S. Senate, 84th Congress, 2nd Session, *Flight Training for ROTC*, 1956, pp. 7-10.

PRINCIPLES AND PROPOSALS

letter to college and university presidents at the same time, the commandant suggested that each institution establish an AFROTC advisory committee to consider the following three possibilities: (1) that civilian faculty members teach selected air science courses, (2) that civilian departments design a course or courses to be offered in lieu of air science courses, and (3) that existing civilian courses which meet the overall objectives of the Air Force program be substituted for portions of the present AFROTC curriculum.[13]

Developments already taken along these lines suggest the opportunities that are available under this new directive. At Harvard, for example, at the time that modifications were made in the Army program in 1956, the Air Force introduced similar modifications in its curriculum, inserting the history of civil-military relations course and the government and defense course. Princeton has also modified its Air Force curriculum along similar lines, incorporating the courses in military history, the economics of national security, and military strategy and national security policies. The new directive makes it possible to go considerably beyond these modest beginnings at Harvard and Princeton and similar ones at a few other institutions, including Ohio State. Accepting the Air Force invitation, Harvard, for one, is inaugurating a new program under which AFROTC instruction will be reduced to the usual drill and laboratory periods, a full year course in the sophomore year, and one semester courses each in the junior and senior years. The student will complete his AFROTC requirements with regular academic courses. In the freshman year, he will elect one full course in the natural sciences, preferably a course entitled the atom and the stars, or possibly the foundations of modern physical sciences, or the historical introduction to the physical sciences. In the junior year he will take a one-semester course in human relations, and in the senior year elect one of three

[13] These proposals were the result, in part, of studies conducted at the Ohio State University under the Mershon bequest. See *Report of the Supervisory Committee for the Ohio State University - Air Force ROTC Civilian Instructor Program* (two volumes, 1955-1956 and 1956-1957), Columbus, Ohio, July 2, 1956 and November 1, 1957.

listed courses in the department of government. At Princeton too, there are new Air Force developments along the lines of the Army program there. In addition to the academic courses in history, military strategy, and military psychology already in its curriculum, the Air Force is now accepting academic courses in logic and public speaking, reducing further the number of courses it offers itself. These programs, like the Army program at Princeton and the Navy program at MIT, clearly suggest how the services can better meet the basic rules of a pre-professional education.

The modifications in the ROTC programs that have been undertaken at such institutions as Harvard, Massachusetts Institute of Technology, Yale, Princeton, and Ohio State show how higher education can accept responsibility for providing sound pre-professional preparation for the military profession. They minimize the blight of the standard centralized curriculum, and the intrusion of the armed services in the academic process. Some suggest that only Harvard, Yale, MIT, and Princeton, or a large state university with special interest in military education, like Ohio State, have the resources to make modifications of this sort. This is not the case, however. Courses of a character similar to those provided by these institutions in lieu of ROTC instruction, or others that will serve the same basic objective of pre-professional education, are available at the majority of colleges and universities maintaining programs.[14] One thing is certain, however: more attention will have to be given to military affairs and defense problems in social science courses than is presently the case. This need not be considered a compromising adjustment to ROTC requirements. With or without ROTC, it is a realistic appreciation of the impact of defense on our political, social, and economic life.

[14] All but 10 of the 178 institutions having AFROTC units, for example, offer a course in international relations, which might be accepted in lieu of the international tensions or world political geography instruction in the Air Force curriculum.

PRINCIPLES AND PROPOSALS

Given the nature of the relationship of most institutions to the military services, it is, nevertheless, unlikely that they will take the initiative in pressing for alterations in the ROTC programs without the encouragement and approval of the services. This does not mean that the services have to abandon the concept of a centrally directed, standard curriculum. Indeed, since the military departments are organized the way they are, it would be somewhat blind to the facts of the situation to think that they could or would. But it would certainly be good sense for the services to strip their curricula of all instruction that either duplicates instruction available in regular academic departments or is instruction of a military kind which is more effectively carried out in military installations during intensive training periods such as summer camps and cruises or post-commissioning basic orientation. Our discussion thus far makes clear what ingredients such a program would include: more and perhaps longer summer camps and cruises, less classroom instruction during the academic year, and more informal laboratory-type activities on the campus.

We do not suggest that the armed services do not belong on the campus at all. This should be clear from our discussion in Chapters v and vi on the need for some kind of recruitment mechanism in close and constant contact with students. But we are convinced that this mechanism should not take the form of formal class sessions, at least as much as it does now. Not only do on-campus ROTC courses generally fail to motivate students to careers in the armed services, but they often tend to discourage enthusiasm that does exist. They also always take time away from other courses and thus cut down the scope of the pre-professional education we have suggested is now needed by young officers.[15]

[15] A recent study of ROTC in eight colleges discloses that two of the main reasons given by students for dropping out of the program are (1) "the time involved in ROTC training" and (2) "disinterest in the content of the ROTC courses." See *The College Student and the ROTC*, A Study of Eight Colleges, prepared for the Human Resources Research Office, The George Washington University, by the Bureau of Social Science Research, Inc., Washington, D.C., September 1958.

3. MOTIVATION TOWARD A MILITARY CAREER

We have discussed ROTC instruction primarily in terms of its pre-professional character. But we also have recognized a second and equally important objective of the on-campus program: motivation toward service in one of the armed forces. Certainly the kind of curricula changes that we have recommended can be accepted only if they support this objective as well as provide an appropriate pre-professional education.

By far the most highly-motivating factor for a student during the academic year is contact with the officers in his ROTC unit. We do not mean the instructor-student relationship, which is often strained because it is of comparatively low quality in the academic setting, but rather the man-to-man, warm relationship developing out of respect for the traditional military qualities of loyalty, sense of duty, and self-discipline. This is a relationship that cannot be developed through any ROTC course, though the military have a passion for "adding another course" if something is missing. It can be developed only through a series of mutual activities, preferably informal, directed by officers whose service record and personal outlook are high, and during which the idea of being an officer and the special things about the military profession slowly find their way to the student through his understanding of men who have devoted their lives to the profession.

Unfortunately, the record of the ROTC programs in this respect is uneven. In some units outstanding officers have been assigned and have won the respect of students and faculty alike. In others, officers of lesser capabilities have done great harm. The services are fully aware of this problem and have attempted in recent years to improve the caliber of ROTC personnel. But other requirements also demand the best officers, and there is never enough of the best available for all claimants.

The answer to this situation is for the services to concentrate upon those activities which they can do well. The undergraduate respects a man who can do a firstrate job in his own field. He quickly spots the man who has the unhappy task of instructing in an area for which he is not qualified. Thus greater attention might well be devoted to non-classroom activities and to programs that exploit the special talents of the military staff. At Dartmouth College, for example, the introduction of voluntary instruction in mountain and winter warfare by a well-qualified instructor has stimulated interest among students already engaged in mountaineering and winter sports. A generation ago the fielding of polo teams by the horse artillery ROTC units at places like Stanford and Princeton served a similar purpose. Today the flight orientation and training program of the Army and Air Force might be more fully exploited along the same lines.

The ROTC courses and laboratory sessions should have two purposes in view: first, career motivation; second, the one rule of pre-professional education which cannot be wholly satisfied by the normal academic experience, instruction which is essential for initial employment and, indeed, to derive full benefit from summer camp or cruise experience. Neither should be pursued by the use of "canned" talks in formal sessions, however. For one thing, the idea of pursuing a career in the military service should be incorporated into the whole freshman orientation and general counseling arrangements the college conducts to ease the student into his educational experience and help him choose his major field of study. For another, what is "essential" for initial employment should be construed in terms of serious entrance into a profession and not in terms of a basic training operation. The organization of military operations, the purposes of the various weapons, the idea of command and responsibility, the meaning and wearing of the uniform, are subjects which should be taught. But they are best taught by demonstration, by actual observation through visits to military installations, through meetings with outstanding officers sent on tours of ROTC units by the services, and not by dull description in formal classroom sessions. Perhaps most important of all, they should be taught with an awareness of the intellectual capacities of the students clearly in mind and an appreciation of the contribution of academic courses to their preparation for a military career.

What we have said might well find objections among our military readers, first, because it seems critical of the quality of military instruction, and, second, because it leaves motivation to a kind of imprecise process of understanding. The military services take justifiable pride in the training techniques they have developed. By use of the standard lesson plan system they have been able to bring millions of untrained men through a basic training process and make successful soldiers, sailors, and airmen out of them. There are limitations to these techniques, however. They are effective only when the instruction is expert and is carried out in an appropriate physical and psychological environment. Neither is available on a college campus. Beyond these limitations, there is the need of the services to drop ideas of *training* during the academic year and concentrate on the objectives of *career motivation* and *pre-professional education*.[16]

This approach, it seems to us, would offer many advantages to the services. By limiting themselves to those activities which they can do well, they would gain increased respect from the student. By minimizing classroom instruction they not only would reduce interference with his regular academic program but would enhance the appeal to him by encouraging him to pursue that program to his full capabilities. Perhaps of greatest significance, this approach would permit acceptance of students into the program at later stages *during* the college experience and not just at the time of matriculation. Such an arrangement would strengthen the motivational aspect of the ROTC. It also would open up the possibility of an officer procurement program with a shorter lead time.

The need to permit ROTC registration at later stages after

[16] This kind of an approach is employed by the Royal Air Force in Great Britain. See *University Air Squadrons, Outline of Conditions of Service*, Air Ministry Pamphlet 198; also *Permanent Commissions in the Royal Air Force, Conditions of Appointment of University Candidates*, Air Ministry Pamphlet 904, and *University and Royal Air Force Technical College Cadetship*, Air Ministry Pamphlet 336.

PRINCIPLES AND PROPOSALS

matriculation is extremely important. At the present time, students at voluntary schools generally have to sign up for ROTC during the first week of freshman year, or not at all. At institutions where military training is compulsory, the student has no choice in the matter until the end of the sophomore year, when he may apply for the advanced course. Where the decision of joining ROTC must be made during the first hectic days of coming to college, it cannot be given the care and consideration that should be given to choosing a career. Nor is there opportunity for the college to be of much help. The exception is the rare case of a young man already oriented, through parental or other influence, toward a military career. Under normal circumstances, however, the threat of the draft can well be a decisive factor. With the heat of the draft at a very low point and even, perhaps, on the point of ebbing, there is a greater need than ever to keep the opportunity to join open, at least until the sophomore year. Such a procedure would allow a more highly developed college counseling system to be effective and would be consistent with the general theory that a student does not begin to "major" until his second or third year.

The services cannot do this, of course, without better cooperation from the colleges and universities than presently exists in most places. Indeed a program that depends more on extracurricular than regular class time, on informal, perhaps voluntary participation rather than prescription, involves an even greater degree of mutual understanding than does the present system. This cooperation and understanding can be achieved only on an institution by institution basis. This is probably the main reason why such a program has to be decentralized. It requires the formation of a faculty committee, on which ROTC commanders sit, to work out programs of studies for students who are seriously interested in the career opportunities of the armed services. The work of the committee should not, as is generally the case now, be simply concerned with procedural matters, leaving the content to the military. Indeed the reasons for maintaining a full standard ROTC curriculum are often given substance by the refusal of civilian educators to wake up to the responsibilities involved in educating young men for service with the armed forces. A faculty committee should be concerned with pre-professional education for a career with the armed forces and apply the same creative force that it would if it were dealing with pre-medical or engineering education.

These comments suggest the degree to which thinking about ROTC by faculties has to change. The lead will have to come from college and university presidents, however. From the practical point of view, they can more easily be approached and organized in an effort through the education associations and especially through the American Council on Education. It is the administrators, moreover, who set the tone by the reasons they sought ROTC units and continue to maintain them on their campuses. Many institutions retain ROTC programs because of a sincere belief that they are essential for the national defense, but unfortunately some of these and others besides appear to retain them more as a hedge against the threat of declining enrollments in time of crisis. Still others, while accepting the national need for the programs, are irritated by the fluctuations of purpose and policy demonstrated by the services and adopt an attitude of tolerance rather than strong support.

In these circumstances colleges and universities, as well as the armed forces, need to clarify the fundamental objective of building a strong professional officer corps and to integrate the programs into the local institution on this basis. No institution should retain an ROTC program as a hedge against some uncertain threat in the future. The experience in the Second World War suggests that in a similar situation they will be replaced by programs of shorter lead time. An ROTC contract in itself is no guarantee of continued male enrollment in case of national emergency.

More important perhaps is the fact that a Second World War type of situation, requiring the rapid mobilization of mass forces, is only one of a number of possibilities and the less likely to recur. In the meanwhile there is the real need for well-educated young officers in the professional service. This is the objective to which any college and university must turn if it commits itself to the program. If it does so, it should then provide the positive leadership and support that is necessary to gain results and not leave the initiative to the military. If it is not prepared to do so, or is not really equipped to do so, it should get out of the program. Whatever pressures the educational associations can exert should be in this direction rather than in the direction of uncritical defense of any institution's desire to maintain a unit whether or not it can help to meet the changing requirements of the armed services.

4. THE ISSUE OF FEDERAL SUPPORT AND PURPOSE

We made the point earlier that "responsibility for achieving a proper relationship of higher education to the needs of society rests with individuals and agencies of the federal government and with leaders in higher education." We also emphasized that "leadership must come ultimately from the former." The kind of on-campus program we have recommended may come about, as it has, at a few institutions. But the complete adjustment of the programs to the changing officer requirements of the services still awaits positive leadership from the federal government. In concluding this examination of the ROTC programs, we therefore return to a central theme of our study: the need for a clear, concise recognition by the federal government of the changing nature of the programs and their essential national purpose.

One obvious manifestation of this recognition would, of course, be realistic financial support. The ROTC programs impose a much more substantial burden upon colleges and universities than is generally recognized. The so-called facilities legislation, which would provide funds for physical construction on a matching basis, would, if endorsed by the Bureau of the Budget and voted by the Congress, lighten this burden only in part. Even if the full cost of construction were provided, as we believe it should be, because of the clear federal purpose of ROTC, the local institution would still have to bear the cost of maintaining the structure, and this may well cost one third to one half as much again as construction cost in capital equivalent. The armed services should bear a considerably larger portion of the costs of operating the ROTC programs, including the maintenance of facilities as well as their construction and administrative supervision. This contribution should be according to a reasonable formula based upon actual costs to the institutions rather than upon tuition and other charges to the student. In other words, state or local tax support or private endowment income, which make it possible for public and private institutions respectively to charge the student a good deal less than the cost of his education, should not be burdened by the federal program. The federal government should be responsible for paying its share of the costs of the educational services that it receives.

It may be argued that the ROTC programs have a value quite apart from their federal purpose, that they constitute a worthwhile educational experience in themselves, that they provide a needed element of discipline or stability on a campus, and they give a certain amount of elementary military training that every young man should have in partial fulfillment of his obligation to his country, and that these are features for which the institutions should willingly bear the costs. Granting that there is some validity to this argument, these purposes now definitely are subsidiary to the central function of the programs as sources of professional officers for the federal armed forces. They do not diminish by much the responsibility of the federal government.

This matter bears directly upon the broader issue of federal aid to higher education. As enrollments rise in the decade ahead, institutions of higher education are going to be hard put to maintain standards, provide adequate faculty compensation, and construct the new facilities that will be required. Financing will become increasingly difficult. In this situation various forms of federal aid are being proposed. But, quite apart from the merits of these proposals, whether for fellowships and scholarships, building aid, revision of the income tax laws to encourage private giving, or what have you, the case for increased federal support of the ROTC programs is simple. The armed services are utilizing the facilities and services of higher education for an unquestioned federal purpose. Adequate reimbursement for this use violates no principles of decentralized educational administration or institutional autonomy. Moreover, by reducing present burdens on colleges and universities in this manner, the government would free financial resources for other purposes and reduce the need for outside help, including federal aid, for these purposes.

It is nevertheless important to emphasize that the federal government should not be burdened with the costs of ROTC activities that do not contribute directly to the objective of the programs as sources of professional officers. Here we come face to face with the issue of compulsory military training. We do not consider that compulsory training is needed to meet the changing officer requirements of the armed services. As we said earlier, the only practical advantage of retaining the compulsory feature is that it tends to broaden the selection base where it exists. We are convinced, however, that compulsory training is an intrusion on the educational process and that it is a negative factor in career motivation. It is also bound to become increasingly expensive as enrollments in the land-grant and state universities soar under the impact of the population bulge and the prerequisite of college training for more and more employment opportunities. It is also bound to create more difficult and frustrating problems in seeking to encourage young men to make their careers in the military profession. The more students, the less chance there is to conduct the kind of on-campus counseling efforts we feel are most likely to gain effective results.

We are nevertheless convinced that the selection base cannot be left to chance. It must be maintained on a broad basis. We are therefore in favor of a scholarship program accompanied by a four- or five-year active duty obligation for all three services and indeed consider it absolutely necessary if the services are going to gain the kind of officers they need. A scholarship program under which awards are made through nationwide testing would, in fact, create a selection base that extended beyond the land-grant and state universities. The details of such a program need not be spelled out here. There is ample background for its development in the Holloway Plan, the recommendations of the Gray Committee in 1948 and the Service Academy Board in 1949, the work that went into the omnibus bills actually presented to the Congress in 1951, 1952, and 1953, the recent plan of the Army Ordnance Corps, the specialized talent scheme drawn up by Assistant Secretary of Defense Carter Burgess in 1955, and, beyond the military establishment itself, the development of a national education policy culminating in the education bill of 1958 which clearly recognizes the responsibility of the federal government to encourage young men to enter professions where there is a gap between "national needs and individual desires."

The ROTC programs will not begin to take on some of the features we have recommended, however, without strong direction from the defense establishment itself. For reasons we suggested in Chapter v, initiative must come from this point. But it is equally clear that it will not be forthcoming without administrative reorganization within the services and particularly within the Department of Defense. Within the services, the situation in the Navy and the Air Force, whereby supervision of the NROTC and AFROTC are centered in the Bureau of Naval Personnel and Headquarters AFROTC respectively, offers advantages over the situation in the Army, in which ROTC affairs are scattered among a number of different agencies. But even in the Navy and Air Force there appear at times to be inadequate coordination between the offices concerned with the educational aspects of the programs in the Bureau and at Maxwell Field and those charged with personnel planning and operations, budgeting, and so forth elsewhere in the Departments of the Navy and the Air Force. In all three services, but particularly in the Army, the programs suffer by association with planning and administration of matters relating to the reserve forces. Their present significant role as the principal source of regular and active duty officers should be recognized in appropriate administrative arrangements.

These matters, however, are of much less consequence than the lack of adequate arrangements at the defense level to coordinate the programs of the three services with each other and with the broader programs of the Department of Defense and of the government at large. The Reserve Forces Policy Board has failed to provide the necessary direction and leadership. Indeed the programs should be dissociated, at every level, from reserve matters and treated from the broader manpower perspective that their changing objectives warrant.

The provision of officers from civilian colleges and universities cannot be treated in isolation. It should be considered in relation to a military manpower policy conceived at the defense level and designed to guide the operations of the military departments. The Cordiner Committee which developed the plan that became the military pay bill of 1958 was an *ad hoc* group that was dissolved when its report was submitted to the Secretary of Defense. Some kind of continuing manpower advisory council is, however, needed by the Secretary if he is going to provide policy guidance in this area of operations. It might well work in the same way the scientific advisory groups do. Each service has its own scientific council, made up of individual experts, to assist in its research and development activities. But there is also a board at the defense level, which provides a mechanism for policy guidance and coordination. By creating a similar advisory system in the field of military manpower, the Secretary of Defense would provide himself with the means of carrying out the professionalization of the services that the present situation requires. Within such a system, the provision of officers from civilian

THE FUTURE

colleges and universities would be one particular area of concern and might well be dealt with by a special subpanel of the main council.

At every level of responsibility, from the college campus to the educational associations to the military departments to the Department of Defense, the real need is to begin to think of the ROTC in terms of the changing nature of our military manpower requirements. Organizational change is only a first step, but it is an essential one. It will be easier for changes in attitude and approach to follow. A change at the defense level will also set a pattern that could then be adopted throughout the system. It would also give assurance to the colleges and universities that the federal government was really clarifying the objectives of the programs and putting itself in the position to support them. All the problems with which this book has been concerned, thus return, in many ways, to the desk of the Secretary of Defense.

A NOTE ON METHOD AND SOURCES

A NUMBER of research methods have been used in the preparation of this book. In the brief history of the ROTC included as Part Two, we relied heavily on the printed record and the experienced advice of a number of experts in the field of military history. We were most fortunate in being allowed to examine the official Department of the Army records for the important period from 1945 to 1955. These records are located at the Departmental Records Branch (DRB), the Office of the Adjutant General (TAGO). Reference to them has been designated by the War Department (WD) or (after 1947) Department of the Army (DA) file number followed by the initials "DRB, TAGO" to indicate their location. Although we did not have an opportunity to examine Navy and Air Force records in the same way, we had the benefit of comments on the historical and other sections of the book from staff of the Bureau of Naval Personnel, and of Headquarters AFROTC. In some cases, copies of Navy and Air Force documents were to be found in the Army files, particularly in matters of interservice concern and, in the case of the Air Force, particularly for the years prior to its separation from the Army in 1947. Mr. Robert Thurston, presently on the Commandant's staff at Headquarters AFROTC and formerly with the Army's ROTC division in the Office of the Executive for Reserves and ROTC Affairs, kindly made available to us invaluable historical documentation from his personal files.

In preparing our analysis of current issues in the ROTC, the research problem was more complex. The full picture does not come through from the printed record, although we took care to examine whatever material was available: in Congressional hearings, in published and, where available, unpublished reports and studies prepared by the armed services and by educational and professional associations, in official regulations and instructions, and in professional military and educational journals. A good deal of our research was conducted through interviews and observation. Much of our time was given to field work. We made numerous visits to appropriate offices in the Pentagon and elsewhere in the armed services. For the Army these included the office of the Assistant Chief of Staff for Reserve Components and the Chief of Army Reserve and ROTC Affairs (CARROTC), and Headquarters, Continental Army Command, Fort Monroe, Virginia; for the Navy, the education and training division of the Bureau of Naval Personnel; and for the Air Force, the office of the Director of Personnel Procurement and Training at Headquarters USAF, and Headquarters Air Force ROTC, Maxwell Air Force Base, Alabama. We also visited colleges and universities throughout the country, selected to include representative examples of the types of institutions that make up the diverse pattern of American higher education. We have discussed ROTC affairs with administrators, teachers, and military instructors at these institutions, as well as with professional colleagues generally over a period of several years.

After investigating all these sources, we prepared a preliminary analysis of current issues for presentation to the Conference held in Hanover in June 1958 and discussed in President Dickey's Foreword. The lively and incisive criticism of our preliminary papers was of invaluable help to us in preparing these pages for final publication.

As far as we know, there are no published books of a general character dealing with the three ROTC programs. Although numerous articles have appeared in military and educational journals from time to time, they have usually been relatively short descriptive accounts, or have dealt with certain narrow features of the programs. Likewise, the ROTC has been the subject of numerous unpublished master's and doctor's theses in recent years, but these have also been of limited or specialized scope. The serious student of ROTC affairs should turn for bibliographical assistance to the Library of Congress, the Air University Library, the libraries of the service war colleges, and the Office of the Chief of Military History, of the Department of the Army.

STATISTICAL APPENDIX*

LIST OF TABLES

1. Officers commissioned through the Army and Navy ROTC programs: 1920-1945.
2. Army officer production by sources: 1950-1957.
3. Navy officer production by sources: 1950-1957.
4. Air Force officer production by sources: 1953-1957.
5. Annual costs of Army, Navy, and Air Force ROTC programs by major items of expenditure: 1954-1957.
6. Army, Navy, and Air Force Personnel on Fulltime ROTC duty: 1957-1958.
7. Officers commissioned through the Army, Navy, and Air Force ROTC programs by civilian institutions of origin: 1955-1957.

* The data for these tables has been secured through the Office of the Assistant Chief of Staff for Reserve Components of the Department of the Army, the Office of the Chief of Naval Personnel, and the Office of the Director of Personnel Procurement and Training of the Department of the Air Force. Although the services report differently on these matters we have grouped the data for comparability. While the figures accurately show the gross dimensions of the programs, individual items should not be used out of context.

TABLE 1
Officers Commissioned through the Army and Navy ROTC Programs: 1920-1945

Year	Army	Navy	Year	Army	Navy
1920	133		1933	6,686	179
1921	934		1934	6,586	213
1922	2,465		1935	6,345	226
1923	3,786		1936	5,628	234
1924	4,048		1937	4,838	194
1925	4,884		1938	5,338	226
1926	5,728		1939	4,964	235
1927	5,839		1940	6,508	144
1928	6,030		1941	7,145	217
1929	6,139		1942	10,039	309
1930	5,890	125*	1943†		570
1931	5,984	126	1944		2,399
1932	6,450	167	1945		979

* The First NROTC class entered college in 1926 under legislation passed the previous year and was graduated in 1930.
† Army ROTC was suspended during the war years.

TABLE 2
Army Officer Production by Sources: 1950-1957

Source	1950	1951	1952	1953	1954	1955	1956	1957
USMA	497	352	394	375	446	324	356	40•
ROTC (RA)	644	819	968	696	375	516	525	68
ROTC (USAR)	8,859	9,464	12,857	10,447	14,500	18,246	13,296	12,98'
OCS	546	2,095	12,541	4,829	1,898	1,315	743	62
Others, inc. Med. Corps, JAG, etc.	12,395	15,232	12,755	11,890	7,150	8,037	7,580	5,71
Total	22,941	27,962	39,515	28,237	24,369	28,438	22,500	20,41

TABLE 3

Navy Officer Production by Sources: 1950-1957

Source	1950	1951	1952	1953	1954	1955	1956	1957
Naval Academy	462	481	518	621	559	496	457	572
NROTC Regular	958	1,649	1,614	1,422	1,354	1,331	1,300	1,209
NROTC contract	235	251	634	634	1,102	1,398	1,344	1,110
Naval Cadet (aviation)	753	1,070	610	1,253	1,193	1,209	1,290	1,401
Enlisted men integrated into Officer Corps	17	1,566	4,386	5,404	5,306	302	1,505	2,698
OCS						1,685	2,608	3,758
Direct commissions inc. Med. Officers	749	3,202	2,124	2,362	2,656	2,889	1,514	2,169
Total	3,174	8,219	9,886	11,696	12,170	9,310	10,018	12,917

TABLE 4

Air Force Officer Production by Sources: 1953-1957*

Source	1953	1954	1955	1956	1957
Service Academies			325	288	341
ROTC (USAF)			83	127	222
ROTC (USAFR)	5,910	9,210	8,997	13,353†	6,179
Air Cadet	6,400	6,600	6,110	2,710	1,583
OCS‡			979	933	1,187
Others, inc. Med. Corps, etc.			3,399	3,100	3,369
Total	*	*	19,893	20,511	12,881

* Figures were not available for the years 1950, 1951, and 1952. Only partial figures were available for the years 1953 and 1954.

† Included are 3,500 graduates called to active duty for two years from Air National Guard status for purpose of fulfilling their remaining active duty obligation.

‡ Includes officers commissioned from warrant officer and enlisted man status.

TABLE 5
Annual Costs of Army, Navy, and Air Force ROTC Programs by Major Items of Expenditure: 1954-1957

Item of Expenditure	Army ROTC 1954-1955	Army ROTC 1955-1956	Army ROTC 1956-1957	Navy ROTC 1954-1955	Navy ROTC 1955-1956	Navy ROTC 1956-1957	Air Force ROTC 1954-1955	Air Force ROTC 1955-1956	Air Force ROTC 1956-1957
Personnel, including pay and allowances	$43,066,000	$46,068,000	$47,992,000	$10,212,562	$10,245,051	$11,390,907	$17,088,249	$18,126,356	$16,996,586
Educational testing				128,650	129,630	99,037			
Tuition, fees, and books				3,076,487	3,393,142	3,639,780			
Flight instruction program									561,218
Summer training				10,259	7,406	11,342	2,534,126	2,053,967	1,339,272
General operations and maintenance (including summer camp in the case of the Army ROTC)	10,182,000	12,551,000	12,823,000	283,380	317,460	271,364	10,835,245	10,070,780	7,769,871
Total	$53,248,000	$58,619,000	$60,815,000	$13,711,338	$14,092,689	$15,412,430	$30,457,620	$30,251,103	$26,666,947

TABLE 6

Army, Navy, and Air Force Personnel on Full-time ROTC Duty
1957-1958

	Army ROTC Hqs.*	Units	Navy ROTC Hqs.	Units	Air Force ROTC Hqs.	Units
Major General					1	
Brigadier General					1	
Colonel/Captain	5	117		54	14	87
Lt. Colonel/Commander	13	285	2	54	17	95
Major/Lt. Commander	5	404	1		27	423
Captain/Lt. S.G.		784		273	10	610
1st Lt./Lt. J.G.		175			3	
Warrant Officer		15			5	
Enlisted men		2,622	1	315	85	925
Civilians					63	
Total	23	4,402	4	696	226	2,140

* Includes the ROTC divisions in the Office of the Chief of Reserve and ROTC Affairs, the Headquarters of the Continental Army Command, and the six army headquarters.

TABLE 7

Officers Commissioned through the Army, Navy, and Air Force ROTC Programs by Civilian Institutions of Origin: 1955-1957

NOTES:

1. Colleges and universities marked by an asterisk (*) are those in which ROTC training is *compulsory* during the first two years.
2. Data in the column marked "Male Graduates 1956-1957" were taken from Office of Education Circular No. 527, *Earned Degrees Conferred by Higher Educational Institutions 1956-1957*, April 1958. They designate men who received *bachelor's and 1st professional degrees* during this academic year. This degree level is defined by the Office of Education as *the first degree granted upon completion of a course of study in a given field and must be based on at least 4 years of college work, or the equivalent thereof.* As such, they show the potential supply of college graduates in each institution and offer a ready measuring rod for ROTC production.
3. *Army ROTC*
    a. Data shown in column marked "USA" denote ROTC graduates who were offered and accepted commissions in the Regular Army under the Army's *Distinguished Military Graduate* program.
    b. Data shown in column marked "USAR" denote ROTC graduates commissioned as reserve officers.
4. *Navy ROTC*
    a. Data shown in column marked "USN" denote NROTC graduates commissioned in the *Regular Navy* (under the *regular*, or *Holloway* program).
    b. Data shown in column marked "USNR" denote NROTC graduates commissioned as reserve officers under the *contract* program.
5. *Air Force ROTC*
    a. Data shown in column marked "USAF" denote AFROTC graduates who were offered and accepted commissions in the Regular Air Force under the Air Force's *Distinguished Military Graduate* program.
    b. Data shown in column marked "USAFR" denote AFROTC graduates commissioned as reserve officers.

College or University	Male grads. 1956-57	ARMY ROTC 1955 USA USAR	ARMY ROTC 1956 USA USAR	ARMY ROTC 1957 USA USAR	NAVY ROTC 1955 USN USNR	NAVY ROTC 1956 USN USNR	NAVY ROTC 1957 USN USNR	AIR FORCE ROTC 1955 USAF USAFR	AIR FORCE ROTC 1956 USAF USAFR	AIR FORCE ROTC 1957 USAF USAFR
Alabama										
*Alabama Polytech. Inst.	1,131	8 120	2 122	5 153	16 14	24 28	32 21	3 76	3 57	1 65
*Jacksonville State Teachers	171	3 23	7 16	13 45						
Spring Hill Col.	142	5 42	46	7 49						
*State Teachers, Florence	113	1 33	3 35	1 23						
*Tuskegee Inst.	187	7	3 28	4 27				20	12	19
*Univ. of Alabama	1,003	1 88	2 78	2 91				41	49	22
Arizona										
*Arizona State Col.	535	2 21	2 30	3 31				57	41 1	26
*Univ. of Arizona	653	1 39	1 49	2 59				1 53	2 45	3 33
Arkansas										
*Arkansas Polytech. Col.	82	2 14	4 24	2 25						
*Arkansas State Col.	181	1 46	5 49	12 39						
*Henderson State Teachers	81	6 50	3 29	4 21						
*Ouachita Baptist Col.	99	1 24	16	2 28						
*Univ. of Ark.	732	2 65	5 73	2 101				35	1 23	21

251

College or University	Male grads. 1956-57	ARMY ROTC 1955 USA USAR	ARMY ROTC 1956 USA USAR	ARMY ROTC 1957 USA USAR	NAVY ROTC 1955 USN USNR	NAVY ROTC 1956 USN USNR	NAVY ROTC 1957 USN USNR	AIR FORCE ROTC 1955 USAF USAFR	AIR FORCE ROTC 1956 USAF USAFR	AIR FORCE ROTC 1957 USAF USAFR
California										
California Inst. of Tech.	139							1 35	14 6	11
California State Polytech.	547	1 9	4 26	5 24						
Fresno State Col.	544							1 48	29	7
*Loyola Univ. of L.A.	217							1 49 1	29	23
*Occidental Col.	146							2 21	21	18
Pomona and Claremont Col.	204		1 37	40						
San Diego State Col.	606	1						1 38 2	42 1	26
San Francisco State Col.	671							27	21	18
San Jose State Col.	974	2 24	3 25	5 46				1 20 1	25 1	16
Stanford Univ.	1,176	67	2 52	89				76	49	57
*Univ. of Cal. (Berkeley)	†	1 98	2 102	2 102	38 40	32 38	30 47	1 62 1	59 2	39
*Univ. of Cal. (Davis)	†	2 17	1 25	4 32	33 39	26 44	14 38			
*Univ. of Cal. (L.A.)	†	3 83	3 43	2 76	19 30	32 21	14 26	1 71	4 48	29
*Univ. of Cal. (Santa Barbara)	†	22	1 21	3 17						
*Univ. of San Francisco	282	77	1 73	1 47						

† University of California had 4,793 male graduates on *all campuses*.

College or University	Male grads. 1956-57	ARMY ROTC 1955 USA USAR	ARMY ROTC 1956 USA USAR	ARMY ROTC 1957 USA USAR	NAVY ROTC 1955 USN USNR	NAVY ROTC 1956 USN USNR	NAVY ROTC 1957 USN USNR	AIR FORCE ROTC 1955 USAF USAFR	AIR FORCE ROTC 1956 USAF USAFR	AIR FORCE ROTC 1957 USAF USAFR
*Univ. of Santa Clara	181	1 82	3 83	4 68						
Univ. of Southern Cal.	1,536				25 33	32 32	22 34	53	29	1 20
Colorado										
*Colorado A & M	560	2 65	2 62	1 74				4 36 4	27	6 29
*Colorado Col.	118	1 12	23	7						
*Colorado School of Mines	160	33	2 45	1 40						
*Colorado State Col. of Ed.	1,015	1 67	1 82	5 64	27 20	21 14	21 17	24 3	17	2 15
Univ. of Colorado	733	2 36	1 18	1 19				47 1	29	3 20
Univ. of Denver								2 21	10	6
Connecticut										
Trinity Col.	181							1 39	37	21
*Univ. of Connecticut	882	2 68	4 72	4 68	21 74	35 61	31 29	1 54	37	6 26
Yale Univ.	1,348	116	53	1 66				98	29	19
Delaware										
*Univ. of Delaware	243	42	36	41						
District of Columbia										
*Catholic Univ.	223							30 1	35	1 13
George Washington Univ.	674							24 3	14	3 14

253

College or University	Male grads. 1956-57	ARMY ROTC 1955 USA USAR	ARMY ROTC 1956 USA USAR	ARMY ROTC 1957 USA USAR	NAVY ROTC 1955 USN USNR	NAVY ROTC 1956 USN USNR	NAVY ROTC 1957 USN USNR	AIR FORCE ROTC 1955 USAF USAFR	AIR FORCE ROTC 1956 USAF USAFR	AIR FORCE ROTC 1957 USAF USAFR
Georgetown Univ.	893	2 29	33	4 42				27	26	25
*Howard Univ.	323	2 19	16	1 9				17	16	12
Florida										
*Florida A & M	155	2 26	2 44	3 34						
*Florida Southern Col.	266	5 40	2 27	5 30						
*Florida State Univ.	758	1 15	1 17	16				26	20	13
Stetson Univ.	172	3 20	1 21	3 25						
*Univ. of Florida	1,225	4 84	5 68	6 68				1 49 1	48	31
Univ. of Miami	1,175	1 40	1 53	44				67 3	37	27
Georgia										
Emory Univ.	516							1 22	18	13
*Georgia Inst. of Tech.	945	1 176	2 74	4 157	31 46	39 34	30 32	93 1	108 1	74 8
*Georgia State Col. of Bus. Admin.	301	53	16	1 23						
Mercer Univ.	208	5 62	3 32	5 48						
*North Georgia Col.	66	3 31	12 48	11 39						
*Univ. of Georgia	894	2 104	1 50	4 48				55 1	36	32 3

254

College or University	Male grads. 1956-57	ARMY ROTC 1955 USA USAR	ARMY ROTC 1956 USA USAR	ARMY ROTC 1957 USA USAR	NAVY ROTC 1955 USN USNR	NAVY ROTC 1956 USN USNR	NAVY ROTC 1957 USN USNR	AIR FORCE ROTC 1955 USAF USAFR	AIR FORCE ROTC 1956 USAF USAFR	AIR FORCE ROTC 1957 USAF USAFR
Idaho										
*Idaho State Col.	188	2 17	4 25	3 24						
*Univ. of Idaho	448	2 36	6 58	3 39	20 10	11 13	15 8	44	2 31	2 16
Illinois										
*Bradley Univ.	339							1 55	4 48	5 26
*De Paul Univ.	483	4	36	35						
Illinois Inst. of Tech.	437									
Knox Col.	101	2 61	45	1 63	19 7	23 6	24 3	1 42	1 16	40
Loyola Univ.	617	1 74	48	2 68						
Northwestern Univ.	1,183							67	34	6
*Southern Illinois Univ.	426									
*Univ. of Illinois	3,029	7 223	4 221	9 198	29 20	18 20	21 29	67	35 6	25
*Wheaton Col.	241	3 28	2 26	2 27	32 24		9	1 97	79 12	48

255

College or University	Male grads. 1956-57	ARMY ROTC 1955 USA USAR	ARMY ROTC 1956 USA USAR	ARMY ROTC 1957 USA USAR	NAVY ROTC 1955 USN USNR	NAVY ROTC 1956 USN USNR	NAVY ROTC 1957 USN USNR	AIR FORCE ROTC 1955 USAF USAFR	AIR FORCE ROTC 1956 USAF USAFR	AIR FORCE ROTC 1957 USAF USAFR
Indiana										
Ball State Teachers Col.	325							1 41	23	1 28
Butler Univ.	220							38	1 22	1 12
DePauw Univ.	199							1 41	1 20	1 14
Evansville Col.	140							1 28	2 26	13
*Indiana Univ.	1,402	5 124	8 129	9 151	35 47	25 21	30 23	106	1 63	6 38
*Purdue Univ.	1,691	2 171	3 195	1 231				103	1 90	6 97
*Rose Polytech. Inst.	85									
Univ. of Notre Dame	1,173	5 73	1 95	3 76	35 49	23 54	32 28	108	1 70	37
Iowa										
*Coe Col.	88							30	17	16
*Drake Univ.	365							1 32	24	1 15
*Grinnell Col.	99							17	13	13
*Iowa State Col.	1,024	2 165	4 125	4 130	31 25	27 22	25 18	120	1 70	50
*State Univ. of Iowa	1,083	2 49	3 56	2 60				74	32	2 29
Kansas										
*Kansas St. Col. of A and AS	848	2 115	88	3 93				1 112	1 62	36

College or University	Male grads. 1956-57	ARMY ROTC 1955 USA USAR	ARMY ROTC 1956 USA USAR	ARMY ROTC 1957 USA USAR	NAVY ROTC 1955 USN USNR	NAVY ROTC 1956 USN USNR	NAVY ROTC 1957 USN USNR	AIR FORCE ROTC 1955 USAF USAFR	AIR FORCE ROTC 1956 USAF USAFR	AIR FORCE ROTC 1957 USAF USAFR
*Kansas State Teachers	335	4	5 44	2 41	29 21	29 22	29 19	1 114	68	3 35
Univ. of Kansas	1,013	37	5 44 72	2 41 4 85				1 35	29 3	4 14
Univ. of Wichita	267	54	3 72	4 85				1 35	29 3	4 14
Washburn Univ.	217	17	2 24	20				1 41	24	1 15
Kentucky										
Eastern Kentucky State Col.	211	6 36	9 31	13 23						
*Murray State Col.	216	6	2 27	2 25						
*Univ. of Kentucky	767	1 41	3 49	5 42				2 87	50	1 32
Univ. of Louisville	525				17 6	25 3	19 6	43	21	27
Western Kentucky State Col.	95	1 22	2 26	4 34				43	21	9
Louisiana										
*Centenary Col.	81	2 16	2 16	1 18						
*Louisiana State Univ. & A & M	948	2 99	2 58	7 73				131	100	3 54
Louisiana Polytech. Inst.	297									
Loyola Univ.	251	3 43	3 42	2 46				1 67	49 2	5 35
*McNeese State Col.	93	25	35	30						
*Northeast Louisiana State Col.	96	27	28	6 24						

College or University	Male grads. 1956-57	ARMY ROTC 1955 USA USAR	ARMY ROTC 1956 USA USAR	ARMY ROTC 1957 USA USAR	NAVY ROTC 1955 USN USNR	NAVY ROTC 1956 USN USNR	NAVY ROTC 1957 USN USNR	AIR FORCE ROTC 1955 USAF USAFR	AIR FORCE ROTC 1956 USAF USAFR	AIR FORCE ROTC 1957 USAF USAFR
Northwestern State Col. of Louisiana	155	3 38	4 35	2 30						
*Southern Univ. & A & M Col.	183	3 33	5 37	3 33						
Southwestern Louisiana Inst.	378							95 1	58 3	23
Tulane Univ.	609	1 38	1 36	2 37	26 22	14 14	32 19	45 1	35	14
Maine										
Bowdoin Col.	183	77	1 64	1 65						
*Colby Col.	112							23 2	11 2	10
*Univ. of Maine	484	2 84	3 87	68						
Maryland										
Johns Hopkins Univ.	396	49	3 49	2 37						
*Loyola Col.	128	1 24	2 27	3 31						
*Morgan State Col.	139	3 43	6 34	6 51						
*Univ. of Maryland	1,458							125 2	62 4	54
*Western Maryland Col.	75	1 26	27	1 26						
Massachusetts										
Amherst Col.	257							52	30	1
Boston Col.	791	1 51	1 67	5 56						
Boston Univ.	1,358	1 39	45	4 63				64	29	23
Harvard Univ.	2,317	74	2 57	1 40	23 43	28 36	28 23	57 4	27 3	3

College or University	Male grads. 1956-57	ARMY ROTC 1955 USA USAR	ARMY ROTC 1956 USA USAR	ARMY ROTC 1957 USA USAR	NAVY ROTC 1955 USN USNR	NAVY ROTC 1956 USN USNR	NAVY ROTC 1957 USN USNR	AIR FORCE ROTC 1955 USAF USAFR	AIR FORCE ROTC 1956 USAF USAFR	AIR FORCE ROTC 1957 USAF USAFR
Holy Cross Col.	410				29 46	27 35	24 17	72 16	49 9	14 6
*Lowell Tech. Inst.	88							1		2
*Massachusetts Inst. of Tech.	757	115	2 112	135				1 68	45 5	34
Northeastern Univ.	945	6 133	4 137	14 217				22	18	12
Tufts Univ.	583				25 33	33 30	30 23			
*Univ. of Massachusetts	551	54	3 41	3 45				3 47	30 5	40
Williams Col.	232							50	24	8
Worcester Poly. Inst.	180	48	57	2 81						
Michigan										
*Central Michigan Col. of Education	297	1 16	1 24	3 33						
Eastern Michigan Col.	254		8	3 21						
Michigan Col. of Min. & Tech.	335	29	46	35				2 31	1 26	2 24
*Michigan State Univ.	2,050	277	1 160	6 195				1 136	1 69	6 - 71
Univ. of Detroit	708	9	1 11	29				41	33	3 20
Univ. of Michigan	2,189	3 38	50	1 88	27 21	31 17	22 19	109	79	45
Wayne Univ.	960	4						34	14	3
Western Michigan Col.	559	6 86	44	3 39						

259

College or University	Male grads. 1956-57	ARMY ROTC 1955 USA USAR	ARMY ROTC 1956 USA USAR	ARMY ROTC 1957 USA USAR	NAVY ROTC 1955 USN USNR	NAVY ROTC 1956 USN USNR	NAVY ROTC 1957 USN USNR	AIR FORCE ROTC 1955 USAF USAFR	AIR FORCE ROTC 1956 USAF USAFR	AIR FORCE ROTC 1957 USAF USAFR
Minnesota										
*Col. of St. Thomas	198									
*St. John's Univ.	157	8	1 32	38				35	19 1	25
*St. Olaf Col.	160							24	23 3	24
Univ. of Minnesota	2,444	159	1 137	113	40 17	19 25	17 14	124 3	71	36
Mississippi										
Mississippi Southern Col.	417	37	3 32	25	17 9	14 6	16 9			
*Mississippi State Col.	717	44	2 44	61				1 44 1	52 3	42
Univ. of Mississippi	422	25	1 26	29				22	15 1	16
Missouri										
*Lincoln Univ.	57	1 24	2 9	3 6						
*Southwest Missouri State Col.	219	2 15	10 28	9 28						
*St. Louis Univ.	857									
*Univ. of Missouri	1,650	1 251	5 211	1 207	23 26	28 19	20 24	2 102 3	65 3	30
Washington Univ.	747	70	59	90				2 123	61	62
*Westminster Col.	81	1 8	2 21	19				53	36 2	19

College or University	Male grads. 1956-57	ARMY ROTC 1955 USA USAR	ARMY ROTC 1956 USA USAR	ARMY ROTC 1957 USA USAR	NAVY ROTC 1955 USN USNR	NAVY ROTC 1956 USN USNR	NAVY ROTC 1957 USN USNR	AIR FORCE ROTC 1955 USAF USAFR	AIR FORCE ROTC 1956 USAF USAFR	AIR FORCE ROTC 1957 USAF USAFR
Montana										
*Montana State Col.	333	2 15	2 31	2 24				25	18 5	15
*Montana State Univ.	377	2 34	4 23	27				35	22	13
*Montana School of Mines	37							7	8	6
Nebraska										
*Creighton Univ.	300	1 40	1 30	1 32						
*Univ. of Nebraska	957	3 85	4 82	4 71	22 14	17 9	21 9	74 1	37 2	27
Univ. of Omaha	309							50	27 2	21
Nevada										
*Univ. of Nevada	156	30	38	2 30						
New Hampshire										
Dartmouth Col.	765	2 57	1 28	2 52	32 35	31 41	34 33	1 63	43 5	51
*Univ. of New Hampshire	374	1 35	2 46	2 53				78	30	8
New Jersey										
Newark Col. of Engineering	372							1 82	80 1	57
Princeton Univ.	723	78	3 47	2 50	32 54	30 52	29 34	89 1	35 6	17
*Rutgers Univ.	1,127	72	73	4 54				76	55	30
St. Peter's Col.	264	2 90	2 90	2 49						
*Seton Hall Univ.	607	4 79	2 76	9 81						
Stevens Inst. of Tech.	161							2 18	24 1	19

College or University	Male grads. 1956-57	ARMY ROTC 1955 USA USAR	ARMY ROTC 1956 USA USAR	ARMY ROTC 1957 USA USAR	NAVY ROTC 1955 USN USNR	NAVY ROTC 1956 USN USNR	NAVY ROTC 1957 USN USNR	AIR FORCE ROTC 1955 USAF USAFR	AIR FORCE ROTC 1956 USAF USAFR	AIR FORCE ROTC 1957 USAF USAFR
New Mexico										
*New Mexico Col. of A & MA	201	24	20	32						
Univ. of New Mexico	377		1		20	24	22	16 3	19	29	18
New York										
*Alfred Univ.	122	2 10	51	28	20 14	24 22	16 3	1	19	29	18
Brooklyn Polytech. Inst.	518	1 46	79	3 57					57	31	1 20
Brooklyn Col.	962		1 48								
*Canisius Col.	152	2 46	1 48	55					47	23	20
City Col. of New York	1,912	3 107	2 89	5 67							
Clarkson Col. of Technology	183		50	45	49						
Colgate Univ.	307				22 14	23 21	21 29	20	91	55	35
Columbia Univ.	1,741	7 209	2 172	6 147	19 52	21	41	29 34	39	30	8
*Cornell Univ.	1,402	7 139	6 131	3 110					87 1	67 4	42
Fordham Univ.	997								80 3	86 5	25
*Hobart Col.	a93							2	20 1	19 2	17
*Hofstra Col.	405	3 92	3 64	2 28							
Manhattan Col.	492		1 43	3 50				2	55	43 1	44
*New York Univ.	2,671		1 51	6 30					81 1	49 3	30
*Niagara Univ.	151		1 42	35							
Pratt Inst.	231	1 42									
Queens Col.	591								1 31	16	12

a Represents male graduates in 1955.

College or University	Male grads. 1956-57	ARMY ROTC 1955 USA USAR	ARMY ROTC 1956 USA USAR	ARMY ROTC 1957 USA USAR	NAVY ROTC 1955 USN USNR	NAVY ROTC 1956 USN USNR	NAVY ROTC 1957 USN USNR	AIR FORCE ROTC 1955 USAF USAFR	AIR FORCE ROTC 1956 USAF USAFR	AIR FORCE ROTC 1957 USAF USAFR
New York Cont.										
Rensselaer Polytech. Inst.	702	1	63	70	22 35	24 33	32 36	46 1	37	57
St. Bonaventure Univ.	198	58	49	40						
*St. Bernardine of Siena Col.	155	58	43 2	29						
St. Lawrence Univ.	184	31	51 3	46						
Syracuse Univ.	1,049	63	87 4	86				3 103 4	53 6	46
Union Col.	387	71 5						1 37 2	34 5	32
Univ. of Buffalo	628	1						25	9 1	26
Univ. of Rochester	347				28 17	22 11	20 16	14	18 2	5
North Carolina										
*Davidson Col.	192	61	40 4	48	30 34	24 28	20 28	53	36	24
Duke Univ.	653							30 1	20	6
East Carolina Col.	217									
*North Carolina A & T Col.	176	2 15	1 20	13				13	8 2	15
*North Carolina State Col. of A & E	744	1 108	1 116 2	92				1 86 5	53 10	55
Univ. of North Carolina	952				30 26	23 25	24 24	77 2	41 3	30
Wake Forest Col.	857	1 61	46	55						
North Dakota										
*North Dakota Agri. Col.	313	1 14	18	23				48 2	27 1	14

College or University	Male grads. 1956-57	ARMY ROTC 1955 USA USAR	ARMY ROTC 1956 USA USAR	ARMY ROTC 1957 USA USAR	NAVY ROTC 1955 USN USNR	NAVY ROTC 1956 USN USNR	NAVY ROTC 1957 USN USNR	AIR FORCE ROTC 1955 USAF USAFR	AIR FORCE ROTC 1956 USAF USAFR	AIR FORCE ROTC 1957 USAF USAFR
North Dakota Cont.										
*Univ. of North Dakota	427	19	22 6	6 31				41	30 1	1 14
Ohio										
Bowling Green State Univ.	365	2 48	1 45	1 42						
Case Inst. of Tech.	275	28	6 30	6 34				1 52 3	16 2	2 16
*Central State Col.	92							38 1	48	2 34
*John Carroll Univ.	302	3 99	2 89	4 133						
Kent State Univ.	594	3 30	2 23	2 39				2 34 2	21 1	1 21
Miami Univ.	531				33 31	24 32	17 20	83 1	67 2	2 21
*Ohio Univ.	622	1 64	3 53	3 72				86 2	74 2	2 29
*Ohio State Univ.	2,096	130	116	2 122	30 28	17 23	30 13	4 183 7	115 4	4 80
Ohio Wesleyan Univ.	234									
*Univ. of Akron	245	3 38	3 44	1 55				1 110	116 1	1 77
Univ. of Cincinnati	736	1 112	1 49	2 71				1 26 1	26	4 18
*Univ. of Dayton	853	36	2 32	4 33				71	62	1 35
Univ. of Toledo	377	4 40	1 47	2 50						
Western Reserve Univ.	511									
*Xavier Univ.	271	1 62	1 43	2 50				30	11	
Youngstown Univ.	267	3 20	22	1 21						

264

College or University	Male grads. 1956-57	ARMY ROTC 1955 USA USAR	ARMY ROTC 1956 USA USAR	ARMY ROTC 1957 USA USAR	NAVY ROTC 1955 USN USNR	NAVY ROTC 1956 USN USNR	NAVY ROTC 1957 USN USNR	AIR FORCE ROTC 1955 USAF USAFR	AIR FORCE ROTC 1956 USAF USAFR	AIR FORCE ROTC 1957 USAF USAFR
Oklahoma										
*Oklahoma A & M	1,189	9 164	7 135	7 116	11 33	23 30	26 29	98	95 1	63
*Univ. of Oklahoma	1,296	5 177	10 131	6 134				98	68 5	44
Univ. of Tulsa	337							23	17 1	12
Oregon										
*Oregon State Col.	772	2 52	5 81	8 109	15 11	20 14	24 11	72	62 2	23
	602	2 54	1 48	1 53				3 59	41 1	29
*Univ. of Oregon	145							40	24 5	21
*Univ. of Portland										
*Willamette Univ.	123							31	18 1	11
Pennsylvania										
*Allegheny Col.	121							12	12 1	13
Bucknell Univ.	250	88	1 78	1 107						
Carnegie Inst. of Tech.	512	89	98	101						
Dickinson Col.	137	16	3 20	1 38						
*Drexel Inst. of Tech.	522	1 75	4 87	3 68				27	9 17	
*Duquesne Univ.	333	2 42	34	2 31						
Franklin & Marshall Col.	254							3 25	19	13
*Gannon Col.	88	6 26	1 17	2 33						

College or University	Male grads. 1956-57	ARMY ROTC 1955 USA	USAR	1956 USA	USAR	1957 USA	USAR	NAVY ROTC 1955 USN	USNR	1956 USN	USNR	1957 USN	USNR	AIR FORCE ROTC 1955 USAF	USAFR	1956 USAF	USAFR	1957 USAF	USAFR
Gettysburg Col.	215		32	3	21	5	33												
*Grove City Col.	175													32		36	4	15	
Lafayette Col.	300	2	94	2	75	6	86							16		14	1	16	
*LaSalle Col.	446		21	4	29	6	34												
*Lehigh Univ.	581		83		87	1	79							29		28		34	
*Pennsylvania Military Col.	112	5	85	5	48	4	52												
*Penn. State Univ.	1,769	4	96	5	70	5	80	31	30	31	26	38	23	177		128	14	65	
State Teachers Col. (Indiana)	175	3	29	2	31	2	37												
*St. Joseph's Col.	279																		
Temple Univ.	1,088	3	44	2	33	1	25							44		33		19	
Univ. of Pennsylvania	1,357	2	95	2	68	2	77	27	27	25	33	27	20	66		41		28	
Univ. of Pittsburgh	1,296	10	83	5	50	14	63							87	2	53		37	
*Univ. of Scranton	220	1	18	1	20	1	14												
Villanova Univ.	625							18	42	20	28	29	19						
Washington & Jefferson Col.	132		32		24	2	34												
Rhode Island																			
Brown Univ.	460	3	64	4	61	7	59	32	47	28	40	20	31	47		25		27	
Providence Col.	277																		
*Univ. of Rhode Island	325	4	88	3	79	4	74												

College or University	Male grads. 1956-57	ARMY ROTC 1955 USA USAR	ARMY ROTC 1956 USA USAR	ARMY ROTC 1957 USA USAR	NAVY ROTC 1955 USN USNR	NAVY ROTC 1956 USN USNR	NAVY ROTC 1957 USN USNR	AIR FORCE ROTC 1955 USAF USAFR	AIR FORCE ROTC 1956 USAF USAFR	AIR FORCE ROTC 1957 USAF USAFR
South Carolina										
*Clemson Agric. Col.	412	3 172	3 120	2 101				62	2 47	1 29
*Furman Univ.	156	38	34	1 30						
*Presbyterian Col.	88	42	28	4 33						
*South Carolina State Col.	121	1 23	2 20	8 37				2 69	2 48	5 50
*The Citadel	352	11 137	17 141	13 128				89	81	3 62
Univ. of South Carolina	593				22 16	21 7	19 10			
Wofford Col.	151	35	45	1 46						
South Dakota										
*South Dakota School of Mines and Tech.	115	19	1 17	33				16	3 15	3 10
*South Dakota State Col.	326	48	32	3 40						
*Univ. of South Dakota	286	2 46	39	1 30						
Tennessee										
*East Tennessee State Col.	241	2 32	2 25	4 43				41	1 37	7 21
*Memphis State Col.	313									
Middle Tenn. State Col.	203	2 48	2 35	4 44						
*Tenn. A & I State Univ.	184							8	12	4
Tennessee Polytech. Inst.	266	3 40	31	5 35						

267

College or University	Male grads. 1956-57	ARMY ROTC 1955 USA USAR	ARMY ROTC 1956 USA USAR	ARMY ROTC 1957 USA USAR	NAVY ROTC 1955 USN USNR	NAVY ROTC 1956 USN USNR	NAVY ROTC 1957 USN USNR	AIR FORCE ROTC 1955 USAF USAFR	AIR FORCE ROTC 1956 USAF USAFR	AIR FORCE ROTC 1957 USAF USAFR
The Univ. of the South	89							20	17 1	8
Univ. of Chattanooga	128	23	5 3	17						
*Univ. of Tennessee	1,114	1 71	1 49	4 37				1 54	31 7	20
Vanderbilt Univ.	475	50	63	1 43	19 19	25 16	22 19			
Texas										
A & M College of Texas	1,136	6 349	11 311	13 339				209 19	158 28	153
Baylor Univ.	749							1 88 3	54 4	28
East Texas State Teachers Col.	267									
*Hardin-Simmons Univ.	149	7	1 16	1 18				48 2	20 3	14
*Midwestern Univ.	113	2 6	14	1 11						
North Texas State Col.	645									
*Prairie View A & M Col.	123	2 44	2 55	2 28				86	48 5	26
*St. Mary's Univ.	236	4 33	4 34	2 30						
*Sam Houston State Teachers Col.	275	17	2 19	2 27						
Southern Methodist Univ.	649									
Southern Texas State Teachers Col.	181							82	59 1	33
Texas Christian Univ.	348	1 24	1 19	3 34				1 11	18	8
Texas Col.								27	18	12

College or University	Male grads. 1956-57	ARMY ROTC 1955 USA	USAR	1956 USA	USAR	1957 USA	USAR	NAVY ROTC 1955 USN	USNR	1956 USN	USNR	1957 USN	USNR	AIR FORCE ROTC 1955 USAF	USAFR	1956 USAF	USAFR	1957 USAF	USAFR
Texas Tech. Col.	737	1	63	1	46	4	51							1	74	1	30	3	23
Texas Western Col.	266	1	43	1	31	1	46												
The Rice Inst.	293		27	1	32		35												
*Trinity Univ.	133		8	1	16	1	27												
Univ. of Houston	733	9	96	3	46	3	43							65	1	64	6	53
Univ. of Texas	2,406	8	129	8	135	6	165	16	16	21	30	16	23						
*West Texas State Col.	164	1	10	3	24	4	18												
Utah																			
Brigham Young Univ.	721													102		68	3	50	
Univ. of Utah	851	1	35	2	33	1	31	27	28	17	33	15	34	117		62		23	
*Utah State Agric. Col.	546	5	54	4	51	4	56	20	22	23	20	16	13	48	1	49	3	21	
Vermont																			
*Middlebury Col.	149		22		30	1	47							26	2	19	2	28	
*Norwich Univ.	159	10	136	5	113	22	126							32	3	19	4	17	
*St. Michael's Col.	131													1					
*Univ. of Vermont	304	1	40	2	54	4	40												
Virginia																			
Col. of Wm. & Mary	270		34		26		15												
*Hampton Inst.	85		19		26	1	20												
Univ. of Richmond	257	2	24	1	37	2	20							11		11		15	

269

College or University	Male grads. 1956-57	ARMY ROTC 1955 USA USAR	ARMY ROTC 1956 USA USAR	ARMY ROTC 1957 USA USAR	NAVY ROTC 1955 USN USNR	NAVY ROTC 1956 USN USNR	NAVY ROTC 1957 USN USNR	AIR FORCE ROTC 1955 USAF USAFR	AIR FORCE ROTC 1956 USAF USAFR	AIR FORCE ROTC 1957 USAF USAFR
Univ. of Virginia	661	5 78	7 84	3 89	21 19	18 18	24 21	27 1	17 1	17
*Virginia Military Inst.	171	5 111	7 107	13 107				72 3	34 3	24
*Virginia Polytech. Inst.	697	3 120	4 97	2 92						
		2 65	1 33	2 41				1 42	48 2	33
*Virginia State Col.	78									
Washington & Lee Univ.	214	2 75	60	67						
Washington										
*Central Washington Col. of Education	204							28	18	21
*Col. of Puget Sound	111							8 1	11	10
*East Washington Col. of Ed.	128	1 8	2 5	4 12						
*Gonzaga Univ.	181	2 23	1 27	26						
*Seattle Univ.	232	2 60	1 52	3 43						
State Col. of Washington	624	3 36	4 68	3 72				1 56 1	44 3	30
*Univ. of Washington	1,814	8 84	1 100	3 101	29 35	32 34	17 19	3 142 3	79 3	51
West Virginia										
*Davis and Elkins Col.	83									
Marshall Col.	248	22	1 25	29				19	14	5
*West Virginia State Col.	99	8 34	4 22	2 11						
*West Virginia Univ.	612	2 84	3 75	2 77				1 39 1	33 4	26

College or University	Male grads. 1956-57	ARMY ROTC 1955 USA	1955 USAR	1956 USA	1956 USAR	1957 USA	1957 USAR	NAVY ROTC 1955 USN	1955 USNR	1956 USN	1956 USNR	1957 USN	1957 USNR	AIR FORCE ROTC 1955 USAF	1955 USAFR	1956 USAF	1956 USAFR	1957 USAF	1957 USAFR
Wisconsin																			
*Lawrence Col.	87	1	43	2	37		29												
Marquette Univ.	960		37		20	3	49	33	24		21	19	22	33		18		1	12
*Ripon Col.	64																		
*St. Norbert Col.	129	3	33	1	41	1	33												
*Univ. of Wisconsin	2,150	4	221	5	218	3	233	27	20		25	27	22	92		69	1	2	50
Wyoming																			
*Univ. of Wyoming	389	3	29	1	19	1	29						17	2		12	1	2	12
Others																			
*Univ. of Alaska	29	1	5		3		2												
*Univ. of Hawaii	390	1	53	2	59	9	59							36	1	25	1	1	15
*Univ. of Puerto Rico	919	1	37	1	46	2	50							34	1	16			6

INDEX

academic freedom, 120, 133
academic time, for ROTC instruction, 120, 167, 202-205; *see also* credit, for ROTC instruction
accreditation of institutions of higher education, 136, 175-176
administration of ROTC programs, 152-165, 172-176; Army, 153; Navy, 153, 174; Air Force, 153-154, 174; need for coordination, 240-242
Advisory Committee on Universal Training, 87
"air age citizenship," AFROTC instruction in, 127, 189-192, 227
Air Defense Command, 8
Air Force, and role of reserves, 8
Air Force, Assistant Secretary of, for Manpower, Personnel, and Reserve Forces, 154
Air Force, Department of, established, 65, 87; and ROTC, 90, 91, 118, 241
Air Force, Deputy Chief of Staff of, for Personnel, 154
Air Force, Director of Personnel Procurement and Training, 154
Air Force, officer production by sources, *see* Statistical Appendix, Table 4, 247
Air Force Academy, as source of officers, 17-19; costs of, 18n; establishment of, 88, 91, 140; program, 168, 199, 218
Air Force ROTC, establishment of, 88; as officer procurement program, 89, 94, 112, 152, 183; as source of non-rated officers, 91, 105, 110, 188; enrollment in, 91, 96, 103, 110, 116, 118, 119; number of participating institutions, 91, 96, 103, 105, 107, 108, 116, 118-119, 147, 162; curriculum, 91, 106, 226-231; basic course, 91, 196; advanced course, 91, 192, 196; and reserve officers, 91, 104, 105, 106, 109, 112; as source of active duty officers, 94; purpose (mission), 103, 112, 118; as source of pilots and navigators, 105, 106, 110, 188; commissioning of graduates, 109, 116, 118, 162; active duty obligation of graduates, 110, 118, 147, 192, 228; and direct commissioning program, 152; administration of, 153-154; as source of career officers, 193, 227; *see also* topical listings
Air National Guard, 8
Air Reserve, 8
Air Training Command, 154
Air University, 154, 188, 197, 227
airpower, doctrine of, 87, 88, 140
American Association of Land-Grant Colleges and State Universities, and ROTC, 46, 51, 96, 126, 127, 128
American Council on Education, 56, 58, 236
American Literary, Scientific, and Military Academy (Norwich University), 28
American Medical Association, 175
American Society for Engineering Education, 203, 204
Amherst College, 119
Annapolis, *see* Naval Academy
Armed Forces Committee on Postwar Educational Opportunities for Service Personnel, 135
Armed Forces Policy Council, 127
Armed Forces Reserve Act of 1952, 6, 160
Armor, Army ROTC, 179

273

INDEX

Army, role and mission of, 6, 64-65; and higher education in World War I, 42-43; and role of regular forces, 49, 52, 73, 86; and higher education in World War II, 58, 60, 61
Army, Assistant Chief of Staff of, for Reserve Components, 153
Army, Assistant Secretary of, for Manpower, Personnel, and Reserve Forces, 153
Army, Department of, establishment of, 90; and Army education, 181; and ROTC, 153, 173, 220
Army, Deputy Chief of Staff of, for Military Operations, 153
Army, Deputy Chief of Staff of, for Personnel, 153
Army, officer production by sources, see Statistical Appendix, Table 2, 246
Army-Air Force ROTC enrollment agreement, 108
Army Field Forces, 179
Army Ground Forces, 54, 55
Army ROTC, as source of regular officers, 34, 50, 111; as source of active duty officers, 51-52, 54, 83, 84, 85, 86, 87, 97, 101, 102; enrollments in, 72, 80, 96, 103, 108, 117, 118, 124; and World War II, 72-73; postwar plans for, 74-97; curriculum and instruction, 76-77, 90, 106; administration of, 76-77, 153-154; students, 77; graduates, numbers of, 80, 96, 103, 107-108, 147; reserve concept of, 85, 86, 89, 93-94, 109, 154, 212; number of participating institutions, 96, 103, 116-117; and Korean conflict, 102-112; and six months training duty, 109, 111, 117, 150; source of active duty officers, 154; summer camp, 177; branch material courses, 219; *see also* topical listings

Army Specialized Training Program, 60-62, 66, 67, 72
Artillery, Army ROTC, 179, 233
Association of American Universities, 133
Atomic Energy Commission, 134
aviation cadet program, as source of officers, 19, 20, 88; Navy, 59; Air Force, 105, 147

Bradley, Major General James L., 76-77; *see also* Bradley Committee
Bradley Committee, Army ROTC, 76-77, 80, 83, 84-85
branch affiliated Army ROTC, 178, 179, 181, 183
Bres, Major General Edward S., Executive for Reserve and ROTC Affairs, 86
Bureau of Naval Personnel, 59; and NROTC, 67, 153; 174, 240
Bureau of the Budget, and Holloway Plan, 78, 80, 81; and federal aid for ROTC facilities construction, 122, 237; and ROTC costs, 124, 146; and ROTC coordination, 158
Burgess, Carter, Assistant Secretary of Defense, 163, 240
Bush, Vannevar, and National Science Foundation, 137, 138

Capen, Samuel P., cited, 56
Chief of Army Reserve and ROTC Affairs, Office of, 153
Chief of Military History, Office of, 200
Chief of Naval Operations, Office of, 153
Chief of Naval Personnel, 155
church-affiliated colleges, and ROTC, 123, 168
Citadel, The, 21, 29, 43n
citizen army concept, 3, 5, 8, 9, 28, 62, 65, 73, 112; and ROTC, 27, 101, 123; and mobilization plan of 1912, 34-35

274

INDEX

citizenship, ROTC instruction in, 45, 227; *see also* "air age citizenship"

civil affairs, role of reserve forces in, 5

civil defense, and ROTC, 128

Civilian Conservation Corps, 50

civilian courses, substitution of for ROTC instruction, 184, 222, 223, 224, 225, 229, 230

Clark, General Mark, commanding Army Field Forces, 179

Colgate University, study of ROTC, cited, 194n

Columbia University, 119

commandants of ROTC detachments, responsibilities of, 95, 174-175, 196-197; selection of, 197

Commission on Financing Higher Education, 133

Commission on Higher Education, 132-133, 139, 140

Commission on Organization of the Executive Branch of the Government, *see* Hoover Commission

commissioning of officers, direct, 50, 81

Committee on Civilian Components, *see* Gray Committee

Committee on Education beyond the High School, 143, 156

Committee on Militarism in Education, 46, 47

compulsory military training, and Land-Grant Act, 31, 33

compulsory ROTC training, 37, 44, 123-129, 212, 235, 239; and Land-Grant Act, 38, 45; opposition to and support of, 46-49; at land-grant colleges, 48, 51, 81, 123; at state universities, 123; at private institutions, 123

Congress, and citizen army concept, 9; and military pay bill, 10; and land-grant colleges, 31, 32; and compulsory ROTC training, 47; and Selective Service, 52; and NROTC, 66-70, 77-81, 84; and Army ROTC, 72, 77-82, 86-87; and AFROTC, 119; and GI Bill, 136; and education and science legislation, 140-141; and ROTC legislation, 122, 141, 145-147, 158, 177, 237, 240

Continental Air Command, 154

Continental Army Command, 153, 179

"contract" ROTC students, *see* Naval ROTC

Cordiner, Ralph J., cited, 10; *see also* Cordiner Committee

Cordiner Committee (Defense Advisory Committee on Professional and Technical Compensation), 10, 242

Corps of Engineers, Army, 181

costs, of ROTC, *see* Statistical Appendix, Table 5, 248

counseling of students, and ROTC, 233, 235, 239

credit, for ROTC instruction, 51, 95, 120, 167, 202-205, 223

cruise, summer NROTC training, 177, 225, 231

curricula, ROTC, evaluated, 216-231

curriculum, proposed joint ROTC, 93-94, 170-172; standardized, 173, 175, 204, 221, 230, 235-236; Army, 178-183; NROTC, 183-187; AFROTC, 188-193

Dartmouth College, 233

Defense, Assistant Secretary of, for Manpower, Personnel, and Reserves, 165

Defense, Department of, establishment of, 87; and ROTC, 106, 109, 122, 126, 127, 158-165, 240-242; and higher education, 163

Defense, Secretary of, and reserve forces, 5; and military pay bill, 9-10, 242; and ROTC, 90, 124, 128, 159-165, 242; and manpower policies, 241

Defense Advisory Committee on Professional and Technical Com-

275

INDEX

pensation, *see* Cordiner Committee
deferment, Selective Service, 102, 215; and ROTC, 55, 104, 105, 142
detachment, ROTC, 173-174, 175
Dewey, John, 47
disestablishment of ROTC units, 117, 118-119, 162
draft, *see* Selective Service
drill, ROTC, 176, 223, 229

education, general, need of officers for, 21
education, higher, as source of military officers, 3, 16-17, 21-23, 36, 129, 237, 242, 243; demands upon, 22-23; and the public service, 22-23, 31, 101, 132; and national manpower requirements, 22, 57-58, 104, 119-120, 131, 132, 134-135, 150, 213-214; American system characterized, 31, 120, 131-132, 168-169, 175, 202, 213; and World War I, 41-42, 52-62; and World War II, 57-62, 68; and student enrollments, 97, 116, 125; and relationship to the armed forces, 120, 129, 147, 151, 169, 194, 213, 240; and the federal government, 130-134, 215; and autonomy and freedom of, 133, 136, 140, 239; and national policy, 134-144, 213, 214-215; and national defense, 210; and leaders of, 215; *see also* topical listings
education, military attitude toward, 167-168
education, national policy for, 134-144, 156-157, 165, 213-214, 240
education, postgraduate, and military officers, 16
education, professional, and the military, 120, 129, 168, 188, 194, 195, 213, 210-216, 226, 230-234; and other professions, 216-218

educational associations, 161n, 237, 242
Eisenhower, President Dwight D., and reserve forces, 8, 9
Eisenhower Administration, education and manpower legislation, 142-143
engineering education, 133, 143, 168; and ROTC, 149-150, 163-164, 203, 204, 217
Engineers Council for Professional Development, 173, 175, 176n, 204
Executive for Reserve and ROTC Affairs (Army), and postwar plans for ROTC, 69, 71, 85, 86, 90; and revised curriculum, 180

facilities, ROTC, federal aid for construction of, 68, 77, 121, 122, 126, 158, 237-238
federal aid to higher education, 103, 133, 237, 238
Federal Government, and relationship to ROTC, 37, 51, 120-130, 133-134, 148, 156-157, 172, 215-216; and aid for construction of ROTC facilities, 68, 77, 121, 122, 126, 158, 237-238; and aid to education, 103, 156, 237, 238; and a national education policy, 134-144, 156-157, 165, 213-214, 215, 240
fellowships and scholarships, provision of by Federal Government, 215, 239, 240; and ROTC, 38, 239-240
First Army Plan, ROTC, 221-222
Flemming, Arthur S., Director of Defense Mobilization, 164
Flexner, Abraham, cited, 45
flight orientation, and AFROTC, 177, 233; and Army ROTC, 233
flight training, and AFROTC, 88-89, 177, 228; and Army ROTC, 177
forces-in-being, concept of, 4, 5, 8, 73, 211; and ROTC, 62, 89, 212

276

INDEX

Forrestal, James, Secretary of the Navy, and ROTC legislation, 70, 79, 82, 84, 85; Secretary of Defense, and joint ROTC issues, 92; and Committee on Civilian Components, 140

GI Bill of Rights (veterans' educational benefits), and ROTC, 72; and manpower policy, 135-138, 141-142

Gardner, John W., cited, 13

Garrison, Lindley M., Secretary of War, 38

General Military Science curriculum, Army ROTC, 106, 165, 178-183, 219, 221

General Staff Act of 1903, 33

generalized ROTC curriculum, 94, 120, 183; *see also* General Military Science curriculum

geography, AFROTC instruction in, 189, 192, 193, 195, 196, 200, 201, 202, 226, 227

Gray, Gordon, Assistant Secretary of the Army, 87, 139; *see also* Gray Committee

Gray Committee (on Civilian Components), postwar plans for ROTC, 87-88, 89-90, 92; and subsidized ROTC, 95, 140, 240; and Reserve Forces Policy Board, 159-160

Gurney, Senator Chan, 85

Hamilton v. Regents of the University of California, 239 U.S. 245 (compulsory military training), 48

Hannah, John A., president of Michigan State University, 128, 171n

Harvard University, and Army ROTC, 173, 220-221, 222; and AFROTC, 229

Hay, James, Representative, 39

Headquarters AFROTC, 154, 200, 227, 228, 240

Hershey, Lieutenant General Lewis B., cited, 9n

higher education, *see* education, higher

Holloway, Rear Admiral James L., Jr., and naval officer education plan, 66n, 74-75, 81; *see also* Holloway Board

Holloway Board (on naval officer education), 74-75, 81, 185, 187, 224, 240

Holloway Plan, NROTC, 66n, 74-76, 77-86, 88, 89, 138; *see also* Holloway Board

Hoover Commission (on the Organization of the Executive Branch), 92, 171n

indoctrination, military, 169-172, 177, 193, 194; Army and Navy, 171; Air Force, 189, 192

Infantry, Army ROTC, 45, 179, 180

Inspector General of the Air Force, and AFROTC, 227

instruction, ROTC, quality of, 92, 180, 193, 194, 195-202, 203, 232-233, 234; nature of, 37, 95, 167, 176, 177, 194; Army ROTC, 180; AFROTC, 195-196, 227; extracurricular, 235

instructors, ROTC, selection of, 68, 196, 197; civilian, 77, 194, 196, 201-202, 229, 235-236; military, 94, 196-197, 219, 232-233; faculty status of, 173, 174, 194; preparation of, 197-198, 199

international relations, AFROTC instruction in, 189, 192, 193, 195, 196, 200, 227; problem of teaching, 198; civilian instruction in, 201

inter-service differences and ROTC, 67, 71-72, 76, 79-85, 87, 91, 178, 188

inter-service relations, and postwar ROTC plans, 67-73, 77-85, 87, 89-90; on-campus arrangements, 92-93, 94, 95, 108, 170-172, 174,

277

INDEX

216; administrative procedures, 152-153, 155, 157-165

Jacob, Philip E., cited, 169
Jacobs, Rear Admiral Randall, 75
Jacobs-Barker plan (Naval officer education), 75
Joint Advisory Panel on ROTC Affairs, 159-163, 165
Joint Army-Navy Selective Service Committee, 52
joint ROTC, *see* inter-service relations

Korean conflict, and reserve forces, 8; and ROTC, 97, 102-112, 141; and mobilization, 102

laboratory exercises, ROTC, 176, 177, 193, 223, 229, 231, 233
Land-Grant Act of 1862 (Morrill Act), and military training, 30-32, 38, 45, 48, 126
Land Grant colleges and universities, 30, 31, 32, 40, 43; and military training, 31, 32, 34, 35, 37, 45, 46, 48, 81, 123-126; and ROTC, 32, 51, 95-96, 122, 123, 126, 127, 128, 240
Lane, Winthrop D., cited, 46
Lasswell, Harold, cited, 167
leadership, instruction in, 176-177, 181, 184, 189, 192, 224, 227
legal education, 168, 217, 219
legislation, ROTC, 77, 78, 79, 80-82, 85-87, 90-91, 141, 142, 145, 148, 240
liberal arts educational institutions, 57
limited war, concept of, 4, 211

manpower, and national policy, 5, 36, 39, 40, 165, 242; national requirements for, 12, 13, 22, 57, 131-134, 136, 143, 148, 158, 211, 213; military requirements, 22-23, 55, 57, 60, 61, 66, 73, 119-120, 129, 144-152, 242; stockpiling of, 28, 55, 62; scientific and technical, 136, 137, 141, 142; and ROTC, 152
manpower advisory council, need for, 242
Marine Corps, platoon leader program, 3n, 96-97, 220; and NROTC, 3n, 184n; and armed forces unification, 65
Marshall, General George C., Secretary of Defense, and universal military training, 5; Army Chief of Staff, and ROTC, 52, and OCS, 54, and Army Specialized Training Program, 60
Massachusetts Institute of Technology, and NROTC, 224-226, 230
McElroy, Neil H., Secretary of Defense, and military pay bill, 9-10; and military training, 163
McGrath, Earl J., cited, 218
McKellar, Senator Kenneth, 38
medical education, 134, 168, 217, 219
Mershon, Colonel Ralph D., and Ohio State University, 198n, 229n
Michigan State University, 128
midshipmen, NROTC, status of, 146-147
militarism, 46, 63
Military Academy (West Point), and postgraduate education, 16n, 220; as source of officers, 17-19, 29, 30; nature of, 168; and academic instruction, 199, 218
military code, 168, 169, 170
military colleges, as source of officers, 17, 20-21; and ROTC, 21, 43n; proposal for, 38, 39
military coordinator, ROTC, 174
military history, ROTC instruction in, 169, 180, 183, 195, 198, 200, 201, 202; and Ohio State University, 198; and Princeton University, 222-223; and Yale University, 222; and Harvard University, 229

278

INDEX

military manpower, turnover of, 9, 10, 12
Military Pay Bill of 1958, 10, 151, 215, 242
military policy, emergence of, 33-40; and ROTC, 62, 64, 112
military profession, changing nature of, 9, 10, 13-14, 15, 112, 120, 129, 194, 204-205, 210-211; educational preparation for, 120, 129, 194, 195, 210-216, 230-234; characteristics of, 167-168; incentives for, 215, 232-237
military training, and military colleges, 21, 29; in the South, 29; and ROTC, 36-37, 74, 93-94, 123, 193; in World War II, 55; attitude of military toward, 168; as military prerogative, 172; characterized, 173; and Army ROTC, 180-181, 219-220; and AFROTC, 227
militia, 28, 33, 36, 39
Militia Act of 1792, 28; of 1903, 33
Minnesota, University of, 46
mobilization, 3-5, 6, 20, 112; 1912 plan, 34, 35; 1930 plan, 49; and World War II, 52, 54-55, 57; and Korean conflict, 102, 112
Morrill, James L., cited, 96
Morrill, Justin, 30 (*see also* Land-Grant Act)
Morrill Act, *see* Land-Grant Act
motivation, for military service, 171, 172, 201, 228, 232-237, 239; for flying, 171, 177, 188; and ROTC, 38, 216, 217, 219-220, 231-237
municipal educational institutions, 57

National Defense Act of 1916, 33, 36, 39, 40; of 1920, 52
National Defense Education Act of 1958, 240
National Guard, role of, 5, 6, 7n, 33, 34, 35, 36, 37, 39, 52, 73, 89; and ROTC, 40, 50, 86
National Science Foundation, fellowships and scholarships, 134, 137, 138, 141, 142, 158
National Security Training Commission, 103
Naval Academy (Annapolis), as source of officers, 17-19, 41, 66, 71, 75, 106; nature of, 168; and academic instruction, 184, 185, 200, 224, 226
naval aviation, 65
naval history, NROTC instruction in, 169, 183, 187, 195, 198, 200
naval officer education, *see* Holloway Board; *see also* Pye Board
Naval ROTC, establishment of, 51; number of participating institutions, 51, 67, 78, 96, 107; and postwar plans for, 66-87; enrollments in, 76, 82-83, 96, 107, 155; "regular" students, 76, 106, 107, 155-157, 177, 186-187, 212; "contract" students, 76, 83, 104, 107, 110, 177, 186, 212; as officer procurement program, 78, 79, 89, 94, 106-107; graduates, numbers of, 76, 96, 107, 110-111; graduates, active duty obligation of, 110; graduates, active duty retention rate of, 110-111, 147, 151, 155-156, 212; and Korean conflict, 106-111; military status of midshipmen, 146-147; students evaluated, 148-149; administration of, 153, 154; curriculum of, 223-226; and enrollment of "regular" students at high tuition cost institutions, 129n, 155-157, 162, 216
Naval Reserve Association, 7n
naval subjects, NROTC instruction in, 183-187
Navy, and reserve forces, 7; and higher education in World War I, 42; in World War II, 59-60; role and mission, 64, 65; and unification of the armed forces, 65-66
Navy, Assistant Secretary of, for

279

INDEX

Personnel and Reserve Forces, 153
Navy, Department of, and World War II college programs, 60, 66; and Department of Defense, 87; and ROTC, 241
Navy, officer procurement by sources, *see* Statistical Appendix, Table 3, 247
Nimitz, Admiral Chester W., and NROTC, 79
Northwestern University, NROTC instructors' course, 197-198
Norwich University, 21, 28, 29, 32, 43n
nuclear power propulsion, Navy, 11-12, 225, 226
nuclear war, 4, 73, 88
Nye, Senator Gerald P., 48

Office of Education, U. S., and World War II, 56; and ROTC, 103, 141, 157-158
Officer Augmentation Act of 1956, 10-11
officer corps, changing nature of, 10-11, 148
officer personnel, changing demands upon, 3, 11-12, 15, 16, 101, 148, 204-205, 211; requirements of, 3, 10-12, 15, 21, 54-55, 101, 112, 120, 129, 134, 144, 148, 150, 204-205, 211, 226, 240; higher education as source of, 3, 16-17, 21-23, 36, 129, 242, 243; advancement of, 10, 14, 15, 18, 76; professionalization of, 10, 101, 134, 151, 210-211; term retention of, 14-15, 16, 147; Regular Army, 29; World War II, 54, 55; high rate of resignations, 110, 147; career incentives for, 145, 148, 150; postgraduate training for, 179, 185, 188, 220, 227
officer procurement, Air Force direct commissioning program, 151
officer rank structure, 14, 18
officers, active duty, term retention of, 11, 14-15, 20; need for, 14, 211; motivation toward, 20, 111; ROTC as source of, 51, 52, 54, 83, 84, 85, 86, 87, 91, 94, 97, 101, 102, 104, 105, 106, 109
officers, Air Force, educational level of, 88, 105, 140, 188; direct commissioning of, 151-152
officers, career, ROTC as source of, 3, 23, 34, 50, 54, 81, 84, 88-89, 94-95, 101, 111, 112, 116, 126, 127, 130, 131, 134, 145, 154, 160, 167, 193, 211, 218, 222, 227, 236
officers, commissioned through ROTC programs: 1920-1945, *see* Statistical Appendix, Table 1, 246
officers, commissioned through ROTC, by civilian institutions of origin, *see* Statistical Appendix, Table 7, 250
officers, ROTC, active duty obligation of, 103, 106, 109, 116, 240; AFROTC, 105, 110, 118, 147, 192, 228; NROTC, 110; attrition of, 212
officers, reserve, ROTC as source of, 91, 104, 105, 106, 109, 112, 154, 167, 212
officers candidate schools, as source of officers, 19-20, 65; in World War I, 41; in World War II, 54, 55, 58; Army, 102; Air Force, 102; Navy, 107, 108; in Korean conflict, 102, 119
Ohio State University, and Mershon Fund, 198n, 229n; ROTC instructors' courses, 198; and curriculum revision, 229, 230
Oppenheimer, J. Robert, and science education, 139
Ordnance Corps, Army, plans for subsidized ROTC, 148, 240
Organized Reserves, Army, 7n; policy for, 33, 40, 49, 73, 89; and ROTC, 40, 49, 72, 86
Osborn, Frederick H., Brigadier General, and veterans' education, 135, 136, 144

280

INDEX

pacifism and ROTC, 45, 46, 96, 126

Partridge, Captain Alden, and Norwich University, 28, 30

Patterson, Robert P., Secretary of War, and ROTC legislation, 79-86

personnel on ROTC duty, *see* Statistical Appendix, Table 6, 249

Platoon Leaders Course, *see* Marine Corps

Plattsburg summer training camps, 35-36

political science, AFROTC instruction in, 226

President, Executive office of, and ROTC, 157-158

Princeton University, and NROTC, 187; and Army ROTC, 222-223, 224, 233; and AFROTC, 223, 229, 230; and military history, 222-223

private educational institutions, and ROTC, 43, 63, 95, 96, 104, 119, 121, 122, 123, 221; and World War II, 57, 119; and tuition income, 103, 104, 146, 155-157

professor of air science, 196

professor of military science, and Land-Grant colleges, 31-32; faculty status of, 33, 174; responsibilities of, 44n, 77, 196

professor of naval science, 196

Proper Military Policy, 1915 Statement, 36, 39, 40

psychology, NROTC instruction in, 184; AFROTC, 224, 227

Public Health Service, Fellowships, 134

Pye, Admiral William S., 66; *see also* Pye Board

Pye Board (naval officer education), 66, 67, 75

Quarles, Donald A., Secretary of the Air Force, 118; Under Secretary of Defense, 128; Assistant Secretary of Defense, 163

quotas on ROTC enrollments, and Army and Air Force, 117-118, 124; and NROTC, 129n, 155-157, 162, 216

"regular" ROTC students, *see* Naval ROTC

Reserve Forces Act of 1955, 5, 6, 8; and ROTC, 109, 150

reserve forces, role of, 3-5, 6-7, 8, 10, 11, 33, 49, 62, 87, 89, 129, 140, 211; and ROTC, 27, 28, 62, 65, 81, 83, 101, 109, 120, 160, 162, 167, 212, 222, 241; and federal status of, 34, 36, 39-40, 89

Reserve Forces Policy Board, 159-160, 241

reserve officers, ROTC as source of, 3, 49-50, 55-56, 81, 84, 85, 88-89, 94-95, 101, 111; and active duty, 11, 50; term retention of, 14-15

Reserve Officers Association, 47

retaliatory capability, 4, 211

Rockefeller Brothers Fund, Special Studies Project, cited, 13n, 22

roles and missions of armed forces, controversy over, 88

Roosevelt, President Franklin D., and veterans' education, 135; and scientific talent, 137

Root, Elihu, Secretary of War, 33, 34, 89

Rosenberg, Mrs. Anna, Assistant Secretary of Defense, 106, 109

ROTC, purpose and objectives, 3, 27, 95, 101, 109, 111-112, 120-121, 128-129, 160, 167, 170, 209-210; establishment and early history, 28, 36-37, 39; enrollments in, 28, 97, 124-125; attitudes of educators toward, 28, 42-43, 44, 51, 57, 58, 103, 112, 116, 117, 119, 120, 123, 126, 167, 194, 209, 235-237; educational content and value, 44, 46, 51-52, 55, 238; graduates, numbers of, 51, 54, 56, 97, 212; number of participating institutions, 54, 78,

281

INDEX

96, 116; postwar plans for, 64-73; selection of participating institutions, 70, 72; administration of, 95, 152-165; attitudes of armed services toward, 209, 216; costs of, 222, 237, 238; status of in participating institutions, 173-174, 193-194, 210-216, 231, 232-237

Saltonstall, Senator Leverett, 79
science education, and the federal government, 133-140, 143; and ROTC, 163-164
scientific advisory groups, 242
scientific and technical education, 72
scientific and technical preparation, need of officers for, 11-12, 21
Scientific Research Board, 139, 140
Selective Service, 9, 10, 41, 52; and World War II, 52, 54-55, 56, 60; and ROTC, 52, 54-55, 56, 60, 97, 116, 119, 126, 129, 142, 145, 150-151, 235
Selective Service Act of 1940, 52, 56; of 1948, 97
service academies, as source of officers, 16-18, 88, 97, 134, 216; as advanced schools, 19; proposed combined, 88, 95; resignations of graduates, 147; nature of, 168, 204; and postgraduate training, 178; curricular developments, 218
Service Academy Board, and ROTC, 93-95, 179, 240
Smith, Brigadier General Edward W., Executive for Reserve and ROTC Affairs, 69
Smith, Harold D., Director, Bureau of the Budget, 79
Somervell, General Brehon, Commanding General, Army Service Forces, 69
Soviet Union, education in, 214-215
specialized and technical training, 187, 188, 218, 226-27; and AFROTC, 91, 106, 188; and Army, 94, 220
specialized scientific and engineering, proposed ROTC program, 163-165
specialized talent, need for, 215
Sprout, Harold H., and NROTC, 187
Stanford University, 233
state universities, and ROTC, 122, 123, 125, 240
Statement of Joint ROTC Policies, 1949, 92-93, 95, 174
Statement of Policies Concerning the Postwar Reserve Officers Training Corps, Army, 77, 84-85
Statement of Proper Military Policy, 1915, 36, 39, 40
Stimson, Henry L., Secretary of War, 34, 70
Strategic Air Command, 112
strategic doctrine, concepts of, 3-4, 5, 129, 211; Air Force, 8, 87, 88, 105, 140
students, attitudes toward military service, 15, 144, 150; toward ROTC, 45, 125n, 126, 144, 167, 231n; values held by, 168-169
Students Army Training Corps, 42, 56
subsidized ROTC, Army plans for, 74, 77, 80, 83, 84, 85, 86, 87, 88, 140, 142; Navy program, 76, 82, 83, 138, 145, 146; Air Force plans for, 88, 139, 140, 142; recommended, 90, 95, 140-141, 145-148, 239-240
Summerall, General Charles P., Chief of Staff, Army, 49
summer cruise NROTC training, 177, 225, 231
summer training camp, Plattsburg, 35; and ROTC, 94, 219-220, 221, 231, 233; and AFROTC, 177, 227

talent, military need for, 16, 212, 213; national need for, 13, 22, 215
teachers colleges, 57

INDEX

technical branches, Army, and ROTC instruction, 181
technical specialists, need for, 14, 15, 20, 56
technology, schools of, 203, 225
textbooks and instructional materials, ROTC, 199-201
Thomason Act, and Army ROTC, 50, 81, 86
training techniques, military, 234
Truman, President Harry S, and NROTC, 81, 82, 83; and scientific research, 136-137
Truman Administration, education and manpower legislation, 140
tuition income, 103, 104, 146, 155-157

unification of the armed forces, 64-65, 79
universal military training, 1916 plan, 40-41; and ROTC, 41, 64, 65, 66, 71-72, 73, 74, 76, 78, 87, 88; *see also* Universal Military Training and Service Act of 1951
Universal Military Training and Service Act of 1951, 5, 103; and ROTC, 104-105, 142

V-1 Navy wartime program, 60
V-5 Navy program, 61, 82
V-7 Navy program, 60
V-12 Navy program, and NROTC, 60, 61, 66, 67, 71, 73, 76, 78, 82
veterans' educational benefits, *see* GI Bill of Rights
Virginia Military Institute, and ROTC, 21; and military training, 29, 43

War Department, and military training in Land-Grant colleges, 31, 32-33, 38, 45; and ROTC, 38, 42, 48, 49, 50-51, 55, 58, 65, 84, 86; and higher education in World War II, 58, 60, 61; and unification of the armed forces, 64-65; and Universal Military Training, 73
War Manpower Commission, 58
warfare, changing nature of, 10, 123, 126, 210-211, 226
weapons development, 4-5, 109, 210-211; and training requirements, 12, 64, 88
West Point, *see* Military Academy
Williams College, 119
Wilson, President Woodrow, and military policy, 39
Wisconsin, University of, 45, 46
Wood, General Leonard, Army Chief of Staff, and military policy, 34, 35, 36
World War I, and ROTC, 40-43; and higher education, 41-43, 55, 56, 61
World War II, mobilization planning, 52; and ROTC, 54-61; and higher education, 54-62, 236
Wyman, General Willard G., Commanding General, Continental Army Command, cited, 5n

Yale University, and AFROTC, 119; and Army ROTC, 222

LYONS, GENE M. Education and military leadership; a study of the ROTC, by Gene M. Lyons [and] John W. Masland. Princeton, Princeton University Press, 1959. 283 p. illus. 23 cm. 1. U. S. Army. Reserve Officers' Training Corps. I. Masland, John Wesley, 1912- joint author. II. Title. U428.5.L9 (355) 59-9227 ‡ Library of Congress